JANICE VANCLEAVE'S

A+
Science Fair
Projects

WILEY

John Wiley & Sons, Inc.

Published by John Wiley & Sons, Inc., Hoboken, New Jersey
Published simultaneously in Canada

Design and production by Navta Associates, Inc.

The publisher and the author have made every reasonable effort to ensure that the experiments and activities in the book are safe when conducted as instructed but assume no responsibility for any damage caused or sustained while performing the experiments or activities in this book. Parents, guardians, and/or teachers should supervise young readers who undertake the experiments and activities in this book.

For general information about our other products and services, please contact our Customer Care Department within the United States at (800) 762-2974, outside the United States at (317) 572-3993 or fax (317) 572-4002.

Wiley also publishes its books in a variety of electronic formats. Some content that appears in print may not be available in electronic books. For more information about Wiley products, visit our web site at www.wiley.com.

Library of Congress Cataloging-in-Publication Data:
VanCleave, Janice Pratt.
  [A+ science fair projects]
  Janice VanCleave's A+ science fair projects.
    p. cm.
  Summary: A collection of thirty-five science fair projects in astronomy, biology, chemistry, earth science, and physics, plus suggestions for designing original projects.
  Includes bibliographical references and index.
  ISBN 0-471-33102-3 (pbk. : acid-free paper)
  1. Science—Experiments—Juvenile literature. 2. Science projects—Juvenile literature. [1. Science—Experiments. 2. Experiments. 3. Science projects.] I. Title. II. Title: A plus science fair projects.
  Q182.3.V352 2003
  507.8—dc21   2002032427

Printed in the United States of America

10 9 8 7 6 5 4 3 2 1

DEDICATION

It is my pleasure to dedicate this book to a very knowledgeable and talented teacher, whose help in writing this book was invaluable. What a joy it has been to work with my friend and colleague:

Holly Harris.

ACKNOWLEDGMENTS

I wish to express my appreciation to these science specialists for their valuable assistance by providing information and/or assisting me in finding it.

Dr. Ben Doughty, Robert Fanick, and Dr. Tineke Sexton. Dr. Doughty is head of the department of physics at Texas A & M University—Commerce in Commerce, Texas. Dr. Sexton is an instructor of biology and microbiology at Houston Community College Northwest in Houston, Texas, and Robert Fanick is a chemist at Southwest Research Institute in San Antonio, Texas. These special scientists have provided me with answers to my many questions. This valuable information has made this book even more understandable and fun.

Members of the Central Texas Astronomical Society, including Johnny Barton, Dick Campbell, John W. McAnally, and Paul Derrick. Johnny is an officer of the club and has been an active amateur astronomer for more than 20 years. Dick is an amateur astronomer who is interested in science education. John is also on the staff of the Association of Lunar and Planetary Observers, where he is acting assistant coordinator for transit timings of the Jupiter Section. Paul is the author of the "Stargazer" column in *Waco Tribune-Herald*.

Dr. Glenn S. Orion, a senior research scientist at the Jet Propulsion Laboratory of California Institute of Technology. Glenn is an astronomer and space scientist who specializes in investigating the structure and composition of planetary atmospheres. He is best known for his research on Jupiter and Saturn. I have enjoyed exchanging ideas with Glenn about astronomy facts and experiments for modeling astronomy experiments.

A special note of gratitude to these educators who assisted by pretesting the activities and/or by providing scientific information: Anne Skrabanek, homeschooling consultant in Perry, Texas; Connie Chatmas, Sue Dunham, and Stella Cathey, consultants in Marlin, Texas.

CONTENTS

HOW TO USE THIS BOOK

cience is a system of knowledge as well as the pursuit of knowledge about the nature of things in the universe. It is the result of observing, questioning, and experimenting to test one's ideas. A **science fair project** is an investigation that is designed to find the answer to one specific science question. Because science fair projects are done for a contest called a **science fair** (an organized contest in which science fair projects are compared and judged on the basis of predetermined criteria), you must follow certain rules in preparing your project. One of the main requirements is that your project must follow the scientific method. You'll find information on this as well as other basic rules generally required of all science fair projects in this book, but you should also consult your teacher and fair director about the specific rules for your local fair before you start planning your project.

Developing a science fair project is like being a detective. It requires that you plan well, carefully collect facts, and then share your findings. Preparing and presenting a science fair project can be a fun and rewarding experience. But trying to develop the project and/or assemble the display at the last minute usually results in frustration.

Start your project with curiosity and a desire to learn something new. Then proceed with a purpose and a determination to solve the problem selected. Even if your project doesn't turn out exactly as you planned, it is likely that your scientific quest will end with some interesting discoveries.

This book will give you guidance in developing your project from start to finish, including information on the basic scientific tools and techniques needed to develop and present a project. Before you start your project, read all of Part I. It explains nine important points you need to know for science fair success:

1. *The scientific method.* A systematic way of gathering and pursuing scientific knowledge is what the **scientific method** is all about. Chapter 1 describes the steps of the scientific method and how they can be used in developing a science fair project.

2. *Topic research.* Selecting a topic is the first hurdle to jump in getting started on your project. The research suggestions in Chapter 2 will help you choose a topic. **Research** is the process of collecting information and data. **Data,** as used in this book, are observations and/or measured facts obtained experimentally. **Topic research,** as defined in this book, is research done with the objective of selecting a **project topic** (subject of a science fair project).

3. *Categories.* You should identify the category in which your project falls at the beginning of your research. Judges base their evaluation of the content of your project on the category in which you enter it. For example, an A+ earth science project incorrectly entered in the chemistry category most likely will receive a lower rating. Chapter 3 provides a list of some common categories that are used in science fairs.

4. *Project research.* Once a topic has been selected, research begins with the objective of identifying a **project problem,** which is the scientific question to be solved. **Project research** is an in-depth study of the project topic with the objective of expressing a project problem, proposing a **hypothesis** (a prediction to the solution to a problem, based on knowledge and research), and designing a **project experiment** (an experiment designed to test the hypothesis) to test the hypothesis. This research should involve more than just reading printed materials. It should include interviews of people knowledgeable about the topic as well as exploratory experiments. **Exploratory experiments** as defined in this book, are experiments in which the data are used as part of the project research. Chapter 4 provides suggestions and directions for gathering project research.

5. *Project overview.* Chapter 5 provides a brief overview of a specific science fair project from start to finish. This chapter guides you step-by-step through the collection of research and its use

in identifying a project problem, proposing a hypothesis, and designing a project experiment. The objective of the chapter is to provide a model of how you can organize and plan your science fair project.

6. *Experimental data.* Data are observations and/or measured facts obtained experimentally. Chapter 6 provides ways to organize and display data, including examples of different types of graphs. This chapter includes information about the **project journal** (written progress record of your science fair project).

7. *Project summaries.* Chapter 7 includes information on how to prepare an **abstract** (brief overview of a scientific project) and a **project report** (written report of an entire project from start to finish).

8. *The display.* Your display is your way of communicating to others what you did and what you learned. It's important that you use the space you're given wisely to represent your project in the best way possible. Chapter 8 provides ideas for designing a project display that will not only catch the eye of observers but hold their attention.

9. *Presentation and evaluation.* Although your presentation and evaluation come at the end of the process, you should be thinking about them throughout the development of the project. It is important to consider how you will be evaluated so that your project entry meets the necessary criteria. Chapter 9 helps prepare you to be judged and gives hints of what to expect at the fair. Your teacher can provide more specific information.

Part II provides A+ project ideas for 35 science fair topics. An A+ idea is not a guarantee that you will receive an A+ grade on your project. Your grade will depend on you. You must do your part by designing your project, investigating, and collecting and organizing the data to the best of your ability. The point is not to copy the projects in this book but to use them as exploratory experiments and as models in developing your own project. The objective of a science fair project is for you to make your own discoveries. Whether or not you win a ribbon at the fair, all science fair participants who do their best earn the prize of being first-place scientists. This is your opportunity to be a winner! Let's get started!

I

A GUIDE TO SCIENCE FAIR PROJECTS

1

The Scientific Method

A science fair project requires the use of a set of steps called the scientific method to discover the answer to a scientific problem. This chapter uses examples to illustrate and explain the basic steps of the scientific method. Chapters 2 through 4 give more details about these steps, and Chapter 5 uses the scientific method in an overview of a sample project.

The steps needed in developing a science fair project are, in this order: doing topic and project research, identifying the project problem, stating a hypothesis, conducting project experimentation, and reaching a conclusion. It is important to note that scientists don't always follow these exact steps or do them in this order. However, scientists do follow some type of step-by-step method, using some or all of the steps.

RESEARCH

Research is the process of collecting information about a subject. It is also the facts collected, which include information from personal experiences; information from knowledgeable sources, including printed works and interviews with professionals; and observational information from exploratory experiments. Your preliminary research, called topic research, is used to select a project topic. For example, you observe that grass growing around a brick is green, but when you move the brick, the grass under it is yellow. This makes you wonder why the grass changed color. Your topic will be about what makes grass change color. You may choose botany as your overall topic, since this is the study of plants.

Once the topic is selected, you begin what is called project research. This research will help you understand the topic, express a problem, propose a hypothesis, and design a project experiment. From your research into the loss of coloring in grass, you discover that grass is green because of the presence of a green **pigment** (coloring substance) called **chlorophyll.** You also discover that light affects the produc-

tion of chlorophyll, and the loss of the green color in plants due to the loss of chlorophyll is called **chlorosis.**

Another type of research is an exploratory experiment. Examples of such experiments are given in Part II of this book. Exploratory experiments are not to be confused with the project experiment. Instead they provide information about your topic that helps you to identify the project problem and may give you ideas for your science fair project experiment. An example of an exploratory experiment for the grass color topic would be to place an object on top of a section of grass and observe the color of the grass under the object over a period of time. The results of other project research and this exploratory experiment give you the needed information for the next step—identifying a project problem.

Research Hints

Do use many references from printed sources with current dates like books, journals, magazines, and newspapers, as well as electronic sources such as computer software and on-line sources.

Do gather information from professionals—instructors, librarians, and scientists, such as researchers, physicians, nurses, and veterinarians.

Do perform exploratory experiments, such as those in the 35 science project ideas in Part II.

PROJECT PROBLEM

A project problem is the scientific question for a science project that will be solved. This question is the foundation of your whole project, so it's very important to be specific about what you will be investigating. It must identify the independent and dependent variables. **Variables** are the changing **factors** (conditions contributing to the results of an experiment) in an experiment. The **independent variable** is the factor in an experiment that you purposely manipulate (change). The **dependent variable** is the factor being observed in an experiment that changes in response to the independent variable. Always make sure there is only one independent variable, so you'll know what causes any change you observe in the one dependent variable. There is no right or wrong way of expressing the project problem, but an "open-ended" question, which is answered with a statement, not just a yes or a no, can increase the complexity of the project experiment required to answer it. This makes the project more acceptable for entry in the senior division of a science fair. For example, an open-ended problem for your grass color project might be "What effect does the absence of sunlight have on chlorosis of lawn grass?"

Problem Hints

Do limit your problem. Note that the previous question has one independent variable—light—and one dependent variable—chlorosis. To find the answer to a question such as "How does the absence of light affect the chlorosis of grass?" would require that you test different kinds of light and an extensive variety of grasses. Identifying the type of light and the kind of grass further limits the topic, making it easier to find the answer to the problem. You might even add the name of a specific grass used, such as St. Augustine grass.

Do choose a problem that can be solved experimentally with measurable results. For example, the question "What is the cause of chlorosis?" is a question that can be answered by finding the word *chlorosis* in the dictionary. But "What effect does the absence of sunlight have on the chlorosis of lawn grass?" is a question that can be answered by experimentation. The degree of chlorosis can be measured.

HYPOTHESIS

A hypothesis is a prediction of the solution to a problem, based on knowledge and research. All of your project research is done with the goal of expressing a problem, proposing an answer to it (the hypothesis), and designing a project experiment to test the hypothesis. The hypothesis should make a claim about how the independent and dependent variables relate.

There are two types of science fair hypotheses: a research hypothesis and a null hypothesis. A **research hypothesis** is the expected result of an experiment. It is a specific and testable prediction, and must contain the independent and dependent variables. It can be a declarative statement or an "If . . . then . . ." type of statement. Here are two examples of a research hypothesis for the sample project question:

"Chlorosis of lawn grass increases as the time without sunlight increases. This is based on the fact that green grass turns yellow if covered by an opaque object for a time."

OR

"If lawn grass does not receive sunlight, then the degree of chlorosis increases with time. This is based on the fact that green grass turns yellow if covered by an opaque object for a time."

A **null hypothesis** is a statement of no predicted change as to the outcome of an experiment. It is often the opposite of what you believe. Your goal is to experimentally reject or fail to reject the null hypothesis. Here is an example of a null hypothesis for the sample project question:

"The absence of sunlight does not affect chlorosis of lawn grass."

Hypothesis Hints

Do state facts from research, including past experiences or observations on which you based your research hypothesis.

Do write down your hypothesis before beginning the project experimentation.

Don't change your hypothesis even if experimentation does not support it. If time permits, repeat or redesign the experiment to confirm your results.

PROJECT EXPERIMENTATION

A project experiment is an experiment designed to test a hypothesis. For example, you want to test the effect of the absence of sunlight on chlorosis. The independent variable for the experiment is absence of light and the dependent variable is the color of the grass (which indicates the amount of chlorosis). *Note:* the dependent variable needs to be measureable. The factors that are not changing are called **constant factors** or **constants.** The constants should include the type of grass, the time of year, the time of day, atmospheric conditions, and so on. It's important to think of all the possible constants when setting up your experiment to be sure they won't change. A possible experiment to compare the effect of the absence of sunlight over a period of time on the chlorosis of lawn grass would be to cover 10 areas of grass with an **opaque** (light cannot pass through) material, such as opaque plastic cups. Secure the cups by partially pushing them into the ground. Remove one cup every 24 hours and observe the grass that was covered by the cup as well as the uncovered grass around the cup. Take a photograph of the grass that the cup covered. Take a photograph of the grass not covered by the cup for comparison. Repeat this procedure until all 10 cups have been removed. The photographs can be compared to determine the degree of chlorosis with a measured amount of absence of sunlight.

A **control** is a standard for comparison. In a control, all constant factors are identical to the experimental setup (cups placed over grass). Only the independent variable is changed from that of the experimental setup. In the experiment, the independent variable is the absence of light, so a control with full light is needed to determine if in fact it is the absence of light that causes chlorosis. Ten **transparent** (light passes through) cups could be used to allow light to reach the grass. Like the opaque cups in the experiment, the transparent cups would cover the grass, and every 24 hours one of the control cups would be lifted and the grass photographed.

Note that in some experiments, a control is not a separate experimental setup. Instead it can be the independent variable selected as the basis for comparison. For example, if the problem is "How does the angle of the Sun's rays at noon affect seasonal temperature?" the experiment would be to determine air temperature and Sun angle at noon during different seasons. Using the data, the control can arbitrarily be determined to be the Sun at its midpoint angle. Then the temperature for Sun angles greater than or less than the control angle can be compared to the temperature of the control angle.

Project experiments include **observations** (information about events or things). The two types of observations are quantitative and qualitative. A **quantitative observation** is a description of the amount of something. Numbers are used in a quantitative description. Instruments such as a scale, a ruler, or a timer are used to make quantitive descriptions. This means that the amount of the property being observed, such as mass, height, or time is described.

Metric measurements are generally the preferred units of measurement for science fair projects, for example, the quantitative observation of length in meters, mass in grams, volume in milliliters, and temperature in Celsius.

A **qualitative observation** is a description of the physical properties of something, including how it looks, sounds, feels, smells, and/or tastes. Adjectives are used in a qualitative description. The qualitative description of grass might relate to its color and include words such as green, yellow, and pale.

Experimentation Hints

When designing your project experiment, remember:

Do include a way of measuring the results. For example, to measure the amount of chlorosis, you can create a color scale from 1 to 10 that measures the degree of color change the grass undergoes. Be sure to specify what 1 to 10 represent, as in: where 1 equals dark green and 10 equals white.

Do use only one independent variable during the experiment.

Do collect more than one set of data to verify your results. Note that for the sample experiment, four or more setups could be started at the same time. This allows the constant factors to be the same for each experiment.

Do have a control.

Do repeat the control along with the rest of the experiment.

Do carefully record and organize the data from your experiment. (See Chapter 6, "Experimental Data," for information on organizing data from an experiment.)

Do have adult supervision for safety assurances.

PROJECT CONCLUSION

The **project conclusion** is a summary of the results of the project experiment and a statement of how the results relate to the hypothesis. If applicable, you should include reasons for experimental results that are contrary to the hypothesis. The conclusion can end with ideas for further testing. *If your results do not* *support your hypothesis, you still have accomplished a successful science fair project. Remember that an experiment is done to test the hypothesis. Your experimental results will either support or not support your hypothesis. So:*

Don't change your hypothesis.

Don't leave out experimental results that do not support your hypothesis.

Do give possible reasons for the difference between your hypothesis and the experimental results.

Do make note of ways that you might experiment further to confirm the results of your original experiment. These ideas can be recorded as ideas for future experimenting.

If your results do not support your hypothesis, you might say:

"As stated in the hypothesis, if lawn grass does not receive sunlight, then the degree of chlorosis increases with time. The experimental results did not clearly support the idea that without sunlight, chlorosis increases with time. While there was some chlorosis under the opaque cups, there was no clear-cut evidence of an increase in chlorosis with time. These results may have been due to the cups that I considered to be opaque. In an effort to control constants, the same transparent cups were used, but for the opaque cups, a paper lining was used. For further testing, I would use a different type of paper lining or a cup made of opaque material."

If your results do support your hypothesis you might say:

"As stated in the hypothesis, if lawn grass does not receive sunlight, then the degree of chlorosis increases with time. The data obtained from experimentation support the idea that the absence of sunlight causes an increase in chlorosis. The grass covered for the longest period of time by the opaque cups had the greatest amount of chlorosis and the grass covered by the transparent cup in the control had no chlorosis. For further testing, I would select light as the independent variable and test the effect of different types of light, such as sunlight, fluorescent light, and incandescent light, on chlorosis."

2

Topic Research

Now that you have the basic tools for doing a science fair project—the systematic steps of the scientific method—you are ready to learn about the specifics of developing a science fair project.

PROJECT JOURNAL

Your project journal is a written record of the progress of your science fair project. The type of book to use for your journal is your choice. It can be a bound book or a loose-leaf binder with tabbed dividers and some pocket pages. Every journal entry should be as neat as possible and dated. A neat, orderly journal provides a complete and accurate record of your project from start to finish for judges, and it can be used to write your project report. It is also proof of the time you spent searching out the answers to the problem you undertook to solve.

You will want a special section in the journal for handouts provided by your teacher, including the science fair's rules and regulations as well as the timetable that lists when different parts of the project are due. The journal should contain notes on your topic and project research, not only your original ideas but also ideas you get from printed sources or from people. It should also include descriptions of your exploratory and project experiments as well as diagrams, graphs, and written observations of all your results. If it is allowed at your science fair, display the journal with your completed project.

SELECTING A TOPIC

Obviously you want to get an A+ on your project, win awards at the science fair, and learn many new things about science. Some or all of these goals are possible, but you will have to spend a lot of time working on your project, so choose a topic that interests you. It is best to pick a topic and stick with it, but if you find

after some work that your topic is not as interesting as you originally thought, stop and select another one. Since it takes time to develop a good project, however, it is unwise to repeatedly jump from one topic to another. You may, in fact, decide to stick with your original idea even if it is not as exciting as you had expected. You might just uncover some very interesting facts that you didn't know.

Remember that the main objective of a science project is to learn more about science. Your project doesn't have to be highly complex to be successful. Excellent projects can be developed that answer very basic and fundamental questions about events or situations encountered on a daily basis that relate to science. There are many easy ways of selecting a topic. The following are just a few of them.

Ask Questions about the World around You

You can turn everyday experiences into a project topic by asking **inquiry questions** (introductory problems for investigation about a topic). For example, you may have seen a potted plant sitting near a window looking healthy in the morning, but the same plant looking wilted in the afternoon. If you express this as an inquiry question—"What causes the stems of a plant to be stiff?"—you have a good question about plants. But could this be a project topic? Think about it! What is it in the plant that makes it stiff? Did the Sun have any effect on the plant's stiffness? By continuing to ask inquiry questions, you zero in on the topic of water movement through plants via **xylem tubes** (plant structures that transport water from the roots to other plant parts) as well as the cause of **turgor pressure** (internal pressure of plant cells due to the presence of water) in plants.

Keep your eyes and ears open, and start asking yourself more inquiry questions, such as "Do certain types of dyes fade faster than others?" "Could I test the fading of different kinds of dye on small pieces of cloth?" To know more about these things, you can research and design a whole science fair project about the topic of the durability of different kinds of dye. You will be pleasantly surprised at the number of possible project ideas that will come to mind when you begin to look around and use inquiry questions.

You and those around you each day make an amazing number of statements and ask many questions that could be used to develop science project topics. Be alert and listen for a statement like "She's a clone of her mother." This statement can become an inquiry question, such as "Why do children look like their parents?" or "Why do some children look more like their grandparents than their parents?" These questions could lead you to develop a project about heredity.

Choose a Topic from Your Experience

You may think that you don't have much experience with science topics, but remember that this doesn't have to be rocket science! For example, you have experienced foods changing temperature. You may remember that while you were eating a bowl of ice cream some of the ice cream melted and the melted ice cream tasted sweeter than the still-frozen ice cream. Ask yourself, "Was this because the melted ice cream was warmer?" With research information about receptor cells for taste, you could design a project to determine the effects of temperature on taste. The project problem might be, "How does temperature affect taste?" Propose your hypothesis and start designing your project experiment. For more on developing a project, see Chapter 5, "Project Overview."

Find a Topic in Science Magazines

You can often get ideas for topics in science magazines, but don't expect magazines to include detailed instructions on how to perform experiments and design displays. What you can look for are facts that interest you and that lead you to ask inquiry questions. An article about the Barringer Meteor Crater near Winslow, Arizona, might bring to mind these inquiry questions: "Why don't all meteors cause craters?" "Are Earth's meteor craters like those on the Moon?" Wow! Impact craters is another great project topic you might discover in a science magazine.

Select a Topic from a Book on Science Fair Projects or Science Experiments

Science fair project books, such as this one, can provide you with many different topics to choose from as well as some inquiry questions that can lead to an interesting project. Even though science experiment books do not give you as much direction as science fair project books, many can provide you with exploratory "cookbook" experiments that tell you what to do, what the results should be, and why. But whether you use a science fair project book or a science experiment book, it will be up to you to pick a topic and develop it into a science fair project. The 35 project ideas described in this book can further sharpen your skills at expressing inquiry questions. A list of different project and experiment books can be found in Appendix 8.

SPECIAL TOPICS

Before beginning your project experiment, discuss your plans with your teacher. He or she will be familiar with the regulations that govern potentially dangerous experiments. These may include chemical and equipment usage, experimental techniques, experiments involving live animals, cell cultures, microorganisms, or animal tissues. For some experiments, an adult sponsor trained in the area of your topic will be required to supervise your project. Your safety, as well as the safety of any other people or animals, is the most important thing. In addition, if you have not adhered to the rules of the fair, you may not be allowed to enter your completed work. Before you begin you should have your project topic approved by your teacher. This prevents you from working on an unsafe project and from wasting time on a project that would be disqualified.

3

Categories

Every science fair has a list of categories, and you need to seek your teacher's advice when deciding which category you should enter your project in. Since science fair judges are required to judge the content of each project based on the category in which it is entered, you would be seriously penalized if you were to enter your project in the wrong category. The list provided here includes the science fair categories represented by the project ideas in Part II with a brief description of each category. Other possible categories not included in Part II include **medicine and health** (study of diseases and health of humans and animals), **engineering** (application of scientific knowledge for practical purposes), **mathematics** (development and application of formal logical systems of computations), and **computer science** (study and development of all aspects of computers, including hardware and software). Ask your teacher for a more comprehensive list of categories and descriptions for the science fair you are entering.

Some topics can correctly be placed in more than one category; for example, the study of soil texture could be in geology or agricultural chemistry. Since you are competing against others, it is to your advantage to select a category that might have fewer competitors. Each of the 35 project ideas in Part II is labeled with the category in which the project could be entered. The categories are

- **Astronomy.** The science dealing with all the celestial bodies in the universe, including the planets and their satellites, comets and meteors, the stars and interstellar matter, the star systems known as galaxies, and clusters of galaxies.

  1. **Astrometry.** The observational study concerned with the measurement of the position of celestial bodies.

  2. **Astronautics.** The science and technology of space exploration.

  3. **Astrophysics.** The study concerned particularly with the production and expenditure of radiation in systems such as stars and galaxies and in the universe as a whole.

  4. **Celestial mechanics.** The study of the motion of **celestial bodies** (the natural objects in the sky, such as stars, moons, suns, and planets) due to gravity.

  5. **Heliology.** The study of the Sun.

  6. **Planetary satellite science.** The study of moons, the natural satellites of planets. **Lunar** refers to Earth's moon.

  7. **Meteoritics.** The study of meteors.

  8. **Planetology.** The study of the planets of the solar system and especially of how they differ.

- **Biology.** The study of organisms and their life processes.

  1. **Botany.** The study of plants and plant life. Subtopics may include the following:

     a. **Anatomy.** A branch of botany dealing with the structural organization of plants, such as cells and seeds, and the functions of their parts.

     b. **Morphology.** The study of plant forms, development, and life histories. Plant developmental morphology is the study of plant growth and development.

     c. **Physiology.** The study of the physical and chemical processes that take place in living organisms during the performance of life functions, such as photosynthesis and respiration.

  2. **Zoology.** The study of animals and animal life including their structure and growth. Subtopics may include the following:

     a. **Anatomy.** The study of the structure of animals and the function of their body parts.

b. Behaviorism. The study of actions that alter the relationship between an animal and its environment.

3. Ecology. The study of the relationships of living things to other living things and to their environment.

4. Microbiology. The study of **microbes** (microscopic living things) or parts of living things.

- **Chemistry.** The study of the composition, structure, properties, and interactions of matter. Subtopics may include the following:

  1. Agricultural chemistry. The science that deals with farming concerns, such as the makeup of soil, the application of fertilizer and insecticides, the analysis of agricultural products, and the nutritional needs of farm animals.

  2. Analytical chemistry. The science of determining the qualitative and/or quantitative amounts of the chemical components of a substance.

  3. Biochemistry. The study of the substances found in living organisms, and of the chemical reactions involved in life processes.

  4. Inorganic chemistry. The study of the structure, properties, and reactions of the chemical elements and their compounds (except for hydrocarbons).

  5. Organic chemistry. The study of hydrocarbons (compounds composed of carbon and hydrogen) and their reactions.

  6. Physical chemistry. The study of the physical properties of substances, such as viscosity and molecular structure.

- **Earth science.** The study of the Earth, from the outermost limits of its atmosphere to the innermost depths of its interior.

  1. Physical geology. The study of the nature of Earth in its present state. Subtopics may include the following:

  a. Hydrology. The science concerned with the quality and distribution of water on Earth.

  b. Mineralogy. The study of the composition and formation of minerals.

  c. Petrology. The study of the composition and formation of rocks.

  d. Soil science. The study of **soil,** the part of the **regolith** (all the loose rock particles that cover the Earth) that can support rooted plants.

  e. Topography. The study of the layout of natural and artificial features on the surface of the Earth.

  2. Meteorology. The study of Earth's atmosphere and especially of Earth's weather.

  3. Oceanography. The study of oceans and marine organisms. (The study of marine organisms is generally called marine biology.)

- **Physics.** The study of forms of energy and the laws of motion.

  1. Acoustics. The study of sound.

  2. Electrodynamics. The study of electric and magnetic force fields; the behavior of electrically charged particles in electromagnetic fields; and the propagation of electromagnetic waves.

  3. Elementary particle physics. The study of properties of elementary particles (smallest parts of matter) such as electrons in static electricity.

  4. Fluid dynamics. The study of the properties and behavior of moving fluids.

  5. Mechanics. The study of the forces, interactions, and motions of material.

  6. Optics. The study of light.

  7. Thermodynamics. The study of temperature and energy; heat flow; the transformation of energy; and phases of matter.

4

Project Research

Once you have completed the topic research and selected a topic, you are ready to begin your project research. This research is generally more thorough than topic research. Project research is the process of collecting information from knowledgeable sources, such as books, magazines, software, librarians, teachers, parents, scientists, or other professionals. It also includes data collected from exploratory experimentation. Read widely on the topic you selected so that you understand it and know about the findings of others who have researched the topic. Be sure to give credit where credit is due and record all information and data in your journal.

How successful you are with your project will depend largely on how well you understand your topic. The more you read about your topic and question people who know something about it, the broader your understanding will be. As a result, it will be easier for you to explain your project to other people, especially a science fair judge.

There are two basic kinds of research, primary and secondary.

PRIMARY RESEARCH

Primary research is information you collect on your own. This includes information from exploratory experiments you perform, surveys you take, interviews you conduct, and responses to your letters to professionals, specialists, and the like.

One way to obtain information about your topic is to interview people who have special knowledge. These can include teachers, doctors, scientists, or others whose careers require them to know something related to your topic. Let's say your topic is about petrified wood. Who would know about petrification? Start with your science teacher. He or she may have a special interest in fossils or know someone who does. Is there a museum nearby with an exhibit of petrified wood? Is there a web site that provides information about how to contact a scientist knowledgeable about

petrification? Owners of rock and mineral shops may have an interest in fossils and could provide information. You could also try the geology department of a local university. Once you start thinking about your topic, you will discover many people who will serve as valuable resources.

Before contacting the people you want to interview, be prepared. Make a list of questions you want to ask. Try discussing what you know about your topic with someone who knows nothing about it. This can force you to organize your thinking, and you may even discover additional questions to add to your list. Once your list is complete, you are ready to make your call. Simple rules of courtesy, such as the following, will better ensure that the person called will want to help.

1. Identify yourself.

2. Identify the school you attend and your teacher.

3. Briefly explain why you are calling. Include information about your project and explain how the person can help you.

4. Request an interview time that is convenient for the person. This interview could be by telephone, face-to-face, or by e-mail. Be sure to say that the interview will take about 20 or 30 minutes. It may be that the person is free when you call, so be prepared to start the interview.

5. Ask if you may tape-record the interview. You can get more information if you are not trying to write down all the answers.

6. Be on time and be ready to start the interview immediately. Also, be courteous and end the interview on time.

7. If the interview is via e-mail, make sure your questions are understandable and grammatically correct. You might ask someone to edit your e-mail before you send it.

8. At the conclusion of the interview, thank the person for his or her time and for the information he or she provided.

9. Even if you send an e-mail thank you, you may wish to also send a written thank-you note as soon as possible after the interview, so be sure to record the person's name and address.

You may write letters requesting information instead of interviewing, or write letters in addition to interviewing. Check the end of articles in periodicals for lists of names and addresses where you can obtain more information. Your librarian can help you find current periodicals related to your topic. If your project deals with a household product, check the packaging for the address of the manufacturer. Send your letter to the public relations department. Ask for all available printed material about your topic. Send your letter as soon as possible to allow time for material to be sent to you. You can use a form letter similar to the one shown here to make it easier to send your questions to as many different relevant people and organizations as you can find.

Kimberly Bolden
123 Lovers Lane
Travis, TX 00000

June 23, 2003

Rust-Away
223 Iron Street
Metal, NM 11111

Dear Director:

I am a ninth-grade student currently working on a science fair project for the Jenny Lynn High School Science Fair. My project is about conditions affecting the rusting of metals. I would greatly appreciate any information you could send me on the antirusting properties of your product. Please send the information as soon as possible.

Thank you very much.

Sincerely,

Kimberly Bolden

SECONDARY RESEARCH

Secondary research is information and/or data that someone else has collected. You find this type of information in written sources (books, magazines, and newspapers) and in electronic sources (CD-ROM encyclopedias, software packages, or on-line). When you use a secondary source, be sure to note where you got the information for future reference. If you are required to write a report, you will need the following information for a bibliography or to give credit for any quotes or illustrations you use.

Book
Author's name, title of book, place of publication, publisher, copyright date, and pages read or quoted.

Magazine or Periodical
Author's name; title of article; title of magazine; volume, issue number, and date of publication; and page numbers of article.

Newspaper
Author's name, title of article, name of newspaper, date of publication, and section and page numbers.

Encyclopedia
Name of encyclopedia, volume number, title of article, place of publication, publisher, year of publication, and page numbers of article.

CD-ROM Encyclopedia or Software Package
Name of program, version or release number, name of supplier, and place where supplier is located.

On-line Document
Author of document (if known), title of document, name of organization that posted document, place where organization is located, date given on document, and on-line address or mailing address where document is available.

USE YOUR RESEARCH

Now you are ready to use the project research information to express the problem, propose a hypothesis, and design and perform one or more project experiments. The project research will also be useful in writing the project report. The following chapters, 5 through 9, guide you step-by-step through a sample project from start to finish. You may want to read these chapters more than once and refer back to them as you progress through your project.

Project Overview

Before you start your project, acknowledge that you are preparing an entry for a contest that has rules. One preliminary rule is that your science fair project must represent the work that you do this year. This means that if your project is a continuation of a previous year's project, you must test the variable in a new way or test a new variable.

There are other science fair project rules that must be followed. Your teacher is the source for a list of all of the rules for your fair.

A science fair project is an investigation that uses the scientific method as a tool to discover the answer to some scientific problem. The following information contains a basic outline for using the scientific method in developing a science fair project. While the sample project in this overview is about the Moon, the procedure can be used to assist you in designing a project about any topic. See Chapter 1, "The Scientific Method," for more information about the scientific method.

RESEARCH

"Tinkering" research, when you don't know what topic to choose, is the first type of research to be done. Begin by reading different science publications, asking questions of knowledgeable people, and checking out information on the Web. You can also perform exploratory experiments about topics that interest you, such as those listed in Part II of this book. From your research, decide on a topic that you want to discover more information about. (See Chapter 2, for more information about topic research.) For our sample, we'll pick the Moon as our project topic.

Project research, when you have a topic but aren't yet sure what kind of problem you can solve, is the next kind of research to be done. If your topic is the Moon, you would find out as much as possible about this celestial body such as its rates of **rotation** (turning of a body about its **axis**—imaginary line through the center of a body) and **revolution** (one turn of a body about its **orbit**—a curved path about another body). Search astronomy books, periodicals, and the Web for information. As you research, write down inquiry questions, such as these:

- How do lunar rotation and revolution rates compare? (Lunar is a term that pertains to the Moon.)
- How does Earth's rotation affect lunar motion?

When you're finished writing down questions, select one that most interests you and proceed to the next step.

PROJECT PROBLEM

When you have selected an inquiry question that most interests you, determine whether it can be your science fair problem by asking yourself these questions:

- Is it about animals? If the answer is yes, you will need to check with your teacher about the rules for working with animals.

- Does it compare products? If the answer is yes, check with your teacher to make sure product comparison is an acceptable project. While some local fairs have a special section for product comparisons, others may not allow them.

- Can you state a hypothesis for the question? If the answer is no, then reword the question or select another one.

- Can the question be answered experimentally with measurable results?

How does the sample inquiry question rate as a project problem?

1. "How do lunar rotation and revolution rates compare?" can be determined by reading, but you also could experiment and confirm this for yourself.

2. "How does Earth's rotation affect the motion of the Moon?" can also be determined by reading. If you reword the question as "How does Earth's rotation affect the position of lunar surface features during its apparent daily motion?" you have a question whose answer you could discover for yourself experimentally. This could be done by observing

and measuring any angular change in the position of the points of a crescent-shaped moon each day as it moves from the eastern to the western horizon.

HYPOTHESIS

While the hypothesis is a single statement, it is the key to a successful project. The project experiment will be designed to test the hypothesis, so be sure to propose a hypothesis that is testable with measurable results. For the sample project problem on the effect of Earth's rotation on the position of lunar surface features during the Moon's apparent motion across the sky, an example of a null hypothesis might be, "Earth's rotation has no effect on the position of lunar surface features."

A research hypothesis might be, "If Earth rotates toward the east, then there will be an apparent clockwise rotation of the position of lunar features each day." This is based on the fact that since Earth rotates, the Moon is viewed by observers on Earth from a different direction during the rotation. (See Chapter 1, "The Scientific Method," for more information about research and null hypotheses.)

PROJECT EXPERIMENT

Can you think of a way to test your hypothesis experimentally with measurable results? If the answer is no, then you need to go back to the previous step and reword your hypothesis or select another one.

At this stage the project experiment needs to be only a basic design in your mind. A possible experiment for the sample Moon problem might be to observe and photograph a crescent Moon at different times to determine whether there is any rotational change in the lunar features during the Moon's apparent movement from the eastern to the western horizon. This can be done by comparing photographs and the position of the pointed ends of the crescent moon at different times. The control will be the position of the Moon when it is at its **zenith** (highest point) in the sky. Compare the position of the pointed ends of the crescent moons in the photographs taken during an observation time of eight or more hours between moonrise and moonset to determine if any rotational change has occurred. Think about the experiment and ask yourself the following questions. If the answer to any of these questions is no, you need to redesign the experiment.

- Does the experiment have measurable results (results that can be measured with an instrument such as a ruler, scale, stopwatch, or other type of scale, such as angular measurements using your hands as the measuring tool)? For the sample experiment, you could take angular measurements of the position of the crescent points to a line perpendicular to Earth in order to determine whether it appears to rotate each day.

- Does the experiment have an independent variable? For the sample experiment, the length of time of observations is the independent variable.

- Does the experiment have a dependent variable? For the sample experiment, the dependent variable is the angle of the crescent moon.

- Does the experiment have a control? For the sample experiment, the control could be the angle of the crescent moon at its zenith position. The observations recorded before and after this position could be compared to this.

- Does the experiment have constant factors? For the sample experiment, the constant factors include the location of the observer and the type of measuring tool used to make the angular measurements. (See Chapter 1 for more information about variables.)

GET STARTED!

Once you have a general plan for testing your hypothesis experimentally and recording the data, then you can design the experiment step-by-step and get started. You should be prepared to perform the experiment four or more times, so that you have at least four sets of data. In the sample Moon experiment, you could make observations on four consecutive nights or select four nonsequential nights during a month. For some experiments in which time is a factor, such as one requiring the growth of plants, four or more identical sets of plants and the control could be started at the same time. For all experiments, you should record all the results in your project journal, dating and, if applicable, recording the time of each entry.

DATA

Data from your experiment and what you do with it are the main ways that a judge evaluates your experiment. Judges like to see **charts** (data or other information in the form of tables, graphs, or lists) of the measured results. If data are displayed clearly, then judges are likely to conclude that the student understands how to properly develop a science fair project. (For more information about data, see Chapter 6, "Experimental Data.")

6

Experimental Data

Data for a science fair project are the quantitative (numerical measurements) observations as well as qualitative (physical characteristics) observations that you obtain experimentally. The information you collect in your project journal is called **raw data.** That simply means data you record during the study. You want your journal to be organized and neat, but you should not recopy the raw data for your journal. Do not be concerned about any stains that might get on the paper while collecting raw data. A clean copy of the raw data can be prepared for your display. As long as you don't change the data, you may represent the information in a different way on your display (such as organized in tables or graphs) so that it is more easily understandable to an observer. (See Chapter 8 for information about the project display.)

TABLE

Data is generally recorded in a table. In a **table** data is organized into words and numbers in columns and rows. If you picture the table as a grid, the spaces between the vertical lines are called **columns** and the spaces between the horizontal lines are called **rows.** There is no uniform way of designing a table, but all tables should have a title and rows and columns that are labeled. If your table shows measurements, the units of measurement, such as minutes or centimeters, should be part of the column's or row's label. The title generally describes the dependent variable

of the experiment, such as "Ants' Attraction to Food," in an experiment where different foods (independent variable) are used and the number of ants attracted to each food is counted (dependent variable). But the title could express what is being compared, in other words the independent variable versus the dependent variable, "Food Types vs. Attraction of Ants." Your table can also include qualitative notations and drawings to illustrate the data.

Table 6.1, an ant data table, shows the data from an experiment in which the number of ants attracted to foods of different sweetness was examined. In the experiment, four circles of equal diameter were drawn at the same distance from the opening of an anthill and 90° from one another. Three food samples of varying sweetness—very sweet, medium sweet, and unsweetened—were placed in three of the circles. The fourth circle, the control, remained empty. After a period of 5 minutes, the number of ants in each circle was counted and recorded in Table 6.1. The experiment was repeated three times on days with as close to the same constant factors as possible, such as the time of day, temperature, atmospheric conditions (sunny or cloudy), humidity, and so on. In this table the independent variable is the type of food and the dependent variable is the number of ants.

Table 6.2 shows data from a different study in which the problem was to determine if ants communicate by laying a scent trail for other ants to follow. This was done by studying four different anthills. For each anthill, 32 identical pieces of food were placed, eight pieces in each direction—north, south, east, and west—but at equal distances from the anthill opening. A circle of similar diameter was drawn around each food sample. The paths between the food circles and the anthills were called "A," "B," "C," and "D." After 15 minutes, the number of ants found in each circle was counted and part of the ground between the food circles and the anthill on paths A, B, and C were cleaned by rubbing them with a stick. The width of the rubbed section for each path was: A = ½ cm, B = 2 cm, C = 4 cm. The

TABLE 6.1 ANTS' ATTRACTION TO FOODS DATA					
Type of Food	Number of Ants on Food				
	Test 1	Test 2	Test 3	Test 4	Average
Candy	8	7	9	9	8.25
Fruit	7	7	6	9	7.25
Chips	7	6	7	5	6.25
Control (no food)	3	2	4	4	3.25

control path, D, was not rubbed. This procedure was done every 15 minutes for a total of 60 minutes. Note that the unit of time, minutes, is part of the column labeled "Time." The independent variable is the width of the rubbed path and the dependent variable is the number of ants in the food circles. The data for hill number 1 shows the number of ants for paths B and C are about the same and are less than those on paths A and D. It might be concluded that small-width rubbing across path A has little to no affect, thus the total number of ants are about the same as path D, which has no rubbing. A final conclusion would be made by averaging the data from each of the four anthills.

TABLE 6.2 ANT COMMUNICATION DATA—HILL #1

Time, minutes	Number of Ants in Food Circle			
	Path A	Path B	Path C	Path D
0	0	0	0	0
15	9	9	10	8
30	15	8	9	16
45	21	9	7	22
60	32	10	9	33
Total	77	36	35	79

ANALYZING AND INTERPRETING DATA

When you have finished collecting the data from your experiment, the next step is to **analyze** (critically examine) and **interpret** (restate) the data. Interpreting the data involves reorganizing it into a more easily understood form, such as by graphing it. A **graph** is a diagram used to compare independent and dependent variables. Graphs give a quick visual comparison of data. All graphs should have:

1. A title for the graph.

2. Titles for the x-axis (horizontal) and y-axis (vertical).

3. Scales with numbers that have the same interval between each division.

4. Labels for categories being counted. Scales often start at zero, but they don't have to.

The three most common graphs used in science fair projects are the bar graph, the line graph, and the circle graph.

In a **bar graph,** solid bars are used to show the relationship between two variables. Bar graphs can have vertical or horizontal bars. The width and separation of each bar should be the same on the graph. The length of a bar represents a specific number such as 8.25 ants. The width of a bar is not significant and can depend on available space due to number of bars needed. A bar graph has one scale, which can be on the horizontal or vertical axis. This type of graph is most often used when the independent variable is qualitative, such as food types in the ant data in Table 6.1. The independent variable for the Ants' Attraction to Food Data table is food type—candy, fruit, chips, no food (control)—and the dependent variable for this data is the number of ants on each food. A bar graph using the data from Table 6.1 is shown in Figure 6.1. Since the average number of ants from the data varies from 3.25 to 8.25, a scale of 0 to 10 can be used with each unit of the scale representing 0.25 ants. The heights of the bars in the bar graph show clearly that some ants were found on the area of the ground without food, but the greatest number were present in the area where the sweetest food was.

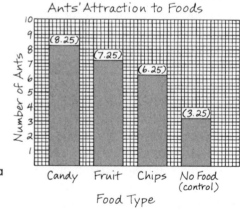

Figure 6.1
Example of a bar graph.

A **line graph** uses a line to compare the relationship between two variables and to show a pattern of change. While a bar graph has one scale, a line graph has two scales. Figure 6.2 shows how the data from Table 6.2 would be arranged on a line graph. Generally the independent variable is on the **x-axis** (horizontal axis) and the dependent variable on the **y-axis** (vertical axis). So for this example, the independent variable of time is on the x-axis and the dependent variable of number of ants in path A's food circle is on the y-axis. One unit on the time scale represents 1 minute and units are marked off in groups of 15 up to a total of 60 units. One unit on the number of ants scale represents 1 ant. Since the largest number counted was 32 ants, the scale for ants is numbered by 5s from 0

Figure 6.2 Example of a line graph.

Path A: Ant Communication Data

Number of Ants (y-axis: 0, 5, 10, 15, 20, 25, 30, 35)

Time (minutes) (x-axis: 15, 30, 45, 60)

(9), (15), (21), (32)

through 35. On the graph, the increase in the slope (incline) of the line over time shows that as time increased more ants were found on the food in path A's food circle.

A **circle graph** (also called a **pie chart**) uses a circle divided into wedge-shaped sections to display data.

To plot your data on a circle graph, you need to calculate the size of each section. An entire circle represents 360°, so each section of a circle graph is a fraction of 360°. For example, data from Table 6.1 was used to prepare the circle graph in Figure 6.3. To determine the size of each section in degrees follow these steps:

Ants' Attraction to Foods

8.25 Ants Candy

119°

7.25 Ants Fruit

104°

3.25 Ants No Food (control)

47°

90°

6.25 Ants Chips

Figure 6.3 Example of a circle graph.

1. Express the ratio of each section as a fraction, with the numerator equal to the average number ants counted on each type of food and the denominator equal to the average total number of ants counted on all the food.

Candy = $^{8.25}/_{25}$, Fruit = $^{7.25}/_{25}$, Chips = $^{6.25}/_{25}$, Control = 3.25/25

2. Multiply the fraction by 360°

Candy	$8.25/25 \times 360° = 119°$
Fruit	$7.25/25 \times 360° = 104°$
Chips	$6.25/25 \times 360° = 90°$
Control	$3.25/25 \times 360° = 47°$

To prepare the circle graph, first decide on the diameter needed, then using a compass, draw the circle. Then draw a straight line from the center of the

circle to any point on the edge of the circle. Using a protractor, start at this line and mark a dot on the edge of the circle 104° from the line. Draw a line to connect this dot to the center of the circle. The pie-shaped section you made represents the number of ants found on the candy. Start the next section on the line for the candy section. Continue until all the sections are represented. Each section should be labeled, as shown in Figure 6.3.

Each section of a circle graph represents part of the whole, which always equals 100%. The larger the section the greater the percentage of the whole.

To determine the percentage for each section, follow these steps:

1. Change the fractional ratio for each section to a decimal by dividing the numerator by the denominator.

Candy	$8.25 \div 25 = .33$
Fruit	$7.25 \div 25 = .29$
Chips	$6.25 \div 25 = .25$
Control	$3.25 \div 25 = .13$

2. Change the decimal answers to percent. *Percent* means "per hundred." For example, for candy, .33 is read 33/100 or 33 per 100, which can be written as 33%.

Candy	$.33 = 33/100 = 33\%$
Fruit	$.29 = 29/100 = 29\%$
Chips	$.25 = 25/100 = 25\%$
Control	$.13 = 13/100 = 13\%$

You could color each section of the circle graph with a different color and make a **legend** (words written on a graph or diagram to explain it) for the chart as in Figure 6.4. The legend can give the number of ants counted and/or the percentage of the total number of ants.

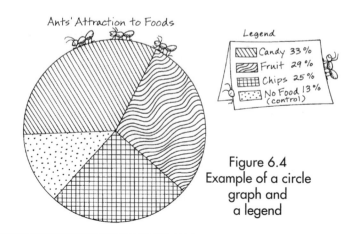

Ants' Attraction to Foods

Legend
Candy 33%
Fruit 29%
Chips 25%
No Food 13% (control)

Figure 6.4 Example of a circle graph and a legend

7

Project Summaries

Most science fairs require that science fair projects include what are called project summaries. The project summaries include the project journal, an abstract, and a project report. (For information about the project journal, see Chapter 2, "Topic Research.") This chapter gives information on, and examples of, a project abstract and a research paper. Before writing your project summaries, check with your teacher about the requirements for your local science fair as well as those for the International Science and Engineering Fair (ISEF).

ABSTRACT

An abstract is a brief overview of the project. It should be no longer than one page and contain a maximum of 250 words. It includes the title "Abstract," the project title, a statement of purpose, a hypothesis, a brief summary of your experiment procedure, data collected from project experiments, and conclusions. The abstract is generally required to be part of the display. (See Chapter 8 for information about the display.) Contact your teacher for other required uses of the abstract. Most fairs require that a copy of your abstract be displayed on the exhibit. This gives judges something to refer to when making final decisions. It might also be used to prepare an introduction by a special award sponsor. The abstract is a very important representation of your project, so be sure to do a thorough job on this part of your project summary.

The **project title** (a descriptive heading), which appears on your abstract, on the title page of your research paper, and prominently on your display backboard, should capture the theme of the project and be intriguing. Its purpose is to attract the attention of an observer and make him or her want to know more. There are no set rules for the length of the title, but it should be short enough to be read at a glance. A rule of thumb for length is about 10 words or less. A good title for the sample project detailed in Chapter 5 is shown in the sample abstract in Figure 7.1.

Abstract
East to West:
Motion of Lunar Surface Features

[No school or student name should appear on the abstract.]

The purpose of this project is to determine if there is an apparent rotation of the Moon's surface features each day as viewed by an observer from any one specific location on Earth. The hypothesis was that from any specific location on Earth, the Moon is observed from different directions during the day due to Earth's rotation, thus there should be an apparent clockwise rotation of the lunar features each day. The project experiment involved recording the position of the concave side of the crescent moon phase in relation to the Earth's surface as the Moon moved from the eastern to the western horizon. This was done by taking pictures of the Moon at different times before and after it passed its zenith. The pictures were compared to determine any change in position.

The position of the concave side of a crescent phase Moon confirmed the hypothesis that the lunar features on the Moon seen from the Earth apparently rotate in a clockwise direction.

Figure 7.1 Abstract.

PROJECT REPORT

Your project report is a written report of your entire project from start to finish. The project report should be clear and detailed enough for a reader who is unfamiliar with your project to know exactly what you did, why you did it, what the results were, whether or not the experimental evidence supported your hypothesis, and where you got your research information. This written document is your spokesperson when you are not present to explain your project, but more than that, it documents all your work.

Because you'll be recording everything in your journal as the project progresses, all you need to do in preparing the project report is to organize and neatly copy desired material from the book's contents.

Check with your teacher for the order and content of the report as regulated by the local fair. The following is generally true. The report should be typewritten, double spaced, and bound in a folder or notebook. It should contain a title page, table of contents, introduction, experiment, discussion, conclusion, acknowledgments, and references. The rest of this chapter describes these parts of a project report and gives examples based on the sample project in Chapter 5.

Title Page: This is the first page of the report. The project title should be centered on the page, and your name, school, and grade should appear in the lower right-hand corner.

Table of Contents: This is the second page of your report. The table of contents should contain a list of everything in the report that follows this page, including a page number for the beginning of each section, as shown in Figure 7.2.

Contents

Figure 7.2 Table of Contents.

Introduction: This section sets the stage for your project report. It is a statement of your purpose, along with some of the background information that led you to make this study and what you hoped to achieve from it. It should contain a brief statement of your hypothesis. If it is a research hypothesis, it should state what information or knowledge led you to your hypothesis. If your teacher requires footnotes, then include one for each information source you have used. The sample introduction shown in Figure 7.3 does not use footnotes.

Introduction

The Moon appears to move from east to west each day. Before starting the project, known facts about the Moon included that its revolution and rotation times result in the same side of the Moon always facing Earth. But neither personal knowledge of the effect of Earth's rotation on the motion of the Moon nor observations of the Moon's lunar features during the day had been made.

After reading about the effect of Earth's rotation on the Moon's motion as well as the appearance of lunar features, it was discovered that the Moon's daily east-to-west motion is an apparent motion. It was also discovered by an observer that the Moon's lunar features as viewed from the Northern Hemisphere are rotated clockwise 180° in the Southern Hemisphere. Questions arose about the effect of the direction of the viewer on the apparent rotation of the lunar features.

Curiosity about the upside-down view of the Moon in the Southern Hemisphere resulted in a project that has as its purpose to determine if there is an apparent rotation of the Moon's surface features each day as viewed by an observer from any one specific location on Earth. Based on previously stated research, the hypothesis was that from any specific location on Earth the Moon is observed from different directions during the day due to Earth's rotation, thus there should be an apparent clockwise rotation of the lunar features each day.

Figure 7.3 Introduction.

Experiment: This part of the report contains information about the project experiment. Describe in detail all methods used to collect your data or make your observations. It should include the project problem followed by a list of the materials used and the amount of each, then the procedural steps in outline or paragraph form as shown in Figure 7.4. Note that the experiment described in Figure 7.4 includes instructions for measuring the angle of the Moon's position using photographs. Include instructions for making self-designed equipment or materials in addition to the rest of the experimental procedure. Include any needed photographs and/or drawings of the equipment. All instructions should be written so that anyone could follow them and be expected to get the same results.

Experiment

Problem

How does the Earth's rotation affect the position of lunar surface features as the Moon moves from the eastern to western horizon?

Materials

camera
fine-point permanent black marker
ruler
protractor

Procedure

1. During the **waning** (getting smaller) crescent moon phase, use the camera to take three or more pictures at one- to two-hour intervals of the Moon during its motion along an **arc** (segment of a circle) across the sky from the eastern horizon to its zenith position. Hold the camera so that it is parallel with the ground while taking each photograph and record the time each photo is taken.
2. Repeat step 1 taking pictures of the Moon from its zenith position to the western hemisphere. *Note:* The picture taken at the Moon's zenith will be considered the control.
3. On each photo, use the marker to mark the time the photo was taken.

4. With the marker and ruler, draw a line across the photo that connects the two points of the Moon. Where this line meets the bottom edge of the photo, draw a second line across the photo perpendicular to the bottom edge of the photo.
5. Label the area to the left of the perpendicular line "East" and the area to the right "West".

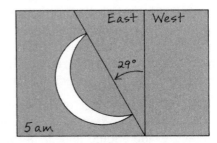

6. Use the protractor to measure the angle between the two lines. Record the measured angle on the photo as well as in a Lunar Feature Angle Data table as shown.
7. Compare the angles of each photo with the control to determine any rotation.
8. Repeat steps 1 through 6 three or more times on consecutive nights or during other Moon phases, such as first and third quarter or **waxing** (growing larger) crescent.

Figure 7.4 Experiment.

Discussion: The discussion of your experimental results is a principal part of your project report. It describes the outcome of your efforts. Include experimental data tables to confirm results, such as Table 7.1. When applicable, determine **random error of measurements** (uncertainty of experimental measurements) and **relative error** (percentage error as compared with a known value). (See Appendix 1 for information about random error of measurement and Appendix 2 for information about relative error.) Include qualitative as well as quantitative results. Never change or omit results because they don't support your hypothesis. Be thorough. You want your readers to see your train of thought, letting them know exactly what you did. Compare your results with published data, commonly held beliefs, and/or expected results. Include a discussion of possible errors. Were your results affected by uncontrolled events? What would you do differently if you repeated this project?

	TABLE 7.1 RESULTS LUNAR FEATURE ANGLE DATA									
	Time									
	5 A.M.	6 A.M.	7 A.M.	8 A.M.	9 A.M.	10 A.M.	11 A.M.	12 P.M.	1 P.M.	2 P.M.
Rotation angle	29°E									

Conclusion: The conclusion is a brief summary, in about one page or less, of what you discovered based on your experimental results, as shown in Figure 7.5. The conclusion states the hypothesis and indicates whether or not the data supports it. If your results are not what you expected, *don't panic.* Assuming that your research led you to your hypothesis, state that while your research backed up your hypothesis, your experimental results did not. Refer to any published data that you based your hypothesis on. Say what you expected and what actually happened. Give reasons why you think the results did not support your original ideas. Include errors you might have made as well as how changing variables other than the independent variable might have affected the results. Discuss any changes you would make to the procedure if you repeated the project and include any ideas for experiments to further investigate the topic of your project. All information in the conclusion should have been reported in other parts of the report so no new material should be introduced in the conclusion.

Acknowledgments: The acknowledgments section is a short paragraph stating the names of people who helped you, with a brief description of their contributions to your project, as shown in Figure 7.6. It should not be just a list of names. Note that when listing relatives, it is generally not necessary to include their names. Identify individuals with their titles, positions, and affiliations (institutions). Note anyone who gave financial support or material donations. Do not reveal monetary amounts of donations.

Conclusion

As stated in my hypothesis, due to the rotation of Earth, there will be an apparent clockwise rotation of the lunar features each day as viewed from any specific location on Earth. The experimental observation over a period of nine hours each day for two days, showed a clockwise rotation of the crescent-shaped Moon, thus a rotation of its lunar features. This data supported my hypothesis and indicated that an observer on Earth sees the moon from a different direction during the day as Earth rotates on its axis.

Figure 7.5 Conclusion.

Acknowledgments

I would like to thank the members of my family who assisted me with this project: my mother, who copy-edited my report, and my father and sister, who assisted in the construction of the display board.

A special note of thanks to Dr. David Russell, professor of astronomy at Calvin University, and to Judith Michael, his assistant, for their expert guidance.

Figure 7.6 Acknowledgments.

References: Your reference list is a bibliography of all the sources where you obtained information. See "Secondary Research" in Chapter 4 for information about bibliographies.

8

The Display

Your science fair display represents all the work that you have done. It should consist of a backboard and anything else that supports your project, such as models, exhibits or examples, photographs, surveys, and the like. It must tell the story of the project in such a way that it attracts and holds the interest of the viewer. It has to be thorough, but not too crowded, so keep it simple, well organized, attractive, and most of all informative. Your teacher can advise you about which materials that cannot be displayed as well as those that are required, such as your abstract.

The size and shape allowed for the display backboard can vary, so you will have to check the rules for your science fair. Most displays are allowed to be as large as 48 inches (122 cm) wide, 30 inches (76 cm) deep, and 108 inches (274 cm) high (including the table the display stands on). Of course your display may be smaller than this but most participants prefer to take advantage of all the possible space. A three-paneled backboard is usually the best way to display your work. Some office supply stores and most scientific supply companies sell inexpensive backboards. See Appendix 9 for science supply companies from which you can order inexpensive backboards. You can purchase the backboard or build your own. Just remember when building to use materials that are not likely to be damaged during transportation to the fair. Sturdy cardboard or wooden panels can be cut and hinged together.

Purchased backboards generally come in two colors—black and white. You can make them different colors by covering the backboard with self-stick colored shelving paper or cloth. For items placed on the backboard, select colors that stand out but don't distract the viewer from the material being presented. For example, if fluorescent colors are used for lettering and/or background, the bright colors will be what catches the eye instead of your work.

The title and other headings should be neat and large enough to be read at a distance of about 3 feet (1 m). A short title is often eye-catching. For the title and headings, self-stick letters of various sizes and colors, can be purchased at office supply stores and stuck to the backboard. You can cut your own letters out of construction paper or stencil letters directly onto the backboard. You can also use a computer to print the title and other headings.

Some teachers have rules about the position of the information on the backboard. If your teacher doesn't, put the project title at the top of the center panel, and organize the remaining material in some logical order neatly on the rest of the board. Typical headings used are: Problem, Hypothesis, Experiment (materials and procedure), Data, Results, Conclusion, and Next Time. Figure 8.1 shows one way of placing the material. The heading Next Time, although not always required, would follow the conclusion and contain a brief description of plans for future development of the project. Alternately, this information could be included in the conclusion rather than under a separate heading.

Typed material can be secured to colored backing such as construction paper. Leave a border of about $\frac{1}{4}$ to $\frac{1}{2}$ inch (0.63 to 1.25 cm) around the edges of each piece of typed material. Use a paper cutter to cut papers so that the edges will be straight.

You want a display that the judges will remember positively. So before you glue everything down, lay the backboard on a flat surface and arrange the materials a few different ways. This will help you decide on the most suitable and attractive presentation. Figure 8.1 shows what a good display might look like.

HELPFUL HINTS

1. Make sure the display represents the current year's work only.

2. The title should attract the interest of a casual observer. Not only should the title itself be interesting but it should stand out visually.

3. Organization is a very important part of designing a display. You want a logical order so that observers (especially judges) can easily follow the

Figure 8.1 Example of a good display.

development of your project from start to finish. Before you actually stick anything to the board, make a diagram of where each part will be placed.

4. One way to arrange the letters on the backboard is to first lay the letters out on the board without attaching them. Then use a yardstick (meterstick) and pencil to draw a straight, light guideline where the bottom of each letter should line up. This will help you keep the lettering straight. Before adhering everything, you may wish to seek the opinion of other students, teachers, or family members.

5. If you need electricity for your project, be sure the wiring meets all safety standards.

6. Bring an emergency kit to the science fair that includes anything you think you might need to make last-minute repairs to the display, such as extra letters, glue, tape, construction paper the color of the backboard, a stapler, scissors, pencils, pens, touch-up paint, markers, and so forth.

7. If allowed, before standing your backboard on the display table, cover the table with a colored cloth. Choose a color that matches the color scheme of the backboard. This will help to separate your project from other projects displayed next to yours.

Do's and Don'ts

Do adhere to the size limitations and safety rules set by the fair you are entering. Generally the size limitations are 30 inches (76 cm) deep, 48 inches (122 cm) wide, and 72 inches (183 cm) high (does not include table height).

Do use computer-generated graphs or neatly hand-drawn ones.

Do display photos representing the procedure and the results.

Do use contrasting colors.

Do limit the number of colors used and do not use fluorescent colors.

Do display models when applicable. If possible, make the models match the color scheme of the backboard.

Do attach charts neatly. If there are many, place them on top of each other so that the top chart can be lifted to reveal the ones underneath.

Do balance the arrangement of materials on the backboard. This means to evenly distribute the materials on the board so that they cover about the same amount of space on each panel.

Do use adhesives, such as a glue stick, rubber cement, or double-sided tape to attach papers. Liquid glue generally causes the paper to wrinkle.

Do check spelling, math calculations, and chemical formulas.

Do have one or more adults, such as teachers and/or parents, review all of your work before you put it on the backboard.

Don't leave large empty spaces on the backboard.

Don't leave the table in front of the backboard empty. Display your models (if any), report, copies of your abstract, and your journal here.

Figure 8.2 Example of a bad display.

Don't hang electrical equipment on the backboard so that the electric cord runs down the front of the backboard.

Don't make the title or headings hard to read by using uneven lettering or words with letters of different colors.

Don't hand print the letters on the backboard.

Don't attach folders that fall open on the backboard.

(Figure 8.2 shows how *not* to set up your display.)

SAFETY

Anything that is or could be hazardous to other students or the public is *prohibited* and cannot be displayed. The following is a list of things that are generally unacceptable for display. Your teacher has access to a complete list of safety rules from your local science fair officials. Models or photographs can be used instead of things that are restricted from display.

Unacceptable for Display

1. Live animals

2. Microbial cultures or fungi, living or dead

3. Animal or human body parts, except teeth, hair, nails, and dried animal bones

4. Liquids, including water

5. Chemicals and/or their empty containers, including caustics, acids, and household cleaners

6. Open or concealed flames

7. Batteries with open-top cells

8. Combustible materials

9. Aerosol cans of household solvents

10. Controlled substances, poisons, or drugs

11. Any equipment or device that would be hazardous to the public

12. Sharp items such as syringes, knives, or needles

13. Gases

9

Presentation and Evaluation

Your teacher may require that you give an oral presentation on your project for your class. Make it short but complete. Presenting in front of your classmates may be the hardest part of the project. You want to do your best, so prepare and practice, practice, practice. If possible, tape your practice presentation on a tape recorder or have someone videotape you. Review the tape and/or video and evaluate yourself, then review your notes and practice again.

Practicing an oral presentation will also be helpful for the science fair itself. The judges give points for how clearly you discuss the project and explain its purpose, procedure, results, and conclusion. Judges are impressed with students who can speak confidently about their work. They are not interested in memorized speeches—they will want to have a conversation with you to determine if you understand the work you have done from its start to its finish. While the display should be organized so that it explains everything, your ability to discuss your project and answer the judges' questions convinces them that you did the work and understand what you have done. Practice a speech in front of friends, and invite them to ask questions. If you do not know the answer to a question, never guess or make up an answer or just say "I don't know." Instead, say that you did not discover that answer during your research, and then offer other information that you found of interest about the project. Be proud of the project, and approach the judges with enthusiasm about your work.

As you progress through developing your project, keep in mind that you may be asked about different developmental stages. Take note of some of the ideas that you had while working on your project. These can be used to hold an audience's interest and impress judges.

You can decide on how best to dress for a class presentation, but for the local fair it is wise to make a special effort to look nice. You are representing your work. In effect, you are acting as a salesperson for your project, and you want to present the very best image possible. Your appearance shows how much pride you have in yourself, and that is the first step in introducing your product, your science project.

JUDGING INFORMATION

Most fairs have similar point systems for judging science fair projects. You may be better prepared if you understand that a judge generally starts by assuming that each student's project is average. Then he or she adds or subtracts points from that level. A student should receive points for accomplishing the following.

1. Project Objectives

   - Presenting original ideas
   - Stating the problem clearly
   - Defining the variables and using controls
   - Relating background reading to the problem

2. Project Skills

   - Being knowledgeable about equipment used
   - Performing the experiments with little or no assistance except as required for safety
   - Demonstrating the skills required to do all the work necessary to obtain the data reported

3. Data Collection

   - Using a journal to collect data and research results
   - Repeating the experiment to verify the results
   - Spending an appropriate amount of time to complete the project
   - Having measurable results

4. Data Interpretation
   - Using tables, graphs, and illustrations in interpreting data
   - Using research to interpret data collected
   - Collecting enough data to draw a conclusion
   - Using only data collected to draw a conclusion

5. Project Presentation (Written Materials/Interview/Display)
   - Having a complete and comprehensive report
   - Answering questions accurately
   - Using the display during the oral presentation
   - Justifying conclusions on the basis of experimental data
   - Summarizing what was learned
   - Presenting a display that shows creative ability and originality
   - Presenting an attractive and interesting display

If the project lacks any of these things, then points are taken away.

DO'S AND DON'TS AT THE FAIR

Do bring activities, such as puzzles to work on or a book to read, to keep yourself occupied at your booth. There may be a lengthy wait before the first judge arrives, and even between judges.

Do become acquainted with your neighboring presenters. Be friendly and courteous.

Do ask neighboring presenters about their projects, and tell them about yours if they express interest. These conversations pass time and help relieve nervous tension that can build when you are waiting to be evaluated. You may also discover techniques for research that you can use for next year's project.

Do have fun!

Don't loudly laugh or talk with your neighbor.

Don't forget that you are an ambassador for your school. This means that your attitude and behavior influence how people at the fair think about you and the other students at your school.

II

35 A+
SCIENCE FAIR
PROJECT IDEAS

ASTRONOMY

Solar System Scale
Miniature Model

1

Our solar system consists basically of the Sun, the nine planets and their moons, and space debris. The boundary of the solar system is called the heliopause, which is the limit the solar winds reach. Solar winds are streams of charges escaping from the Sun's atmosphere—gaseous layer surrounding it—and flowing into the solar system. From the heliopause, the solar system is about 18.6 billion miles (29.8 billion km) across. The Sun is the largest celestial body in the solar system, having a diameter of about 870,000 miles (1,392,000 km). Pluto is the smallest planet at about 1,434 miles (2,294 km) across. All of the millions of asteroids and comets are much smaller than Pluto.

In this project, you will make a 3-D model to represent the sizes of celestial bodies in the solar system. You will also learn how to represent the distances between planets and between planets and their moons.

GETTING STARTED

Purpose: To build a 3-D scale model of Earth.

Materials

drawing compass	scissors
metric ruler	index card
sheet of colored poster board	pen

Procedure

1. The diameter of Earth is about 7,973 miles (12,757 km). Using the metric scale of 1 cm/3,000 km, calculate the diameter of the model Earth as follows.

   Earth's actual diameter ÷ 3,000 km/cm

   = model Earth's diameter

   12,757 km ÷ 3,000 km/cm = 4.252 cm

   Rounding the number to the closest centimeter, the model Earth's diameter would be 4 cm.

2. Use the compass to draw two circles with diameters of 4 cm (radius 2 cm) on the poster board.

3. Cut out the circles, then cut along a straight line (radius) from the circumference to the center of each circle.

4. Fit the two circles together at a 90° angle to each other (see Figure 1.1).

Figure 1.1

Earth
1 cm / 3,000 km

5. Prepare a legend showing the scale of the model by folding the index card in half. Write the scale, "1 cm/3,000 km," on one side of the card. Stand the card alongside the model.

Results

You have made a scale model of Earth.

Why?

Celestial bodies are groups of natural objects in the sky, such as suns, stars, planets, and moons. A **solar system** is a group of celestial bodies that **revolves** around the sun. This means they move in a curved path around another object, which is also called **orbiting**. A **sun** is a **star** (glowing sphere of gas) that is the celestial body at the center of a solar system. If capitalized, Sun is the central body in our own solar system. Basically our solar system is made up of nine **planets** (celestial bodies that orbit a sun and shine only by reflected light), **moons** (small bodies in orbit around a planet) and other space **debris** (scattered pieces of something that has been broken). If capitalized, Moon refers to Earth's moon.

In this experiment you made a **scale model** (replica made in proportion to the object it represents) of the Earth, one of the planets of our solar system. A **scale** is a ratio between the measurements of a model and the actual measurements of an object. In a scale ratio the model measurement comes first. If the first value of the ratio is smaller, the scale drawing or model is reduced, such as the 1 cm/3,000 km in this experiment. Scale models of bodies in our solar system, such as Earth, are valuable because they allow an observer to compare the relative sizes and distances of large things more easily.

TRY NEW APPROACHES

How does the size of Earth compare with the other planets in the solar system? Make more scale models, using the diameters of the planets given in Appendix 3. **Science Fair Hint:** Attach threads to the models and suspend them from a 4-foot (1.2-m) or longer dowel. Support the ends of the dowel, then take a picture of the models. Use the photo and models in your science fair display.

DESIGN YOUR OWN EXPERIMENT

1. A **satellite** is a body that revolves about a celestial body. A **natural satellite** is a celestial body that revolves about a larger celestial body. Earth has one natural satellite, the Moon. Design a scale model that accurately represents the size of both Earth and the Moon and the average distance between them. The Moon's diameter is 2,173 miles (3,476 km). The average distance between the centers of Earth and the Moon is about 240,250 miles (384,400 km). Use the scale 1 cm/3,000 km. Make one sphere to scale for Earth and another for the Moon. Label the models "Earth" and "Moon." Calculate the length of string needed to represent the distance between them. Measure and cut string of the necessary length. Tape one end of the string to the center of the model Moon and the other end to the center of the model Earth. Ask helpers to hold the models, stretching the string taut between the models, while you take a photo (see Figure 1.2). Display the photo along with a legend indicating the actual sizes and distances along with the scale you used.

Figure 1.2

2. The planet Jupiter has many moons. Its four largest are collectively called the **Galilean satellites** (any of the four largest moons of Jupiter: Io, Europa, Ganymede, and Callisto) because they were discovered in 1610 by Galileo (1564–1642). Make a model of Jupiter and the Galilean satellite called Ganymede. The diameter of this moon is 3,293 miles (5,268 km). It orbits 668,750 miles (1,070,000 km) from Jupiter. Jupiter's diameter is 89,875 miles (143,800 km).

3a. The average distance between Earth and the Sun is about 93 million miles (149 million km). This distance is called an **astronomical unit** (AU) and is used as a measure of distance in the solar system. The AU measurement for any planet can be calculated by dividing the planet's distance in miles (km) by 93 million miles (149 million km). For example, Mercury is about 36 million miles (58 million km) from the Sun, thus the AU distance between the Sun and Mercury is:

36,000,000 miles ÷ 93,000,000 miles = 0.387 AU
58,000,000 km ÷ 149,000,000 km = 0.389 AU

Rounding the answer to the nearest tenth, Mercury is 0.4 AU from the Sun.

Prepare a data table like Table 1.1, giving the average distances of the planets in miles (km) from the Sun (distances shown are from Appendix 3) and in AU units. Calculate the AU distance to the nearest tenth as in the preceding example.

b. Use the AU distances to draw a scale model of the solar system.

TABLE 1.1 PLANET'S AVERAGE DISTANCES FROM THE SUN		
Planet	**Average Distance, millions of miles (millions of km)**	**Distance, AU**
Mercury	36 (58)	0.4
Venus	68 (108)	
Earth	93 (149)	1.0
Mars	143 (228)	
Jupiter	486 (778)	
Saturn	892 (1,427)	
Uranus	1,794 (2,870)	
Neptune	2,810 (4,497)	
Pluto	3,688 (5,900)	

GET THE FACTS

1. By definition, natural satellites (moons) are smaller than the planets they orbit. Even the smallest known planet in our solar system, Pluto, has a moon called Charion. Pluto is smaller than Earth's moon, and Charion is even smaller. Find out more about the natural satellites of the planets. Do all the planets have satellites? How do their sizes compare with the size of the planets they orbit? Make models of the planets and their satellites. For information, see Patrick Moore's and Will Tirion's, *Guide to Stars and Planets* (Cambridge: Cambridge University Press, 1993).

2. The sixth planet from the Sun, Saturn, is known for particles that orbit the planet, creating what looks like rings as observed from Earth. Make a model of Saturn. How many rings are there? What are they made of? How large are they? What causes them to change in visibility? For information, see Ann-Jeanette Campbell's *New York Public Library Amazing Space* (New York: Wiley, 1997), pp. 124–128.

2 Angular Separation
Angular Distance between Celestial Bodies

The apparent distance between celestial bodies is how large the linear measurement between bodies appears to be from Earth. Angular separation or angular distance is the apparent distance expressed in radians or degrees.

In this project, you will build a cross-staff resembling the instrument used by early navigators and astronomers. You will use it to measure both angular separation and angular diameter of celestial bodies including the Moon.

Getting Started

Purpose: To use a cross-staff to measure angular separation.

Materials

cross-staff (see Appendix 5)

Procedure

1. Use the cross-staff to measure angular separation. You can take measurements inside or outdoors.

- Stand 4 yards (4 m) from a closed door or other object. Record this sighting distance in column 1 of an Angular Separation (Wide Sight) Data table like Table 2.1.

- Rest the zero end of the measuring stick against one of your cheekbones. Open the eye over this cheekbone and close the other eye. Use your open eye to sight along the length of the stick. With the bottom of the crosspiece

parallel with the floor, slide the crosspiece until the left side of the door lines up with the left-hand edge of the wide side and the right side of the door lines up with the right-hand edge of the wide sight (see Figure 2.1). The width of the wide sight is d_1 and is equal to 4 inches (10 cm). Record this sight width in column 2 of your data table as shown.

Figure 2.1

- Read the value on the measuring stick where the bottom of the labeled side of the crosspiece touches the measuring stick. This measurement is d_2, the distance from the sight to your eye. Record measurement d_2 in column 3 of your data table for trial 1.

		TABLE 2.1 ANGULAR SEPARATION (WIDE SIGHT) DATA							
Sighting Distance	**Distance: Width of Sight (d_1), inches (cm)**	**Distance: Sight to Eye (d_2) inches (cm)**						**Angle Separation Da,°**	**Random Error of Measurement**
		Trial 1	Trial 2	Trial 3	Trial 4	Trial 5	Average		
4 yards (4 m)	4 inches (10 cm)								

2. Repeat step 1 four times, for a total of five independent measurements of the same distance.

3. Calculate the angular separation between the left and right sides of the door in degrees, 0°, using the average of your five measurements for d_2 and this equation:

$$D_a = 57.3° \times (d_1 \div d_2)$$

where D_a is the angular separation, d_1 is the width of the sight, and d_2 is the distance from the sight to your eye. D_a is expressed in degrees. Both d_1 and d_2 must be expressed in the same unit—either inches or centimeters. *Note:* $d_1 \div d_2$ yields a number without a unit of measurement. When no unit of measurement is indicated in giving the measure of an angle, the angle is understood to be expressed in radians. To express the angle in degrees, the conversion 57.3° per 1 radian is used.

For example, for the wide sight, if d_1 = 4 inches (10 cm) and d_2 = 20 inches (50 cm), then

$$D_a = 57.3° \times d \ (4 \text{ inches } (10 \text{ cm}) \div 20 \text{ inches } (50 \text{ cm})) = 11.45°$$

4. Using the method in Appendix 1, determine the random error of measurement. Record the error in column 10 of your data table.

Results

The angular separation will vary with door width. The author's measurement was 11.45°.

Why?

Like a circle, the sphere of sky surrounding Earth measures 360°. But only about half the sphere is visible above the **horizon** (imaginary line where the sky appears to touch Earth). So the sky you see covers an **arc** (segment of a circle) of about 180° from one side of the horizon to the other. As an observer from Earth, you look at celestial bodies from a great distance. The **apparent distance** between celestial bodies is how large the linear measurement between the bodies appears to be from Earth. The **angular separation** or **angular distance** is the apparent distance expressed in radians or degrees. **Altitude** is the angular distance above the horizon.

The **cross-staff** is an instrument used to determine angular separation. At a specific distance from an object, you measure the apparent width of an object (the width of the sight of the crosspiece) and the distance of the crosspiece from your eye. The ratio of apparent width to distance multiplied by 57.3° expresses the angular separation in degrees.

TRY NEW APPROACHES

1a. Does the width of the cross-staff's sight affect the results? Repeat the experiment twice, using the medium, "M," and small, "S," sights. Compare your calculations.

b. Assess the accuracy of your cross-staff by determining the true angular separation between the sides of the door (D_A). Do this by using a ruler to measure the actual width of the door, d_a, and using the sighting distance, d_s, of 4 yards (4 m) and this equation:

$$D_A = 57.3° \times (d_a \div d_s)$$

For example, if door measurement d_a equals 29 inches, then

$$D_A = 57.3° \times (29 \text{ inches} \div 144 \text{ inches})$$
$$= 11.54°$$

c. Determine the relative error of your measurements using the method in Appendix 2.

2a. Does sighting distance (d_s) affect angular separation? Repeat the original experiment, collecting data for distances of 2, 4, 6, and 8 yards (m) using the wide sight. Determine the relative error for each sighting distance measurement.

b. Repeat the previous experiment using the medium and small sights of the cross-staff. Draw a line graph of your findings. Put the sighting distance on the horizontal axis. Put angular separation on the vertical axis. Use points and lines of different colors for the wide, medium, and small sights.

DESIGN YOUR OWN EXPERIMENT

1. Design and experiment to test the accuracy of the cross-staff in measuring angular separation between stars in a **constellation** (group of stars that appears to make a pattern in the sky). For example, you might measure the angular separation of some of the stars in the Big Dipper which is an **asterism** (group of stars with a shape within a constellation) in the Ursa Major constellation. See separation A shown in Figure 2.2 from Alkaid to Dubhe, separation B from Megrez to Dubhe, and separation C from Dubhe to Polaris. Record your measurements in a table like Table 2.2. If it is too dark to read your cross-staff, stand with the light from a building behind you. Make five measurements for each separation and average them. Compare your average with known (true) angular separations given and record the difference. If the difference is more than the known value, record a positive (+) error. If the difference is less, record a negative (–) error. For more information about the angles between the stars of the Big Dipper, see Terence Dickinson's, *Night Watch* (Willowdale, Ontario: Firefly Books, 1998), p. 30.

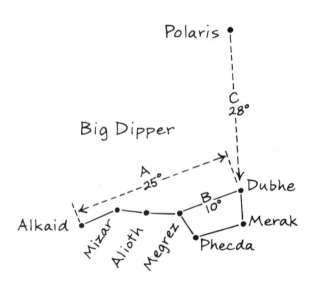

Figure 2.2

2. Design an experiment to determine if the angular separation of celestial bodies changes. Perhaps you can repeat the measurements between the stars of the Big Dipper at different times in one night or at the same time on different nights.

3. Use your cross-staff to measure the angular diameter of a celestial body such as the Moon. Since the Moon's diameter appears to be relatively small, use the smaller notch, S_2, on the left side of the crosspiece. If it is not a full moon, measure the Moon's height rather than its width.

GET THE FACTS

The cross-staff was the first practical instrument for measuring the altitude of the Sun from the deck of a ship. The cross-staff measured the distance between the horizon and the Sun quite well, but it had problems. The user had to look directly at the Sun, risking eye damage or blindness. Another problem was aligning the crosspiece so that one end appeared to touch the Sun while the other touched the horizon. In 1594, John Davis (1550–1605), a British navigator, published his book *The Seaman's Secrets,* in which he described an improved instrument called the backstaff. What advantages did the backstaff have over the cross-staff? How were these two instruments different? For information about these and other navigational instruments, see Richard Moeschl's *Exploring the Sky* (Chicago: Chicago Review Press, 1993), pp. 115–123. Another resource is Dennis Fisher's *Latitude Hooks and Azmuth Rings: How to Build and Use 18 Traditional Navigational Instruments* (New York: TAB/McGraw-Hill, 1994).

TABLE **2.2** MEASURING ANGULAR SEPARATIONS WITH A CROSS-STAFF								
Location	Measured Angular Separation,°						Known Angular Separation, °	Error
	Trial 1	Trial 2	Trial 3	Trial 4	Trial 5	Average		
A							25°	
B							10°	
C							28°	

3 Orbital Period
Time of Revolution

German astronomer Johannes Kepler (1571–1630) in his third law of planetary motion expressed the relationship between the orbital period of a planet and its average distance from the Sun. An orbital period is the time it takes a planet to make one revolution, which is once around its orbit.

In this project, you will discover how mass and distance affect a celestial body's orbital period. You will model the effect of the barycenter on the period of a planet. You will also discover how Bode's law predicts the distances of planets.

GETTING STARTED

Purpose: To determine the effect of distance on the orbital period of an orbiting planet.

Materials

³⁄₈-inch (0.93-cm) metal washer
6-foot (1.8-m) cord
ruler

2 pairs of safety goggles
timer
helper

Procedure

Note: This activity is to be performed outdoors.

1. Tie the washer to the end of the cord.

2. On the cord, measure 18 inches (45 cm) from the washer and tie a knot in the cord.

3. Measure 18 inches (45 cm) from the knot and tie a second knot in the cord.

4. Repeat step 3, making a third knot.

5. Put on a pair of safety goggles. In an area away from other people, hold the cord at the first knot—18 inches (45 cm)—from the washer and swing your arm so that the washer spins above your head.

6. Find the slowest speed that will keep the washer "in orbit."

7. Ask your helper to wear safety goggles and be your timekeeper (see Figure 3.1). When your timekeeper says "Start," count the number of revolutions the washer makes. A **revolution** is one turn around an orbit.

Figure 3.1

8. Stop counting when the timekeeper says "Stop," at the end of 10 seconds.

9. Calculate the **orbital period**, T, (time per revolution) of the washer by dividing the time by the number of revolutions. For example, if you counted five revolutions in 10 seconds, the orbital period would be:

T = orbital period = time ÷ number of revolutions

= 10 seconds ÷ 5 revolutions

= 2 seconds/revolution

This is read as 2 seconds per revolution and means that it took 2 seconds for the washer to travel 1 revolution.

10. Repeat steps 5 to 9 four times for a total of five trial measurements.

11. Repeat steps 5 to 10 for the two other distances: 36 inches (90 cm) at the second knot, 54 inches (135 cm) at the third knot.

12. Record the data in an Orbital Period versus Orbit Distance table like Table 3.1.

TABLE 3.1 ORBITAL PERIOD VS. ORBIT DISTANCE						
Orbital Distance inches (cm)	Orbital Period (T), seconds/revolution					
	Trial 1	Trial 2	Trial 3	Trial 4	Trial 5	Average
18 (45)						
36 (90)						
54 (135)						

13. Make a bar graph of the average orbital periods. Place distance (the independent variable that you changed) on the horizontal axis. Place the orbital period (the dependent variable that changes in response to the independent variable) on the vertical axis. For information about constructing bar graphs, see p. 18.

Results

The longer the cord, the greater the orbital period.

Why?

Kepler's **third law of planetary motion** states that the more distant a planet's orbit from the Sun, the greater the planet's orbital period. This experiment shows that the law works for any object spinning in a circular path.

TRY NEW APPROACHES

Matter is the substance from which all objects are made. **Mass** is the measure of the amount of matter in an object. How does the mass of the orbiting object affect its orbital period? Repeat the experiment using two washers. As before, provide just enough energy to keep the washers in a circular orbit. In Chapter 4, "Artificial Satellites," page 41, find the orbital **velocity** (speed in a specific direction) of a satellite. Note that **orbital velocity** (revolutions/sec) is the reciprocal of the satellite's orbital period (sec/revolutions). Is the mass of the satellite part of the orbital velocity formula? Do your experimental results agree with the formula?

DESIGN YOUR OWN EXPERIMENT

Center of mass is the point on a body where its mass seems to be concentrated. **Gravity** is a force of attraction between all objects in the **universe** (everything throughout space including Earth). Two celestial bodies held together by mutual gravitational attraction are called **binary bodies,** such as the Sun and a planet. The **barycenter** is the point between binary bodies where their center of mass is located, which is the point around which the bodies rotate.

1. The farther the barycenter of a planet-Sun system is from the Sun, the greater the orbital period of the planet. Use two dowels of different lengths to illustrate this principle. First, determine the center of mass of each dowel by balancing it horizontally on your finger. Where your supporting finger touches the rods is their center of mass. Mark the center of mass on each dowel. Rest one end of each dowel on a level surface, such as a floor or table, with a few inches (cm) between them. The flat surface represents the Sun. Hold the dowels up vertically, steadying them with the tips of your fingers. Lean both dowels forward the same amount so they will fall in the same direction. Release both at the same time. Which hits the surface first? For your display you may wish to make a drawing like Figure 3.2 showing the results of this experiment.

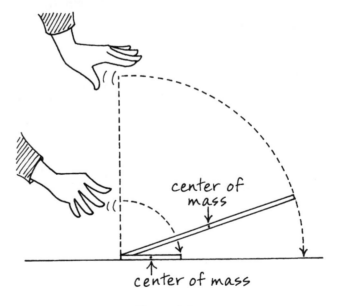

center of mass

center of mass

Figure 3.2

2a. Design an experiment to measure the orbital periods of one of the visible planets. Note that Mercury is too close to the Sun to be seen and the movements of Jupiter and Saturn are very slow. The visibility and relatively fast movements of Venus and Mars make them the best subjects. One experiment is to measure the average angular motion of the selected planet per day. Use this to calculate the orbital period, which is the time for 1 revolution of 360°. Staring on day 1, use a cross-staff (see Chapter 2, "Angular Separation," for instructions on making and using a cross-staff) to measure the angular separation between the planet and a star. Take five measurements on the first day and average them. Take five measurements 7 days later and average them. Record measurements in an Angular Separation Data table like Table 3.2. Calculate the orbital period of the planet using these steps:

- Calculate the difference (D_1) between the average angular separation on the first and seventh day.

- Calculate the time (t_1) for D_1, which is the time between the two sets of measurements. Thus, t_1, = 7 days.

- Calculate the portion of the revolutions (D_2) the planet moved in 6 days by dividing D_1 by the degrees in 1 revolution, which is 360°. $D_2 = D_1/360°$.

- Calculate the orbital period (T) using the following equation:

$$T = t_1/D_2$$

TABLE 3.2 ANGULAR SEPARATION DATA

	Angular Separation, °					
	Trial 1	Trial 2	Trial 3	Trial 4	Trial 5	Average
D_1						
D_2						

b. Kepler's third law of planetary motion states that a planet's orbital period (time of 1 revolution around the Sun) depends on its average distance from the Sun. This equation is:

$$P^2 = k \times r^3$$

where P is the orbital period, r the average distance from the Sun, and k a constant. If P is in years and r is in AU, k equals 1. Using the known radius of the visible planets (see Appendix 3), calculate the orbital period of each. Note that the radius (½ diameter) must be expressed in astronomical units (AU), which can be determined by taking the average distance of the planet from the Sun and dividing by the average distance of Earth from the Sun. For example, for Mercury the radius in AU is 0.39 AU. See page 33 for AU calculations.

c. Using the known orbital period and the experimentally determined orbital periods in the previous experiment, calculate your experimental percentage error. (See Appendix 2 for information about percentage error.) What is retrograde motion and how would it affect your percentage error? For information about retrograde motion, see Dinah Moche's *Astronomy* (New York: Wiley, 2000), pp. 197–200.

GET THE FACTS

The German astronomer Johann Titius (1729–1796) showed that the distances of planets from the Sun follow a fixed formula when measured in astronomical units. The formula is known as *Bode's law*. What is this pattern? Why isn't it called Titius's law? What significant role did the pattern play in the discovery of the asteroids and some of the planets? How accurate are the distances using the formula? For information, see Nancy Hathaway's, *The Friendly Guide to the Universe* (New York: Penguin, 1994), pp. 190–192.

4 Artificial Satellites
Man-made Orbiters

A satellite is a celestial body that orbits another. An artificial satellite is a man-made object that orbits Earth. Artificial satellites are raised to a desired height above Earth and launched by rockets parallel to Earth's surface. This forward velocity (speed of an object in a specific direction) and the force of gravity keep the satellite in orbit around Earth.

In this project, you will learn about launching speed and its effect on a man-made satellite's orbit. You will discover the best times to see satellites and how to measure their angular velocity. You will also find out why satellites are launched in different directions.

GETTING STARTED

Purpose: To model how an artificial satellite is launched into orbit.

Materials

2 equal-size books, each about 10 inches (25 cm) long
index card
transparent tape
3 rulers—2 must be identical and have a groove down the center
walnut-size piece of modeling clay
bath towel
marble

Procedure

1. Lay the books end to end on a table.

2. Lay the index card on the end of the books farther from the edge of the table.

3. Tape the grooved rulers together end to end. Tape only on the ungrooved side. This is your launcher.

4. Lay the launcher on the books so that one end is on the index card. Raise that end 2 inches (5 cm) above the book. Put the clay under the end for support. Let the other end of the launcher extend over the end of the books.

5. Adjust the books so that the extended end of the launcher is 4 inches (10 cm) from the edge of the table.

6. Lay the towel on the floor near the edge of the table. The towel will help stop the marble when it hits the floor.

7. Position the marble on the raised end of the launcher, then release it (see Figure 4.1) The marble should land on the towel.

8. Observe the path of the marble after it leaves the launcher.

Figure 4.1

Results

The marble's path curves after it leaves the launcher.

Why?

An **artificial satellite** (man-made satellite) is any object purposely placed into orbit around a celestial body, including Earth. Since the launching of the first artificial satellite in 1957, thousands of artificial satellites have been placed in orbit around Earth. These satellites have many uses for private companies, governments, and educational facilities. This experiment models the launching of an artificial satellite, called the marble satellite.

In this model, the table represents Earth. The top of the books is a position above Earth's surface where the "marble satellite" is launched horizontally, parallel to Earth's surface. After it separates from its launcher, the satellite moves in a curved path. The curve results from the satellite's forward horizontal velocity and the downward pull of gravity. A real satellite would continue revolving around Earth in a curved path called an orbit that would pass through the launching point.

TRY NEW APPROACHES

If the horizontal velocity of the marble satellite is great enough, gravity pulls it into a curved path past the edge of the table. Demonstrate the effect of different horizontal velocities on the path of the satellite by repeating the experiment, raising the end of the launcher to different heights.

DESIGN YOUR OWN EXPERIMENT

1a. Earth's surface curves away from a line **tangent** (touching at a single point) to its surface at a rate of $3\frac{3}{50}$ miles (4.9 km) for every 5 miles (8 km). So, near Earth's surface, an object traveling at 5 miles (8 km) per second would maintain its altitude and move in a circular path around Earth. Draw a diagram to represent the effect of launching speeds greater than, less than, and equal to 5 miles (8 km) per second.

b. A satellite's horizontal speed depends on its distance above Earth, which affects the strength of gravity acting on the satellite. The gravity at a certain distance from the center of Earth can be calculated by using this equation:

$$g_1/g_2 = r_2^2/r_1^2$$

where g_1 = 9.8 m/s², gravity at distance equal to the radius of earth (at surface)

r_1 = 12,757 km, radius of Earth

g_2 = gravity at distance r_2

r_2 = distance from center of Earth to satellite's orbit

The least velocity a satellite must have to orbit Earth is determined by this equation:

$$V = \sqrt{gr}$$

where V = the velocity of the satellite

g = the acceleration of gravity at distance r from the center of Earth

r = the average radius of the satellite's orbit from the center of Earth

Artificial satellites that stay above one place on Earth as they orbit are called **geosynchronous satellites**. These satellites orbit above Earth at an **altitude** (height above a surface) of 22,300 miles (13,938 km). Use these formulas to determine the velocity of a geosynchronous satellite and the gravity acting on it. **Science Fair Hint:** Prepare a diagram showing satellites at different distances from Earth's surfaces, the calculations used to determine their velocity, and the gravity (force of attraction between all objects in the universe) acting on them. For more information, look up satellite velocity in a physics text.

2. Satellites look like slow-moving stars. Those in orbits at an altitude of 300 miles (480 km) or less are visible to the naked eye. Determine when satellites are most visible. Observe satellites at different times of the night and during different seasons. For more information on satellite motion, see Terence Dickinson's *Night Watch* (Willowdale, Ontario: Firefly Books, 1999), p. 35.

3. Determine the **angular velocity** (angular displacement per unit time of an object moving in a curved path) of satellites by measuring the angular distance traveled during a measured amount of time. Find out which satellites are visible on a certain date from sources such as *Sky and Telescope* magazine or from Web sites such as www.skyandtelescope.com. (See Part II, Chapter 2, "Angular Separation," for information about measuring angular distance.)

GET THE FACTS

Most satellites are launched from west to east, but some are launched to orbit Earth from pole to pole. Why is a launch into a polar orbit more difficult? What are satellites used for? For information, see Dinah Moche's *Astronomy Today* (New York: Random House, 1995), pp. 20–21.

5 Apparent Magnitude
Apparent Star Brightness

Stars vary widely in brightness. Some appear very bright, while others are barely visible to the naked eye. Around 150 B.C., long before the invention of telescopes, the Greek astronomer Hipparchus devised a scale to measure apparent magnitude, the brightness of stars as seen with the naked eye from Earth. He gave a value of 1 to the brightest star and a value of 6 to the dimmest. Today, we use a variation of his scale to measure the brightness of stars. Instead of observing and estimating magnitudes with the naked eye, we now use an instrument called a photometer, which produces more precise measurements. Also, the scale has been extended beyond 1 to 6 so astronomers can measure an even broader range of brightness.

In this project, you will demonstrate the effect of luminosity and distance on the apparent magnitude of a star. You will build an instrument to measure apparent magnitude. You will learn how apparent magnitude differs from intrinsic (natural) luminosity, which is the amount of light a star emits. You will also discover the difference between apparent and absolute magnitude.

GETTING STARTED

Purpose: To demonstrate how distance affects the brightness of an object.

Materials

3 pencils
yardstick (meterstick)

2 identical incandescent flashlights with new batteries
2 helpers

Procedure

1. In an open area outdoors, stick a pencil in the ground to mark the starting point. Use the yardstick (meterstick) to measure two distances from the pencil, one at 10 feet (3 m) and the second at 30 feet (9 m). Mark these distances with pencils in the ground.

2. At night, stand beside the first pencil.

3. Ask your helpers to hold flashlights and to stand side by side at the second pencil, 10 feet (3 m) away.

4. Instruct your helpers to turn on their flashlights and shine them toward you.

5. Look at the lights just long enough to compare their brightness.

6. Ask one of your helpers to move to the third pencil, 30 feet (9 m) away, while continuing to shine the light toward you (see Figure 5.1).

7. Again, compare the brightness of the lights.

8. Ask your other helper to move to the third pencil while continuing to shine the light toward you.

9. As before, compare the brightness of the lights.

Figure 5.1

Results

The lights appear equally bright at an equal distance from you. When they are at different distances, the closer light appears brighter.

Why?

Magnitude is a measure of how bright a celestial body appears to be. **Apparent magnitude** is a measure of how bright a celestial body appears as viewed with the naked eye from Earth. Apparent magnitudes are ranked on a **magnitude scale,** with an inverse relationship between brightness and magnitude numbers, expressed as magnitudes. For example, the magnitude 1 star in Figure 5.2 is brighter than the magnitude 3 star. Apparent magnitude is not a measure of luminosity. **Luminosity** is the amount of light energy a light source such as a star gives off in a given amount of time. When stars have the same luminosity, the closer star, like the closer flashlight, has a greater magnitude.

TRY NEW APPROACHES

The star Aldebaran, in the constellation Taurus, is about 50 times larger and about 100 times more luminous than the Sun. It appears far less bright, however, because it is so far away from Earth. Demonstrate how distance affects the apparent magnitude of stars with unequal luminosity. Repeat the experiment using two flashlights, fresh batteries in one and weak batteries in the other.

DESIGN YOUR OWN EXPERIMENT

1. Design a model to illustrate how distance affects the apparent magnitude of stars with equal luminosity. One way is to make a drawing using lines to indicate luminosity. In Figure 5.2, the three stars emit the same amount of energy, as indicated by the number of lines (6) in the boxes. The numbers show, however, that their apparent magnitude varies, with the closest star appearing the brightest (having the lowest magnitude number).

Figure 5.2

2a. Design an experiment to measure the apparent magnitude of stars. One way is to make a brightness viewer. The following steps provide a method for testing the brightness of a magnitude 1 star.

- Punch two holes near the short edge of an index card. Label the card "Magnitude 1."

Figure 5.3

- Cover one of the holes with a piece of transparent (not frosted) tape (see Figure 5.3). The covered hole is the testing hole. The uncovered hole is the viewing hole.

- To calibrate the viewer:

  (1) Through the viewing hole, look at a star known to be of magnitude 1. For information about star magnitude, see Terence Dickinson's *Night Watch* (Willowdale, Ontario: Firefly Books, 1998), pp. 100–119.

  (2) Look at the same star through the testing hole. The star should be barely visible. If it appears bright, add more layers of tape until the star is barely visible. *Note:* Be careful to keep the layers of tape clean and wrinkle free.

- To use the viewer, find a star by looking through the viewing hole. Then move the viewer so that you look at the same star through the testing hole. If you can barely see the star, it has a magnitude of 1 or less.

b. To identify stars with magnitudes greater than 1, repeat the previous experiment for stars of greater magnitude.

3. The stars that make up the bowl of the constellation Ursa Minor, commonly called the Little Dipper, have magnitudes of 2, 3, 4, and 5 (see Figure 5.4). Use these stars as a "magnitude scale in the sky" against which the magnitudes of other stars can be compared and estimated.

Figure 5.4

GET THE FACTS

Some stars give off much more light than the Sun, but Earth receives thousands of millions of times more light from the Sun than from any other star. Why? To compare the light outputs of the Sun and other stars, astronomers use an *absolute magnitude* scale. How was it developed? How does it work? For information, see the *National Audubon Society Field Guide to the Night Sky* (New York: Knopf, 1995), pp. 24–25.

6 Sunspots
Cooler Surface Regions

In the early 1600s in Paris, a German astronomer and Jesuit priest, Christoph Scheiner (1573–1650), was convinced he saw dark spots on the Sun. He was criticized for that idea because the renowned Greek philosopher Aristotle (384–322 B.C.) had stated that everything in the universe except Earth was perfect and without flaws. Scheiner revised his opinion and stated that the spots were caused by something near but not on the Sun. However, Galileo (1564–1642), an Italian scientist, saw the sunspots, studied their motion, and argued that they originated on the Sun. He is often credited as the first to discover them.

In this project, you will create a model of the layers of the Sun. You will investigate the photosphere, the area that appears to be the Sun's surface. You will observe the movement of sunspots to confirm that the Sun rotates. You will also learn how sunspots cycle and how they affect the Sun's activity.

GETTING STARTED

Purpose: To build a model of the Sun's internal structure.

Materials

serrated knife (use with adult approval)

Styrofoam ball, 6 inches (15 cm) in diameter or larger

2 different colored permanent markers

four 1-by-4-inch (2.5-by-10-cm) white labels

4 round toothpicks

pen

Procedure

1. Use the knife to cut away one-fourth of the Styrofoam ball. Set the ball aside.

2. With one of the markers, paint an area in the center of the ball to represent the Sun's core.

3. Use the second marker to draw a band surrounding the core to represent the convection zone.

4. Prepare four flags using these steps:
   - Touch the two sticky ends of a label together, leaving a gap near the folded end.
   - Insert a toothpick through the gap and press the label onto the toothpick to make a flag (see Figure 6.1).
   - Write the names of the Sun's layers on the flags: "Photosphere," "Convection Zone," "Radiation Zone," "Core."

Figure 6.1

5. Stick the flags in the Sun model as shown in Figure 6.2.

6. Make a Layers of the Sun table like Table 6.1, showing the thickness and temperature of each layer.

Figure 6.2

TABLE 6.1 LAYERS OF THE SUN		
Layer	**Thickness, miles (km)**	**Temperature, °F (°C)**
Core	87,000 (139,200)	27,000,032 (15,000,000)
Radiation Zone	239,250 (382,800)	4,500,032 (2,500,000)
Convection Zone	108,750 (174,000)	1,980,032 (1,100,000)
Photosphere	342 (547)	9,932 (5,500)

Results

You have made a model showing the layers of the Sun and a table describing some of their characteristics.

Why?

The Sun's **core** (center of a celestial body) is its hottest part. In the core, **nuclear fusion** (the combing of the nuclei of atoms) releases enormous amounts of energy (ability of matter to make changes) called radiation. **Radiation** is energy that can move through space, and is not carried by matter. Energy from the hot core moves through the area outside the core called the **radiation zone.** From there, heated gases expand and rise. When they cool, they become denser and sink back down again. Circulating gas forms the **convection zone.** The next layer, the **photosphere,** is actually the first layer of the Sun's **atmosphere** (gaseous layer surrounding any celestial body that has gravity strong enough to prevent the gases from escaping). But from Earth, it looks like the Sun's surface. Your model does not show the layers of the atmosphere above the photosphere: the **chromosphere** and the outermost layer, the **corona.**

TRY NEW APPROACHES

Photographs of the Sun's photosphere show that it has a grainy appearance called **granulation.** Covering the photosphere are bright spots resembling rice grains, called **granules.** A granule is the top of a rising current of hot gases from the convection zone. A single granule measures about 900 miles (nearly 1,500 km) across. Between the granules are dark **intergranular lanes** where the cooler gases return to the convection zone. Also seen on the photosphere are large dark spots called **sunspots.** These are centers of intense localized magnetic fields that are thought to suppress the currents of hot gases. They are dark because they are cooler than the areas surrounding them. Find out more about granules and sunspots and add them to your Sun model. For information about the size of sunspots and their two observable regions, the **umbra** (darkest part) and the **penumbra** (grayish outer part), see Dinah Moche's *Astronomy: A Self-Teaching Guide* (New York: Wiley, 1996), pp. 102–105.

DESIGN YOUR OWN EXPERIMENT

The Sun rotates about once every 4 weeks. Design an experiment to confirm that the Sun rotates. Observe and record the location of sunspots over a period of time, but unlike Galileo, who looked directly at the Sun and in time lost his eyesight, *you must NOT look directly at the Sun.* A safe, indirect method of observing sunspots uses a telescope, but binoculars with one lens covered will work, too. *Without looking through the lens,* point the telescope at the Sun and adjust the position of the instrument until its shadow is as small as possible. Then focus the Sun's image on a sheet of white poster board—the screen. Secure the telescope and screen so that they do not move by setting the telescope on a tripod and tacking the screen to a tree (see Figure 6.3). Cut a hole in a second piece of poster board large enough to fit around the end of the telescope that faces the Sun. This sheet of poster board casts a shadow on the screen, making the Sun's image easier to see. At the same time each day or as many days as possible for 2 weeks or more, tape a clean sheet of paper to the screen. Mark the Sun's image and the location of sunspots on the paper. Compare the drawings. How much do the sunspots move? Do some move faster than others? Does the path of sunspots reveal the location of the Sun's equator and poles? For more information, see Philip Harrington's *Astronomy for All Ages* (Old Saybrook, CT: Globe Pequot Press, 1994), pp. 77–79. **CAUTION:** *Never look directly at the Sun. It will permanently damage your eyes.*

Figure 6.3

GET THE FACTS

At any given moment, the number of visible sunspots can vary from several hundred to none at all. The number increases and decreases in a regular pattern called the *sunspot cycle.* How long does each cycle last? How does the Sun's activity relate to the number of sunspots? Get today's sunspot number at www.spaceweather.com. For more information, see Moche's *Astronomy,* p. 103.

7 Galilean Satellites
Jupiter's Largest Moons

The four largest satellites of Jupiter are called Galilean satellites because they were discovered in 1610 by Galileo. Their names are Io, Europa, Ganymede, and Callisto, from closest to farthest from Jupiter.

In this project, you will discover the motion of each Galilean satellite during an Earth day (24 hours). You will plot the positions of the satellites as they move around Jupiter and determine their locations relative to Jupiter from a bird's-eye view above Jupiter's north pole, as well as from an observer's view from Earth. From actual observations, you will identify the Galilean satellites by name and learn more about each one.

GETTING STARTED

Purpose: To determine the motion of Io during an Earth day (24 hours).

Materials

sheet of white copy paper   pencil
drawing compass   protractor
metric ruler

Procedure

1. The radius of Io's orbit is about 4.9×10^5 km. Using a scale of 6 mm/1×10^5 km, calculate the radius of the orbit for a scale model as follows:

   actual radius of Io's orbit × scale
   4.9×10^5 km × 6 mm/1×10^5 km = 29.4 mm

   Rounding the number to the closest millimeter, the radius of the scale model of Io would be 29 mm.

2. In the center of the paper, use the compass to draw a circle with a radius of 29 mm. The circle represents the orbit of Io.

3. In the center of the circle, make a small circle with a diameter of about 8 mm. This circle represents Jupiter.

4. Label the directions "East" and "West" on the paper as shown, in Figure 7.1 with "Facing South" at the bottom of the paper.

5. Make a dot on the east side of the large circle. Number the dot 1. This dot represents the first observation location of Io.

6. To find the angular distance of Io's movement in one Earth day (24 hours), divide the angular distance of one revolution (360°) by Io's orbital period (1.77 days). Round the answer to the nearest whole number of degrees.

   $$d = 360° \div 1.77 \text{ days} = 203°$$

7. Use the protractor to find a point on the large circle 203° from the first dot. Make a dot on the circle at this point and number the dot 2.

8. Use the protractor to find a point on the circle 203° from dot 2. Make a dot on the circle at this point and number the dot 3. Repeat to find the location of dot 4.

9. Use the compass to draw 203° arcs as shown in Figure 7.1 to indicate the angular distance between the dots.

Figure 7.1

Results

The dots represent Io's position after 0, 1, 2, and 3 Earth days, with observation beginning at position 1.

Why?

A natural satellite is a celestial body revolving around another larger celestial body, such as the moon Io around Jupiter. The orbital radius of Io is about 4.9×10^5 km (3.1×10^5 miles). In this experiment you made a scale model of Jupiter's moons. A scale is a ratio between the measurements of a model and the actual measurements of an object. In a scale ratio the model measurement comes first. If the first value of the ratio is smaller, the scale drawing or model is reduced, such as the 6 mm/1×10^5 km in this activity. At this scale, the small center circle approximates Jupiter's diameter of about 1.4×10^5 km (0.875×10^5 miles). The distance of 29 mm from the center of the circle approximates the orbital distance of Io from Jupiter's center.

The locations of dots 1, 2, 3, and 4 indicate the movement of Io over 3 Earth days (72 hours). During the first Earth day, Io moved counterclockwise from dot 1 to dot 2, moving 203° around Jupiter. During the second Earth day, Io moved from dot 2 to dot 3, another 203°. Then during the third day, Io moved from dot 3 to dot 4, another 203°.

TRY NEW APPROACHES

Assuming all of the Galilean moons start at the same point on the first day of observation, how would their apparent distances from Jupiter appear at the end of 2 Earth days? Repeat the project using a data table like Table 7.1 to determine the angular distance each moon moves during 1 Earth day. Draw orbits at the correct radius from Jupiter's core using the same scale (6mm/1×10^5 km). Use different-colored markers to represent each satellite. One at a time, plot the positions of each of the satellites for day 2.

TABLE 7.1 PROPERTIES OF THE GALILEAN SATELLITES

Name	Orbital Radius (km)	Orbital Period (days)
Io	4.2×10^5	1.77
Europa	6.7×10^5	3.55
Ganymede	10.7×10^5	7.15
Callisto	18.8×10^5	16.69

DESIGN YOUR OWN EXPERIMENT

1. The gravity of Jupiter has pulled the satellites into its equatorial plane, meaning the moons are basically in line with Jupiter's equator. At times the satellites with larger orbital radii appear closer than those with smaller radii. In the previous experiments, you modeled a bird's-eye view of Jupiter's moons, but that's not how we see them from Earth. Find a way to model the edge-on locations of the moons as we do see them from Earth. Since we on Earth are almost perfectly aligned

with the orbital planes of the moons, they seem to line up in a straight line across Jupiter's equator. One way to show this is to lay a sheet of clear plastic over the diagram of the positions of the satellites in the previous experiment. Make a red grape-size ball of modeling clay to represent Jupiter. Place this clay ball on the part of the plastic covering Jupiter. Using four different colors of clay, make four pea-size clay balls representing Jupiter's moons and place one ball on dot 1 of each moon's orbit. Slip a piece of stiff cardboard or a book under the paper with the plastic on top, and raise the cardboard so the plane of the plastic is perpendicular to your face and Jupiter is directly in front of your eyes. Observe the positions of each of the satellites in relation to Jupiter. Two diagrams can be made as in Figure 7.2, one a bird's-eye view of the satellites as seen from above Jupiter's north pole (above the plastic) and the other the edge-on view (as seen by an observer on Earth). Repeat this procedure, moving the satellites to their location after 1 Earth day and then again after 2 and 3 Earth days.

Figure 7.2

2. Observe Jupiter through a telescope for a period of 17 or more days. During this time, most of the satellites will have made many revolutions around Jupiter, but Callisto will have made only one. Design an experiment to plot the position of the satellites from day to day. Make four or more observations at least 1 hour apart to identify the satellites. They can be identified by the rate at which they move: from fastest to slowest, they are Io, Europa, Ganymede, and Callisto. For information on identifying the satellites on any specific day, see astronomy magazines, such as *Sky and Telescope* and *Astronomy,* for the month of the observation.

GET THE FACTS

While the term satellite refers to any object orbiting a celestial body, *planetary satellite* generally refers specifically to moons. The moons of Jupiter are called Jovian satellites. How many Jovian satellites are known to date? How do their distances and orbital periods compare? See an astronomy text and/or search the Web for information about Jovian satellites.

8 Meteors
Streaks of Light in the Sky

What are those points of light moving across the sky? If they blink or glow red, they are probably on an airplane. A white, continuous, slowly moving light is probably an artificial satellite. The bright streaking white light is a "shooting star," which is actually a meteor.

In this project, you will determine why meteor showers occur by modeling the plane of Earth's orbit in relation to that of a comet. You will discover the two types of meteoroid streams and learn how to represent them. You will also compare the number of meteors in "showers" with the numbers of meteors that fall to Earth sporadically.

GETTING STARTED

Purpose: To model Earth's orbit passing through a comet's orbit.

Materials

pen
1-by-3-inch (2.5-by-7.5 cm) strip of poster board
one-hole paper punch
three 12-inch (30-cm) pipe cleaners—2 yellow,
　1 green

Procedure

1. Draw the Sun in the center of the strip of poster board.

2. Punch four holes in the strip, centering them near the edges of the four ends.

3. Thread the green pipe cleaner through the holes on the short ends of the strip. Twist its ends together, and form it into an elliptical shape. This is a model of Earth's orbit.

4. Twist the ends of the yellow pipe cleaners together to form one long piece. Thread it through the remaining holes. Twist the ends together and form it into an ellipse. This is a model of a comet's orbit.

5. Position the two orbits at angles so that Earth's orbit touches the comet's orbit at only one point (see Figure 8.1).

Figure 8.1

Results

The comet's orbit is at an angle nearly perpendicular to Earth's orbit, so they only touch at one point.

Why?

Comets are celestial bodies made of dust, rock, sand, gases, and ices (mainly water and carbon dioxide) that move in an extremely elongated orbit about the Sun. They are often called dirty snowballs. When they get near the inner planets, the Sun's heat vaporizes surface ice, freeing some of the rock, sand, and dust. These pieces become **meteoroids** (solid particles that have broken off a celestial body and that orbit the Sun) scattered along the comet's path. Meteoroids from comets are generally the size of dust specks, while those from **asteroids** (irregularly shaped rocky chunks of matter that rotate as they orbit the Sun, generally between Mars and Jupiter; also called **minor planets**) can be very large.

When a meteoroid enters Earth's atmosphere, it is called a **meteor**. Meteors move so fast that friction with the air causes them to heat up and **vaporize** (change to a gas). The hot vapor is **incandescent** (glowing because of heat). This incandescence is the light of a "shooting star." Any meteor large enough to survive its fall through Earth's atmosphere and actually make it to Earth's surface is called a **meteorite.**

The orbit of Earth and the orbits of most comets never meet. But some comets have orbital paths that do intersect with Earth's orbit. Thus, in its annual trip around the Sun, Earth passes through the orbital paths of several comets at different times throughout the year. Each time this happens, Earth passes through debris the comet left in its path, and a **meteor shower** (an increase in the rate of meteors) is seen by observers on Earth. On any clear night 3 to 15 meteors are generally seen per hour. But during a meteor shower as many as 60 meteors per hour have been seen.

TRY NEW APPROACHES

Since comets approach the Sun from all directions, most of them are on a different orbital plane than Earth. Therefore, Earth generally passes through the path of any given comet only once each year. However, it is possible for Earth to intersect a comet's path twice each year—once where the comet is coming in toward the Sun, and again when it is heading back out away from the Sun. This is the case with the famous Halley's comet, which happens to have an orbital plane similar to Earth's. It produces two annual meteor showers: the Eta Aquarids in May and the Orionids in October. Model this by repeating the experiment, making the four holes in your poster board in line with one another, with two holes on each side of the Sun.

DESIGN YOUR OWN EXPERIMENT

1a. The direction of most meteors is sporadic. The remains of a long-dead comet are spread widely across space. Thus meteoroids from these comets may enter Earth's atmosphere from any and all directions. Design an experiment that compares the number of meteors coming from one direction during a shower to the numbers that come sporadically during a given time period. One way is to make nightly counts during a meteor shower. Do the same when the meteor fall is sporadic. For information about how to observe and count meteors, as well as dates of expected meteor showers, see Fred Schaaf's *40 Nights to Knowing the Sky* (New York: Holt, 1998), pp. 120–127.

b. The meteoroids of a meteor shower are part of a **meteoroid stream** (debris from a comet traveling in or near a comet's orbital path). These meteoroids may be bunched, or concentrated, in one part of the comet's orbit. When Earth passes through such a bunched swarm of meteoroids, observers on Earth are likely to see a **meteor storm** (many meteors occurring in a short period of time). Or the meteoroids may be rather uniformly distributed along a comet's path. This occurs when comets have made many trips around the Sun, and generally produces more sparse meteor showers. Design a display for these two types of meteoroid streams.

GET THE FACTS

Meteors sometimes leave a glowing trail across the sky called a *meteor train*. What causes this trail? How long does it last? For information about meteor trains and other types meteors, such as fireballs and bolides, see Schaaf's *40 Nights,* pp. 118–120.

BIOLOGY

9 Meristematic Region
Growth Zone

Dicots, the popular name for dicotyledons, are one of the two large groups of flowering plants. In dicots the seeds have two cotyledons, which is the leaflike part of the seed containing nutrition for the seed to develop and grow. All types of plants contain areas of rapidly growing tissue, called meristem. The meristem is responsible for growth, both in the length and the width of plant stems.

In this project, you will discover the location of the meristematic region in dicot plant stems responsible for the elongation of the stems. You will discover if there is a change in meristematic growth rate during different times of the day and among different plants. You will determine any effect of light duration on meristematic growth. You will also research how the primary and secondary growth of a plant affects its size.

GETTING STARTED

Purpose: To determine where growth occurs in the stem of a pinto bean plant.

Materials

three 9-ounce (270-ml)   pencil
   paper cups   12 dry pinto beans
potting soil   tap water
ruler   marking pen

Procedure

1. Fill each cup with potting soil to within 2 inches (5 cm) from the top.

2. Use the pencil to punch six or more holes near the bottom of each cup.

3. Lay four beans on the surface of the soil of each cup.

4. Cover the beans with about 1 inch (2.5 cm) of soil.

5. Moisten the soil with water. Keep the soil moist but not wet throughout the experiment.

6. Allow the seeds to germinate and the seedlings to grow to a height of about 6 inches (15 cm) above the top of each cup. *Note:* This will take seven or more days.

7. Select 4 or more of the most healthy looking seedlings.

8. Use the marking pen to draw a line across the stem of each selected plant level with the lip of the cup. Use this mark as the starting line.

9. Mark three equal sections on each stem between the cotyledons (the two remaining parts of the seed) and the starting line (see Figure 9 .1).

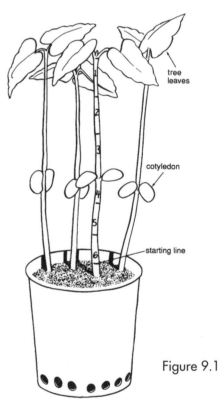

tree leaves

cotyledon

starting line

Figure 9.1

10. Mark three equal sections on each stem between the cotyledons and the true leaves at the top of the stem.

11. Prepare drawings of each plant, numbering each section from 1 to 6, starting at the top of each stem as in Figure 9.1.

12. Measure and record the starting length of each section in a Stem Growth Data table, such as the one in Table 9.1.

TABLE **9.1** STEM GROWTH DATA—PLANT 1						
	Section Length, mm					
	1	2	3	4	5	6
Start						
Final						
Difference						

13. Set the plants near a window with indirect sunlight. Add equal amounts of water to each cup to keep the soil moist but not wet. After seven days, again measure and record the length of each section. Determine any change in the length of each section.

Results

The author's plants showed the greatest elongation in the sections marked 1, only slight changes in the sections marked 2, and no measurable changes in the lower sections marked 3 through 6.

Why?

New plant cells are formed at growing points of actively dividing cells. These growing points are called **meristems.** The specialized clusters of cells in the meristem produce growth by mitosis. In **mitosis,** the cell parts duplicate themselves and then divide into two separate cells. With each division at least one of the new cells, called daughter cells, remains meristematic, thus preserving the meristem. The second daughter cell may be meristematic for a time, but eventually forms a specialized cell.

A bean plant is a **dicotyledon (dicot),** which is one of two groups of flowering plants, characterized by having seeds with two cotyledons. In a dicot, the **cotyledons** are the two parts of the seed, also called seed leaves, that contain stored **nutrients** (nourishing materials needed for life and growth of **organisms**—living things) required for the seed to grow and develop. The **stems** (part of a plant that supports other plant parts, including leaves, flowers, and fruit) of the bean plants in this experiment have meristems located at the **apex** (tip) of their stem, which are called **apical meristems.** Division of apical meristem cells increases the length of the stem, at the top of the stem.

TRY NEW APPROACHES

1. Does the rate of meristematic growth in the bean plants change during different periods of the day? Repeat the experiment marking only the three sections of the stems above the cotyledons. Measure these sections at two-hour intervals during the day, starting early in the morning and stopping at sunset.

2. Does the apical meristem growth rate differ in different dicot plants? Repeat the original experiment using different kinds of bean seedlings such as pinto, lima, and red kidney beans. For a better comparison of the growth, divide the area above the cotyledon of each plant into four or more sections. **Science Fair Hint:** Use the bean seedlings as the control so that growth of the other seedlings is compared to the bean seedlings. Use diagrams showing the changes in the length of each section as part of a project display.

DESIGN YOUR OWN EXPERIMENT

1. The interval in a 24-hour period in which an organism is exposed to light is called a **photoperiod** (length of daylight and darkness). The responses of organisms to changes in the photoperiod is called **photoperiodism.** Design an experiment to determine if light duration affects the rate of meristematic growth. One way is by repeating the original experiment using three test groups of plants with 3 cups of plants in each group. Make every effort to vary only the amount of light that each group receives. Loosely cover the cups in one group with clear cellophane, taping the edges and top of the cellophane together to form a transparent (allows light to pass through) tubelike "hat" over each cup. Use wax paper to prepare a **translucent** (allows some light to pass through, though this light is **diffused**—spread out in different directions) "hat" for the second group, and aluminum foil to prepare an opaque (doesn't allow light to pass through) "hat" for the third group. Let the cups with the opaque hats be the control group. Lift the hats and measure the plants daily.

2. Plants grow in different environments with different nutrients. Design an experiment to determine how nutrients affect meristematic growth. One way is to repeat the original experiment using three sets of plants with the independent variable being nutrient. You will need to determine a method of growing the plants in soils from three different regions. Take care in the design of the experiment to keep all factors constant except for the independent variable, soil, for each set of plants the same.

GET THE FACTS

1. Some plants live for hundreds and even thousands of years. Some bristlecone pines found in eastern California have been documented as being many thousands of years old. Theoretically these plants can grow forever by substituting new cells for aging and nonfunctioning cells. This potential for continuous growth is called *open growth* and involves apical and secondary meristems. Growth from apical meristems is called *primary growth* while growth from *lateral meristems* found in the *cambrium* (growth layer in plant stems) is called *secondary growth*. How does primary and secondary growth affect the size of a plant? What produces growth rings in some plants? Do all plants have cambrium? For more information, see a biology text.

2. Some plants have a main stem that grows taller than other stems on the plant. This is called a *terminal shoot*. What causes a terminal shoot? What is apical dominance? For more information, see *Janice VanCleave's A+ Projects in Biology* (New York: Wiley, 1993), pp. 57–62.

10 Seed Parts
Exterior and Interior

Given the right amount of water, oxygen, and warmth, most seeds germinate and develop into mature plants. Seeds vary in physical appearance both on the outside and on the inside.

In this project you will have the opportunity to identify exterior and interior seed parts. The seed parts of two basic seed types, dicotyledons and monocotyledons, will be compared. You will determine why the cotyledon is necessary and investigate the presence of starch in each seed part.

GETTING STARTED

Purpose: To dissect a bean seed and identify its parts.

Materials

8 to 10 pinto beans
1-pint (500-ml) jar
distilled water
refrigerator
paper towel
magnifying lens (handheld type)

Procedure

1. Place the beans into the jar and cover them with distilled water.

2. Put the jar of beans in the refrigerator to reduce bacterial contamination.

3. Soak the beans for 24 hours.

4. Remove the beans from the jar and place them on the paper towel to absorb the excess water.

5. Inspect the outside of the beans and identify the seed coat and hilum (see Figure 10.1).

6. Use your fingernails to carefully remove the seed coat from one of the beans.

7. Very gently pry the rounded side of the bean open like a book with your fingernail.

8. Spread open the two halves of the bean.

9. Use the magnifying lens to study the inside of each bean half and identify the cotyledon, plumule, epicotyl, hypocotyl, and radicle (see Figure 10.1).

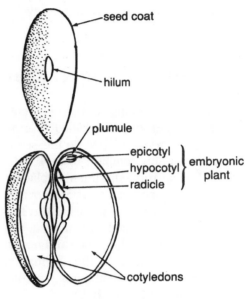

Figure 10.1

10. Open several beans and compare their parts for differences in size, shape, and organization.

Results

The brown seed coat is thin and peels off easily to reveal a white structure with two separate halves connected at the top. Inside is a cylindrical structure with what appears to be folded leaves at the end.

Why?

The bean seed consists of three basic parts: a seed coat, an embryo, and two cotyledons. The surface covering of a seed is called the **seed coat.** This jacket around the seed protects the **embryo** (an organism in its earliest stage of development) from insects, disease, and other damage. The **hilum** is the scar on the seed coat of some seeds, such as beans; it is the point where the seed was attached to the plant during development.

A bean has two halves under the seed coat called cotyledons, so it is called a dicotyledon or a dicot (a plant whose seed has two cotyledons). The end of the embryo that develops into the **shoot** (part of plant that grows above ground) is called the **epicotyl.** The tip of the epicotyl that looks like folded leaves is called the **plumule** (embryonic shoot tip that consists of several tiny, immature leaves that at maturity form the first true leaves). Below the epicotyl is the **hypocotyl,** which attaches the embryo to the cotyledon. The end of the hypocotyl, called the **radicle,** develops into the root.

TRY NEW APPROACHES

la. While dicotyledons have two cototyledons, **monocotyledons,** also called **monocots,** have only *one* cotyledon. How do the seed parts of a monocotyledon compare to those of a dicotyledon? Repeat the experiment replacing the bean seed with corn seed. *Note:* A corn kernel is a fruit. The corn seed is inside the fruit, but the kernel is often called a corn seed. Corn seed is much more difficult to open and may require the use of a scalpel. As in the original experiment, study and identify seed parts (see the corn kernel diagram in Figure 10.2).
CAUTION: *Adult supervision is needed when cutting with a sharp instrument. Always cut in a direction away from your hands and fingers.*

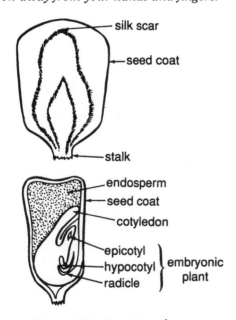

Figure 10.2 Corn Kernel

b. Seeds vary in size, shape, and color. **Science Fair Hint:** Collect and display samples of seeds. Organize the seeds to indicate which are **angiosperms** (flowering seed plants) and which are **gymnosperms** (a nonflowering seed plant). Further classifications, such as how the seeds are transported, can also be used. For information about seeds see Cynthia Overbeck's *How Seeds Travel* (Minneapolis: Lerner Publications Company, 1990).

2. Use a **stereomicroscope** (dissecting microscope that allows thick specimens to be observed) to study, identify, and compare the parts of bean seed and corn seed. **Science Fair Hint:** Diagram the parts of each seed type, label the parts, and display the diagrams.

DESIGN YOUR OWN EXPERIMENT

1. Bean seeds have two cotyledons. Are both cotyledon's necessary for their **germination** (process by which a seed grows)? One way to determine this is to grow bean seeds with different amounts of the two cotyledons. Soak 30 beans for 24 hours in a jar of water. Prepare five or more beans for each of the following five groups:

- 100%—Do not cut away any part of the cotyledons.

- 75%—Cut away the lower half of one cotyledon.

- 50%—Cut away the lower half of both cotyledons.

- 25%—Cut away all but one-fourth of the cotyledons, leaving the section attached to the embryo.

- 0%—Cut away both cotyledons, leaving only the embryo.

Note: Use a scalpel to carefully cut away the indicated parts of the cotyledons (see Figure 10.3). Make every effort not to disturb the embryo. Discard extra beans.

Place the prepared beans on a moist paper towel. Set the towel on a sheet of aluminum foil and fold the foil around the beans. Open the foil

Figure 10.3

package daily and make observations of any evidence of germination. **Science Fair Hint:** Use diagrams and photographs to represent results.

2. Starch is a stored food supply for seeds. Is starch stored in seed parts other than the cotyledons? One way to determine this is to test for the presence of starch using iodine. **CAUTION:** *Keep iodine out of the reach of small children. It is poisonous and is for external use only. It can stain skin, fabric, and furniture.* A positive test for the presence of starch is a dark blue-black color on the material where the iodine is placed. Using bean seeds, determine the presence of starch by using iodine on each of the following seed parts: cotyledon, epicotyl, hypocotyl, radicle, and seed coat. Separate the parts from one another and place them in shallow containers. Add one or two drops of tincture of iodine (found at a pharmacy) to each part. Prepare and display a data table to indicate the presence of starch. Use a plus sign (+) to indicate the presence of starch and a minus sign (–) to indicate its absence.

GET THE FACTS

1. *Endosperm* (the food-storage tissue of a seed) is present at some stage during the development of all seeds. It is present in mature corn seed but not in bean seed. What happens to the endosperm? Why is it present in some mature seeds but not in others?

2. The seed coat of different seeds varies in color, thickness, and texture. Sometimes, it is smooth and paper thin, as on a bean. A coconut's seed coat is rough, thick, and hard. This outer coat protects the embryo from drying out against injury from falls or being struck by objects, and from attacks by insects, some animals, bacteria, and fungi. It also insulates the embryo from extreme temperatures. Germination cannot take place unless the seed coat is cracked. The seed coats of some plants are cracked by alternate freezing and thawing. Not all seeds are affected by temperature changes, and many plants do not live where the temperature drastically rises and falls. How else might a seed coat crack, allowing water and oxygen in and the developing embryo to emerge?

3. Many types of seeds do not germinate regardless of the environmental conditions. They germinate only after a period of rest called the *dormancy period*. Dormancy may be the result of many factors; for example, the seed coat may contain chemical inhibitors that prevent germination. During a period of rest soil moisture leaches out the chemicals or they break down as they react with other chemicals in the soil. When the inhibitors are gone, the seed germinates. Find out more about seed dormancy and the events that result during a rest period.

11 Autotrophs
Food Builders

Respiration is the chemical and physical process by which animals and plants take in oxygen and use it to release energy from glucose molecules. Respiration provides energy necessary for carrying on all essential life processes. Plants are autotrophic—that is, they are able to manufacture glucose through a process called photosynthesis. Photosynthesis is a process in which energy from light is captured and stored in the plant.

In this project, you will use plants to examine the processes of photosynthesis and respiration and determine substances produced and consumed in each. You will study the effect of light on these processes. You will also determine if respiration occurs during the germination of seeds.

GETTING STARTED

Purpose: To test for the production of carbon dioxide by respiration in plants.

Materials

five 6-inch (15-cm) test tubes
distilled water
masking tape
pen
ruler
four 5-inch (15-cm) sprigs of elodea or other water plant the length of the test tube (found at a pet store)

0.04% aqueous solution of bromthymol blue indicator (your teacher can purchase this from a scientific supply company)
5 corks to fit the test tubes
aluminum foil
bowl or container that will hold the test tubes upright

Procedure

1. Rinse the test tubes with distilled water.
2. Place a piece of tape about 2 inches (5 cm) long from the top edge down the side of each tube. Use the pen and ruler to mark a line across the tape 1 inch (2.5 cm) from the top of each tube.
3. Use the pen to label four of the test tubes "1," "2," "3," "4." The fifth tube will be the control. Label this remaining tube "C."

4. Place an equal-size sprig of elodea into test tubes 1 through 4.
5. Fill all the test tubes including C up to the 1-inch (2.5-cm) line with bromthymol blue indicator. Put a cork in each of the tubes.
6. Observe and record the color of the liquid in each tube in a Carbon Dioxide Data table like the one shown in Table 11.1.

Figure 11.1

TABLE 11.1 CARBON DIOXIDE DATA					
Time, hr	**Color of Liquid in Test Tubes**				
	Test tube 1	Test tube 2	Test tube 3	Test tube 4	Test tube C
0					
↓					
24					

7. Cover the test tubes with aluminum foil so that no light can enter.
8. Stand the tubes together in a bowl and place the bowl on a table in an unlighted or dimly lit area.
9. Observe the color of the liquid in each test tube every hour for eight or more hours during the day, then again after 24 hours. Record the color in the data table.

Figure 11.2

Results

The color of the liquid in test tube C remains unchanged and is blue. The color of the liquid in test tubes 1 through 4 changes from blue to green to yellow as time passes.

Why?

Indicators are natural or synthetic chemical substances that change color in response to other chemicals. **Acid indicators,** such as bromthymol blue, change color in the presence of a substance called acid. **Acids** cause the bromthymol blue indicator to turn from blue to green, then to yellow, depending on the **concentration** (amount of one substance dissolved in a given volume of another) of acid present. At a low acid concentration the color is green and at a higher concentration the color is yellow.

A **chemical reaction** is a change that produces one or more new substances. In a chemical reaction, a **reactant** is a substance that is changed and a **product** is a substance that is produced. **Internal respiration** involves a series of chemical reactions that liberate energy from **glucose** (a type of sugar) molecules. Respiration is a catabolic process that occurs inside every animal and plant cell. A **catabolic process,** is a chemical reaction in which larger substances in an organism are broken down into smaller ones. During respiration the catabolic process is the breakdown of a glucose to water and a gas, carbon dioxide, with a release of energy. Internal respiration is also called **aerobic respiration,** which means that oxygen is one of the reactants. The general equation for aerobic respiration is:

glucose + oxygen→water + carbon dioxide + energy

The products of respiration of the elodea plant (carbon dioxide and water) mix with the liquid indicator. Some of the carbon dioxide chemically combines with the water, forming the acid called carbonic acid. The more carbon dioxide that dissolves in the water over time, the greater the concentration of the acid formed. The color of the liquid in each test tube indicates changes in the concentration of acid as a result of the respiration of each elodea plant over time.

TRY NEW APPROACHES

1. Respiration occurs with or without the presence of light, but light is necessary for photosynthesis. **Photosynthesis** is the process by which light energy is absorbed and then converted to the chemical energy of glucose. This conversion occurs in plants that have chlorophyll (pigment that absorbs light). Photosynthesis is an **anabolic process,** in which energy is needed to build larger molecules from smaller ones. During photosynthesis, carbon dioxide and water in the presence of chlorophyll and light energy combine, forming glucose and oxygen. The general equation for photosynthesis is:

carbon dioxide + water $\xrightarrow[\text{light energy}]{\text{chlorophyll}}$ glucose + oxygen

Determine how light affects the concentration of carbon dioxide released by plants into the environment around them. Do this by repeating the experiment but leave off the aluminum foil covering the test tubes. Then place the test tubes 8 inches (20 cm) from a desk lamp. Compare the color of the test tubes in the light with those from the previous experiment that did not receive light.

2. Does the amount of light affect the results? Repeat the previous experiment twice by placing one set of uncovered test tubes closer to the light and a second set of test tubes farther away from the light.

3. Does the source of light affect the results? Repeat the experiment by placing five uncovered test tubes near different light sources such as sunlight, incandescent bulbs, fluorescent bulbs, and plant grow-lights. When using artificial lights, place the test tubes an equal distance from the lights.

DESIGN YOUR OWN EXPERIMENT

1. Seeds do not need light to germinate. Design an experiment to find out whether respiration occurs during seed germination. One method is to fill a small plastic soda bottle one-third full with dry pinto beans and cover the beans with distilled water. Place the jar in a refrigerator to reduce the production of bacteria while the beans soak. (Soaking the beans allows water to penetrate them, which encourages germination.) After soaking overnight, pour off the water and use modeling clay to secure one end of a flexible plastic drinking straw inside the mouth of the bottle. Insert the free end of the straw into a glass of bromthymol indicator (see Figure 11.3). Observe the color of the indicator solution near the end of the straw to determine whether carbon dioxide is exiting the straw.

bromthymol blue

Figure 11.3

2a. The chemical equations for photosynthesis and aerobic respiration are:

Photosynthesis:

$$6\ CO_2 + 6\ H_2O \xrightarrow[\text{Light Energy}]{\text{Chlorophyll}} C_6H_{12}O_6 + 6\ O_2$$

Aerobic Respiration:

$$C_6H_{12}O_6 + 6\ O_2 \rightarrow 6\ CO_2 + 6\ H_2O + \text{Energy}$$

While photosynthesis requires light, aerobic respiration does not. Note that the products of one of the energy equations are the reactants for the other. Plants are **autotrophs,** which are organisms that can make their own food. So plants can live in a closed environment as long as they have access to sunlight, because they can recycle matter (transforming sugar and oxygen into carbon dioxide and water, and back again). They do need access to sunlight, however, because light energy cannot be recycled. Design an experiment to determine how long a plant can live in a closed container without any outside nutrient sources. One way is to prepare eight jars of distilled water and equal amounts of elodea sprigs. Use lids to close four of the jars. Then set all of the jars near a window with indirect sunlight or in a well-lighted area of a room. Observe the plants for one month or more. Compare the plants in the covered jars with those in the uncovered jars.

b. The previous experiment can be performed by filling the jars about one-fourth full with soil. Use plants such as grass or ivy. Moisten the soil in each jar, then do not add any nutrients.

GET THE FACTS

1. *Cellular respiration* is the process by which *adenosine triphosphate, ATP* (a special energy-carrying molecule) is produced by respiration. How is ATP involved in energy production? What part do ADP molecules play in the production of ATP molecules? How much ATP is produced during aerobic respiration? What happens to the ATP molecules? Where does aerobic respiration take place in living organisms? For information about respiration, see a biology textbook.

2. Photosynthesis is said to require light, but it actually involves two processes, one called the light reaction and the other the dark reaction. What is the difference between these two reactions? What is needed for these reactions to occur? A biology text can provide information about photosynthesis.

12 Aquatic Respiration
Breathing Rate of Goldfish

Aquatic (pertaining to water) bony fish extract oxygen from water as terrestrial animal lungs draw oxygen from air. But gills are more efficient at extracting oxygen from water than lungs are at getting oxygen from the air. Gills extract about 80 % of the oxygen in water they take in, while human lungs extract only about 20 % of the oxygen from air they breathe.

In this project, you will determine the breathing rate of a goldfish. You will determine the effect of variables on the rate of breathing, such as fish size and type, water temperature, and the fish's excitement level.

GETTING STARTED

Purpose: To determine the breathing rate of a fish by observing the opening and closing of its mouth and operculum.

Materials

medium-size goldfish in a small fishbowl
timer

Procedure

Note: The goldfish should be in a small fishbowl that has been properly prepared according to instructions from a professional at a pet store or from a fish manual. Feeding the fish should be considered part of the normal maintenance of the fish and not as part of a project experiment.

Figure 12.1

mouth

operculum

1. Locate the fish's mouth (see Figure 12.1).
2. Count the number of times the fish opens and closes its mouth over a period of 2 minutes.

	Mouth openings in 2 minutes				
TABLE 12.1 FISH BREATHING RATE DATA	Test 1	Test 2	Test 3	Test 4	Average
Medium Fish					

Record the number of openings in a Fish Breathing Rate Data table, like the one in Table 12.1.

3. Repeat step 2 three times, then average the number of mouth openings.

4. Calculate the breathing rate of the fish per minute by taking the average rate for two minutes and dividing it by 2. For example, if the average is 210 mouth openings in 2 minutes, the breathing rate per minute would be:

$$\text{breathing rate} = 210 \text{ openings} \div 2 \text{ minutes}$$
$$= 105 \text{ openings /minute}$$

5. Repeat steps 1 through 4 counting the opening and closing of the fish's **operculum** (protective flap of skin over a fish's gills).

Results

The fish's mouth and operculum open and close an equal number of times. The breathing rate in the example is 105 openings per minute.

Why?

External respiration is a process used by organisms to exchange gases with the environment. **Breathing** (mechanical process of moving gases into and out of the body) is an essential part of the external respiration in most animals. The respiratory system of some **aquatic** (pertaining to water) organisms, including bony fish, such as a goldfish, consists of a set of gills beneath a protective flap called the **operculum. Gills** are **organs** (structures in organisms that perform a function) through which fish breathe. One set is on either side of the fish's body. The gills contain many capillaries (tiniest blood vessels). As water flows over the gills, oxygen from the water enters the blood by passing through the walls of these capillaries and the waste gas, carbon dioxide, in the blood leaves the capillaries and enters the water. Thus an exchange of gases occurs in the gills.

A fish opens its mouth to inhale water, not to drink it. "Yawning" movements draw water into the mouth. When the mouth is open the operculum is closed. Then the mouth closes and the operculum opens. The water that came in through the mouth then passes over the gills and out the operculum. The breathing rate, or the number of times the mouth or the operculum open and close per minute, was determined for the fish in this experiment.

Figure 12.2

TRY NEW APPROACHES

1. How does the size of a fish affect its breathing rate? Determine this by repeating the experiment using goldfish of different sizes; use fish that are larger and smaller than the one in the experiment. Let the medium-size fish be the control and compare the breathing rates of the other fish with that of the control fish.

2. Is the breathing rate of different kinds of fish the same? Determine this by repeating the original experiment using different kinds of fish. Select fish that are of comparable size to the medium-size goldfish in the original experiment.

DESIGN YOUR OWN EXPERIMENT

1a. During the winter, a fish's water environment gets colder. Design an experiment to determine if a change in water temperature affects the respiration rate of fish. One way is to prepare a testing tank by filling a 1-quart (1-liter) wide-mouth jar about three-fourths full with distilled water. Allow the water to sit for 30 minutes or more until it is at room temperature. Using a fishnet, carefully transfer the medium-size fish from the original experiment into the test jar. Place a clean thermometer into the jar and set the jar in a bowl half filled with water. Slowly lower the temperature of the water inside the testing jar by adding a few

small pieces of ice to the bowl (see Figure 12.2). When the ice pieces melt, use the thermometer to gently stir the water inside the testing jar so that the water's temperature is the same throughout. Allow the testing jar to remain undisturbed for 5 minutes to allow the fish to calm. Then, determine the respiration rate of the fish at this temperature. Continue cooling the jar by small degree intervals until the temperature is about 41°F (5°C). Do not lower the temperature to freezing at 32°F (0°C). After the experiment is complete, allow the testing jar to sit so that it returns to room temperature before returning the fish to its regular container. Prepare and display a graph showing the average breathing rate of the fish at each temperature (see Figure 12.3).

Breathing Rate of Fish

Number of Times Mouth Opens per Minute

Figure 12.3

b. Repeat the previous experiment to determine the effect of temperature on different sizes of fish as well as different kinds of fish. On a line graph, use a different color line for each different fish tested.

2a. Animals breathe faster when they exercise as well as when they get excited. Design an experiment to determine if being excited affects the breathing rate of a fish. One method is to cover the fishbowl of the medium-size fish with a dark cloth and restrict as much as possible noises and movement outside the bowl. After five or more minutes, quietly position yourself so that you can immediately begin counting mouth movements as you quickly remove the cloth. Calculate the breathing rate per minute of the startled fish.

b. Repeat the previous experiment using fish of different sizes as well as different kinds of fish.

GET THE FACTS

Gas exchange in an organism supports cellular respiration by supplying oxygen and removing carbon dioxide. The source of oxygen, called the *respiratory medium,* is water for fish and air for terrestrial animals. The part of an animal's anatomy where gas exchange with the respiratory medium occurs is called the *respiratory surface,* which is the gills in a fish. The greater the respiratory surface, the greater is the gas exchange. What is the purpose of gill rakers and how do they affect gas exchange? What does ventilation of gills mean? Why is it necessary to keep the respiratory surface wet? What is countercurrent exchange? For more information, see a biology text.

13 Operant Conditioning
The "Aha!" Response

An object that has bilateral symmetry can be divided into mirror images by drawing one vertical line through the center. In other words, if a vertical line were drawn dividing the object in half, the left and right sides would match each other. Most animals, and some plants, have bilateral symmetry. Animals with a bilaterally symmetrical nervous system are those in which the parts of the nervous system on the right and left sides of their bodies are mirror images of each other.

When confronted with alternatives, animals with bilaterally symmetrical nervous systems can learn to make consistent choices. Sometimes, learning is a response to a particular stimulus or to a reward. Other times, learning comes through force of habit, or trial and error, or insight.

In this project you will study the human ability to learn by trial and error as well as through insight. The ability of mice and insects to learn as a result of operant conditioning—that is, to learn as a result of receiving rewards for desired behavior—will be determined. You will also look at factors that may affect the retention and rate of learning, such as practice and distractions.

GETTING STARTED

Purpose: To determine the time it takes for a person to trace the mirror image of a pattern.

Materials

20-by-24-by-36-inch (50-by-61-by-90-cm) cardboard box	felt-tip marking pen
box cutter	10 copies of test sheet (Draw your own. See Figure 13.2)
24-by-16-inch (60-by-40-cm) mirror	10 test subjects
duct tape	timer

Procedure

1. Build a mirror test box (see Figure 13.1). *Note:* The size of the box and mirror are not critical. You want a box and mirror large enough to allow each test subject to see only the mirror image of the pattern and be able to insert his or her hand without restriction to trace the pattern. Here are the steps followed by the author in building a test box using the listed materials.

   a. In the front wall of the box, 4 inches (10 cm) down from the top, use the box cutter to cut a 20-inch (50-cm) slit across the center of the box.

   b. In the back wall of the box, 17 inches (43 cm) down from the top, cut a 20-inch (50-cm) slit across the center of the box.

   c. Insert the edges of the mirror (facedown) through the slits in the front and back walls of the box.

   d. Use duct tape to secure the edges of the mirror to the box.

   e. Cut a 16-by-16-inch (40-by-40-cm) square out of the front wall of the box. Make sure this hole is centered and its top edge is about 4 inches (10 cm) below the edge of the mirror (see A in Figure 13.1).

   f. Cut a 4-by-12-inch (10-by-30-cm) section from the bottom edge of the front wall of the box (see B in Figure 13.1.)

   g. To allow viewing light to enter, cut out one 12-inch (30-cm) square from each side of the box with the lower edge of the square about 4 inches (10 cm) from the bottom of the box (see C in Figure 13.1).

2. Set the mirror test box on a table.

3. Lay the marking pen and one copy of the test sheet inside the box. (see Figure 13.2).

4. Have the test subject sit in a chair positioned in front of the test box.

5. Read the following instructions to one test subject:

   • Follow the instructions as I read them to you.

   • Insert your hand through the opening at the bottom of the box.

Figure 13.1

Figure 13.2

- Look at the mirror through the opening in the center of the box.

- The objective is for you to use the pen to draw a line through the center of the path on the test sheet as fast as possible without crossing the printed lines of the pattern. When I say "Get ready . . . Start," you will begin and I will start the timer. When you finish, say "Stop" and the timer will be stopped.

- Place the tip of the pen on the word "Go" on the sheet.

- Get ready.

- Start.

6. Repeat the procedure for all of the test subjects.

Results

The time varies for each person tested.

Why?

The test subjects learn to trace the pattern of the mirror image of the path by a method called **insight response** or the **"aha!" response.** Insight responses are entirely new responses but depend upon previously learned responses put together in a new way. The faster the test subject learns to compensate for the fact that the up and down movements in the mirror image are backward, the faster is his or her time for completing the path.

TRY NEW APPROACHES

1. Can the test subjects improve their time with practice? To determine whether the amount of practice time affects the results, assign each person a different number of practices from 1 to 10. Allow the subjects to practice and then repeat the experiment. **Science Fair Hint:** Prepare a learning curve for each subject. Use the *y*-axis for the time per path and the *x*-axis for the number of practices (see Figure 13.3).

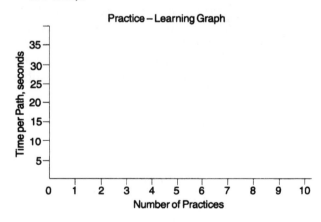

Figure 13.3

2. Do distractions affect the tracing time? Repeat the original experiment using 10 different test subjects. During the timing period, provide the same distractions for each subject, such as playing a radio and/or having someone talk to the person being timed.

3. How does spacing the practice period affect the time of the learner? Use a different set of test

subjects. Allow all subjects to practice for the same amount of time. Have half of the subjects do all their practice in one session and the other half practice over several days. After the practice sessions, repeat the original experiment.

DESIGN YOUR OWN EXPERIMENT

1. Are the test subjects faster at solving mazes that are not mirror images? Design a way to determine this. One way is to not use the mirror box, instead determine the time required for each subject to draw a path through a maze designed by you and printed on a sheet of paper. Provide 10 copies of the maze and record the time for each person to complete each maze in succession. Repeat using the mirror box and the same testing subjects and mazes. Graph the results.

2. The method of using rewards to train an animal to perform tasks that are not **innate behavior** (behavior that is inherited, not learned) is known as **instrumental conditioning** or **operant conditioning.** Through operant conditioning, ants and mice can be trained to solve mazes. They will find their way through a maze in order to find food. After they have gone through the maze once, the speed of solving the maze increases with each subsequent test. Design and construct mazes for these organisms to solve. Determine the number of errors per trial. Graph the trials on the x-axis and the errors on the y-axis. Display as many of the test materials as possible without overcrowding the display area. Use photographs of the subjects during testing. The psychologist B. F. Skinner used this operant conditioning method to train pigeons to play Ping-Pong. Use a psychology or biology text dealing with learned behavior to find out more about the training of animals to perform tasks that are not innate.

GET THE FACTS

1. The movements required to trace the mirror image of the path involve brain activity. Muscular movements are controlled by the parts of the brain called the *cerebellum* and *cerebrum*. Use a biology textbook to find out more about the cerebellum and cerebrum. In which do impulses resulting in muscle movement originate? Where are the impulses coordinated?

2. Insight responses are very creative acts and involve *inductive* and *deductive reasoning*. Use a psychology textbook to find out about these two types of learning processes. Which type of reasoning involves learning the general principle that mirror images are upside down? Down is up? Up is down? Applying the knowledge that the directions are reversed involves which of the processes?

14 Ecosystem
Interactions

In nature, there is a constant interaction among animals, plants, fungi, protists—microorganisms not easily classified as fungi, plant or animal—and their environment. A specific area where living and nonliving things interact is called an ecosystem. In this ecosystem, there is a direct relationship between the community of living organisms and its surroundings. The organisms affect their physical surroundings just as they are affected by them.

In this project you will observe some of these interactions in an open ecosystem and investigate populations within a sector. You will also determine populations of organisms by using the technique of random sampling.

GETTING STARTED

Purpose: To select and lay out a study area.

Materials

compass
measuring tape
hammer

12 wooden or metal tent stakes
300 yards (300 m) of cord

Procedure

1. Select a study area that has a variety of plant life. (A wooded area was chosen by the author, but any ecosystem can be used.)

2. Use the compass to determine which direction is north.

3. With the measuring tape, measure an area 30 × 30 yards (30 × 30 m). The plot of ground should be laid out so that it is aligned in a north-to-south direction.

4. At each of the four corners of the plot, hammer one stake into the ground, leaving about 6 inches (15 cm) of the stake aboveground.

5. Attach the end of the cord to one stake, loop it around the other stakes, and tie it to the starting stake to enclose the plot.

6. Use the measuring tape to divide the sides of the plot into 10-yard (10-m) sections.

7. Drive one stake into the ground at each 10-yard (10-m) interval along all sides of the plot (see Figure 14.1).

8. Using cord to join opposite stakes, divide the plot into nine equal subplots.

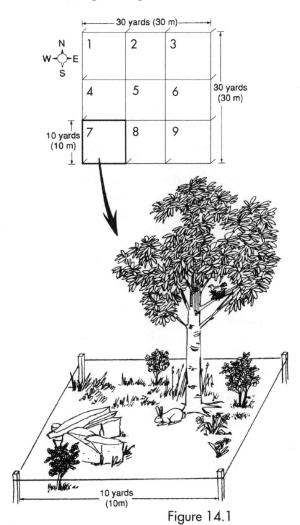

Figure 14.1

Results

A sampling plot of ground is selected, measured, and subdivided.

Why?

An **environment** is all the external factors affecting an organism. These factors may be **biotic factors** (living organisms) or **abiotic factors** (nonliving things including water, soil, climate, light, and air). All organisms living in a particular environment, such as a forest or desert, together with the abiotic factors that affect them, are collectively known as an **ecosystem.** In an ecosystem, energy and nutrients flow between the abiotic and biotic environment.

A **sampling plot** is a select area of an ecosystem that allows you to study the biotic and abiotic factors in it. During a field study, measurements of physical factors and organisms are taken. Separate information taken from each subplot, when studied as a whole, provides a clear picture of the abiotic and biotic factors within the plot and gives clues to the greater ecosystem surrounding the plot.

TRY NEW APPROACHES

On graph paper, sketch the plot. Identify each subplot with a number. Indicate the compass directions on the sketch with arrows. Make separate sketches of each subplot. Note prominent land features such as trails, open areas, erosion, and streams.

DESIGN YOUR OWN EXPERIMENT

1. Measure the angle of the **slope** (steepness of an inclined surface) of each subplot. Do this by con-

Figure 14.2

structing and using an Abney level. Make the level by using masking tape to attach a protractor to the center of a yardstick (meterstick). Tie a 12-inch (30-cm) piece of string to the center of the protractor and attach a washer to the free end of the string (see Figure 14.2). Hold the measuring stick parallel to the ground of each subplot while a helper reads the angle on the protractor made by the hanging string. When the slope is zero, the string hangs straight down across the 90° mark. To determine the angle of slopes, subtract the angle reading from 90°. For example, if the protractor reads 50°, the angle of the slope is 90° − 50°, or 40°.

2a. Observe the types of plants in each subplot. Collect leaf samples from the plants and, using plant field guides, identify the types of each plant present. Land plants are commonly classed as trees, shrubs, herbs, or vines according to the size and type of stem. Land plants are either a **woody plant** (a plant containing stems with a large amount of wood) with relatively hard stems or a **nonwoody plant** (a plant containing stems with a small amount of wood) with relatively soft stems. **Wood** is the part of a plant made of xylem tubes (tubes that transport water and other nutrients from the root throughout a plant and provide support). A description of the four types of land plants follows:

- **Trees**—Plants with a single tall, woody stem called a trunk that grows from the ground and is able to stand erect without support. Other woody stems branch from the trunk.

- **Shrubs**—Short, woody plants usually with several stems branched near the ground that are able to stand erect without support. Also called bushes.

- **Herbs** or **herbaceous plants**—Names for nonwoody plants. The stems of these plants remain relatively soft and include grasses and flowers, such as daisies and dandelions.

- **Vines**—Flexible, weak-stemmed plants whose long, slender, fast-growing shoots rely on other plants or objects for support. Vines may wind around supporting structures, and/or use thorns, **tendrils** (slender spiraling stems), or hooks to climb and anchor to a structure. Vines can be woody or nonwoody (herbaceous).

Science Fair Hint: You could display labeled photographs of the plants from each subplot along with preserved samples of the leaves or leaf rubbings.

b. Observe and record the presence of different fungi and lichens in each subplot. **Fungi** is a group of plantlike organisms that have no leaves, flowers, or chlorophyll, and include mildew, mold, mushrooms, and toadstools. **Lichen** is a plantlike organism made of fungus and **algae** (a plantlike organism with no leaves, stems, or roots, but that has chlorophyll necessary for photosynthesis). See a biology text for more information about fungi and lichen.

3a. Record the actual presence or indications of the presence of animals. Note the presence of tracks, holes, sounds, claw marks, hair, nests, and so on. Cautiously turn over rocks and logs to discover insects, reptiles, and amphibians. Remember that you are an observer and do not want to change this ecosystem, so return rocks and logs to their original positions.

b. Make molds of tracks by pouring plaster of paris into the tracks. Mix this liquid by following the directions on the box. You could use the molds as part of a project display.

GET THE FACTS

1. When an organism feeds upon another living thing, there is a transfer of materials and energy. This transfer from organism to organism is called a *food chain.* Find out more about the food chain. What is a food web? What is a pyramid of energy and a pyramid of numbers? Use the information collected in your plot to construct a pyramid of numbers. For information, see *Janice VanCleave's Ecology for Every Kid* (New York: Wiley, 1996), pp. 37–46.

2. Energy is constantly lost in an ecosystem and has to be replaced by sunlight. There is a fixed amount of matter within the system. Find out how matter is recycled in an ecosystem. For information, see a biology text.

15 Preservatives
Food Additives

In our complex world, food products have to be shipped for long distances and/or stored for periods of time. It would be difficult to transport and store most kinds of food without using preservative additives.

In this project, you will have the opportunity to test the effectiveness of calcium propionate, a food additive that inhibits mold growth in bread. The effect of this additive in different types of bread as well as the effect of temperature on the preservative will be determined. You will also analyze other methods of preserving food.

GETTING STARTED

Purpose: To determine how effective the food additive calcium propionate is in inhibiting the molding of bread.

Materials

paper towels

water

6 plastic 1-gallon (4-liter) size resealable bags

6 slices of white bread with calcium propionate

6 slices of white bread without calcium propionate or any other preservatives

marking pen

masking tape

magnifying lens (hand-held type)

Procedure

CAUTION: *Do not do this project if you are allergic to mold.*

1. Moisten one paper towel with water and lay it inside one plastic bag.

2. Place one slice of bread with calcium propionate and one without side by side on top of the moistened paper towel inside the bag.

3. Zip the plastic bag closed.

4. Use the marking pen and masking tape to label the slices of bread with and without calcium propionate. Place the label on the outside of the bag above the indicated slice of bread.

5. Repeat the procedure (steps 1 through 4) preparing five additional bags with two slices of bread, one slice of bread with calcium propionate and one without, inside each bag. *Note:* Six bags is not a significant number, but it does provide enough samples to verify your results.

6. Keep the six bags of bread closed and at room temperature.

7. Examine the slices each day with the magnifying lens.

8. Continue observing the bread for two weeks or until every slice has become moldy. Record the length of time required for each slice to mold. Discard the unopened bags.

Results

Given enough time, all of the bread slices become moldy. However, the slices with calcium propionate mold more slowly (see Figure 15.1).

Figure 15.1

Why?

Food additives are natural and synthetic chemicals added to food to supply nutrients, to enhance color, flavor, or texture, and/or to prevent or delay spoilage.

Spoilage is the ruining of food as a result of chemical changes often owing to the presence of organisms such as fungi and microbes. A **food preservative** is a food additive, such as calcium propionate, used to maintain freshness and extend the shelf life of package food. Organisms that spoil food are fussy about their diet, and different **species** (group of similar organisms) can be found on specific foods.

Calcium propionate is one of the food additives on the U. S. Food and Drug Administration's **GRAS** ("Generally Recognized As Safe") **list.** At low concentrations, it is considered harmless to humans but inhibits the reproduction and growth of mold. The addition of calcium propionate to bread allows the product to be stored for longer periods of time.

Calcium propionate is a preferred preservative for bread because it retards the rapid growth of bread mold, increases the content of calcium, and avoids the possibility of decreasing gas formation during baking, thus allowing the bread to rise normally.

TRY NEW APPROACHES

1. How effective is calcium propionate in breads other than white bread? Repeat the experiment using different types of bread. such as wheat, rye, and potato. **Science Fair Hint:** Record results of the original as well as this experiment and display the data tables.

2. Does temperature affect the effectiveness of the preservative calcium propionate? Repeat the original experiment using two sets of bread samples. Place one set in the refrigerator and place the second set in a warm area such as on top of a refrigerator. **Science Fair Hint:** Take photographs as each experiment progresses to show the changes in the food as a result of containing or not containing calcium propionate.

DESIGN YOUR OWN EXPERIMENT

Note: Avoid touching the food test samples. The food samples are not edible and should be discarded after the experiments.

1. Drying foods was one of the earliest methods of food preservation. This method is based on the fact that the organisms known to spoil food do not grow and reproduce without water. Find out more about procedures for preserving food by drying. Place dried and fresh food samples in open dishes (beef jerky and strips of fresh beef make good samples). Examine the food samples daily for evidence of spoilage and determine the effectiveness of drying as a method of preserving.

2a. Table salt (sodium chloride) and vinegar (acetic acid) are used as preservatives. Test the effectiveness of these preservatives on inhibiting microbe growth. Dissolve one chicken bouillon cube in 1 cup of (250 ml) of hot water. Divide the solution equally between three clear glasses. Add 1 teaspoon (5 ml) of salt to one glass and 1 teaspoon (5 ml) of vinegar to the second glass. The third glass is the control. Label the glasses accordingly. Place the glasses in a warm place and examine their contents daily. Spoilage due to the presence of microbes results in a solution that looks cloudy, has an odor, and often contains gas bubbles.

b. Does the amount of preservative added change the results? Repeat the experiment two times, first using one half as much salt and vinegar, and then using twice as much salt and vinegar.

3. Many foods are spoiled by the growth of various fungi in the food. Favorable conditions such as moisture and warm temperature encourage rapid reproduction of fungi. Sugar is used as a preservative for fruits because it aids in removing moisture from the cells of the fruit. Fungi are less likely to grow in the dryer fruit. Demonstrate sugar's ability to dehydrate fruit cells by peeling an apple and cutting it into small pieces. Place the pieces into a jar and add ¼ cup (62 ml) of granulated sugar and stir. Secure the lid on the jar. After about 24 hours, the apple pieces will be surrounded by a thick solution of the sugar dissolved in water from the fruit's cells. Use diagrams showing the changes in the jar to represent the dehydrating property of sugar. As part of a display, show pictures of products that use sugar as a preservative. *Note:* Salt also dehydrates and, like sugar, preserves by drying out food such as meat.

GET THE FACTS

1. The U.S. Food and Drug Administration (FDA) regulates the use of food additives. Nitrates and nitrites are used as preservatives for meat; they also give meat a healthy-looking red color. These preservatives are potentially dangerous because they can lead to the production of cancer-causing chemicals in the digestive system. FDA regulations allow foods to contain up to 500 parts per million (ppm) of nitrate and 200 ppm of nitrite. It is considered safe for adults to consume these preservatives at this low level, but foods for babies under one year of age should contain no nitrate or nitrite additives. Find out more about nitrates and nitrites. Could other safer methods of preserving meats be used?

2. The food additive sodium benzoate is on the GRAS list. This chemical occurs naturally (in very small amounts) in many foods, such as prunes and cranberries. It is naturally present and part of the metabolic process in the human body. Find out more about sodium benzoate. What conditions must exist for it to be effective? List foods it is used in. What is considered a harmless level for human consumption?

3. The FDA allows preservatives to be added to foods at specific levels. How are these safe levels of consumption determined?

4. Five types of microorganisms that cause food to spoil are staphylococci, bacilli, molds, streptococci, and yeasts. These organisms feed on much the same substances as do humans and, when present, can bring about undesirable chemical and physical changes in food. With the right conditions, they can double in number every 20 or 30 minutes. Find out more about these food spoilers and how they can be controlled. You could prepare a data table for display showing diagrams of the five types of microorganisms and listing specific types of food spoilage, such as botulism (one of the most serious types of food poisoning) or simple fermentation by yeast. (See the sample data table in Figure 15.2.)

5. Find out more about advancements in preserving foods. Compare home food preservation methods in the past and at present. Some things have changed very little, such as the smoking of meats on an open fire. You could use diagrams to compare old and new techniques.

6. In the late eighteenth century, Napoleon offered 12,000 francs for a new way of preserving food. Nicolas Appert, a Parisian chef, won the money with his heat-preserved foods. Find out how this man without any knowledge of microbes and their role in food spoilage was able to preserve food.

Figure 15.2

CHEMISTRY

16 The Best Plant Food

Nutrient Differences in Soils

Fertilizer is a natural or synthetic chemical substance or mixture of substances used to add nutrients to soil so as to promote plant growth.

Plants can grow in natural environments without the assistance of commercial fertilizers. The soil seems to provide all the nutrients the plants need. Is there a difference in the nutrients in soils from one location to another?

In this project you will test the effects on plant growth of nutrients leached from soil samples taken from different environments. You will also discover which nutrients are best for plants.

GETTING STARTED

Purpose: To determine whether nutrients leached from potting soil are sufficient for plant growth.

Materials

2-quart (2-liter) food colander

two 2-gallon cooking pots or containers with openings large enough to support the colander

two 2-by-2-foot (60-by-60-cm) pieces of cheesecloth

2 quarts (2 liters) of potting soil

1-quart (1-liter) jar

4 gallons (16 liters) distilled water in plastic jugs

funnel

marking pen

masking tape

8 house plants (same kind and size and each with five or more leaves) in similar containers

Procedure

1. Place the food colander over the opening in one pot so that the rim of the pot supports the colander.

2. Line the inside of the colander with one piece of cheesecloth.

3. Fill the cloth-lined colander with potting soil.

4. Use the jar to pour 2 gallons (8 liters) of distilled water evenly over the soil (see Figure 16.1).

Note: It will take time for all of the water to drain through the soil, so add the water slowly. The water that has drained through the soil is called the filtrate.

water
cheesecloth filter
potting soil
filtrate

Figure 16.1

5. After all the filtrate has drained through the soil, lift the soil-filled colander and place it over the empty pot.

6. Pour the filtrate through the soil again.

7. Repeat steps 5 and 6 three times. Keep the washed soil.

8. Use the funnel to pour the filtrate into the two empty water jugs. Cap the jugs.

9. With the marking pen and tape, label these jugs "Nutrient Filtrate."

10. Label the remaining jugs of water "Water Only."

11. Fill one of the cooking pots about three-fourths full with tap water.

12. Remove the plants from their containers. Gently shake the soil from their roots and stand the plants in the pot of water to soak off more soil.

13. Remove all the soil from the plant containers, rinse them with tap water, and repot the plants using the washed soil from step 7.

14. Use the marking pen to label four of the plant containers "Water Only" and the remaining four "Nutrient Filtrate."

15. Place all the plants together in a spot where their environment (temperature, amount of sunlight, and so on) is the same.

16. Keep the soil moist, but not dripping wet, consistently using the liquid indicated on the plant container's label. Add the same amount of liquid to each plant, and water them all at the same time.

17. Observe and record the growth of the plants for four or more weeks.

Results

Your results may vary, but the author found that at the end of four weeks the nutrient-fed plants had stronger stems and greener leaves.

Why?

Many nutrients needed for plant growth are **soluble** (able to break up and thoroughly mix with another substance) in water. Thus, when mixed with water they form an **aqueous solution,** which is a mixture in which one or more substances are dissolved in water. (**Dissolve** means to break into very small particles and mix thoroughly with a liquid.) Nutrients in soil can be removed by a process called leaching. **Leaching** is the removal of soluble chemicals from a material, such as soil, by filtering water through the material so that water-soluble substances are extracted. In this experiment, the cheesecloth acts as a **filter** (material that allows a liquid, but not solids, to pass through) and the liquid passing through the cheesecloth is called the **filtrate** (liquid that passes through a filter). The filtrate collected by leaching is rich in nutrients. Plants grown with this nutrient liquid grow better than plants grown in the washed soil without nutrients. Plants without soil nutrients continue to make food in their leaves by photosynthesis, but photosynthesis alone is not enough to sustain the plants. The nutrients taken in by the roots are necessary for proper growth and maintenance of plant cells. Lack of nutrients results in many problems, including yellow leaves, wilting, thin foliage, small leaves, and generally poor growth.

TRY NEW APPROACHES

Do all soils contain the same nutrients? Repeat the experiment using samples of soils taken from different locations. Remove any ground covering, grass, and/or plants growing in the soil. Be sure to label the soil samples and make notes of the types of plants growing in the soil and in the general area from which each sample is taken (see Figure 16.2). This information can be used later to determine the nutrients needed by these plants. Use leached water from the different soil samples to grow plants. Determine which nutrient filtrate is the best for the plants used.

Figure 16.2

DESIGN YOUR OWN EXPERIMENT

The types of nutrients in soil can be determined with an inexpensive soil-testing kit. (Your teacher can order this from a plant nursery or a science supply company. See Appendix 9 for a list.) Design an experiment to compare the effect of specific nutrients, such as nitrates and phosphates, on plants. One way is to repeat the original experiment, but test for and identify the presence of some of the nutrients. Record your testing results in a Nutrient Soil Data table like Table 16.1. You may wish to include information in the table about where the soil was found, as shown in Table 16.1.

TABLE 16.1 NUTRIENT SOIL DATA

Soil Sample	Nitrate Test	Phosphate Test	Soil Location
1	yes	yes	potting soil
2	yes	no	open field with only crabgrass growing in it
3			
4			

GET THE FACTS

Plants look unhealthy when they do not have proper nutrients. Use a gardening book to determine the nutrients needed for proper plant growth for the plants in your experiments and the symptoms that indicate a deficiency of each nutrient.

17 Acid-Base Indicators
Color Changers

Acid/base indicators are chemicals that help you compare or estimate the strength of an acid or base by changing color depending on the pH value of a tested liquid. The lower the pH value, the more acidic the liquid. The higher the pH value, the more basic, or alkaline, the liquid.

In this project, you will make indicators from foods, such as red cabbage and various plants. You will determine the affect of acids and bases on the color of indicators and create color scales for the different indicators. You will also investigate the effect of soil pH on the color of flowers containing an acid-base indicator.

GETTING STARTED

Purpose: To determine the effect of acids and bases on red cabbage indicator.

Materials

pen
masking tape
1-tablespoon (15-ml) measuring spoon
white vinegar, 5%
distilled water
½ teaspoon baking soda

three 10-ounce (300-ml) clear plastic cups
sheet of white copy paper
red cabbage indicator (see Appendix 6)
4 stirring spoons

Procedure

1. Use the pen and tape to label the cups "Acid," "Base," "Neutral."

2. Add 1 tablespoon (15 ml) of vinegar to the Acid cup, 1 tablespoon (15 ml) of distilled water and ½ teaspoon (2.5 ml) baking soda to the Base cup, and 1 tablespoon (15 ml) of distilled water to the Neutral cup. *Note:* Wash the spoon in distilled water and dry it after each use so that you do not contaminate or dilute the contents of the different cups.

3. Set the cups on one of the sheets of white paper so that it will be easier to detect color changes.

Figure 17.1

4. Add 1 tablespoon of red cabbage indicator to each cup. Using different spoons, stir the contents of each cup. Then observe and record their color in a Red Cabbage Indicator Data table like Table 17.1.

TABLE 17.1 RED CABBAGE INDICATOR DATA	
Solution	**Color of Indicator**
Acid (vinegar, 5%)	red
Water (distilled)	purple
Base (baking soda)	blue

Results

The red cabbage indicator turns red in vinegar, remains purple in water, and turns blue in baking soda.

Why?

Chemicals are substances made of a combination of **elements** (basic chemical substance of which all things are made). Each element is made of **atoms** (building blocks of matter), and only one kind of atom makes up each specific element. Indicators are natural or synthetic chemical substances that change color in response to other chemicals. **Acid/base** indicators change colors in the presence of acids or bases. **Acids** are aqueous solutions containing hydronium ions—H_3O^{+1} and **bases** are aqueous solutions containing hydroxide ions—OH^{-1}. Generally the characteristics of acids and bases are opposite. The special scale for measuring the acidic or basic nature of a substance is called the **pH scale.** The values on the **pH** (a number used to indicate the acidic or basic nature of a solution) scale range from 0 to 14, with the pH value of 7 being **neutral** (having no acidic or basic properties). Acids have a pH of less than 7 and bases have a pH greater than 7.

Red cabbage contains a chemical that is one of a class of compounds called **anthocyanins** (red pigment found in some foods). The anthocyanin pigment in red cabbage is an acid/base indicator. Vinegar is known to be an acid with a pH of about 2.8 and baking soda is a base with a pH of about 8.5. So from the results of this experiment, cabbage indicator is red at pH of 2.8, purple at pH 7, and blue at pH 8.5. For more information about color changes of anthocyanins in red cabbage due to changes in pH, see pages 10–11 in Dianne N. Epp's *The Chemistry of Food Dyes* (Terrific Science Press: Middletown, Ohio, 1995).

TRY NEW APPROACHES

Anthocyanins are found in red poppies, blue cornflowers, grapes, beets, blueberries, and apple skin. Repeat the experiment using a different plant and/or fruit to make anthocyanin indicator. How do the colors differ from the colors in the original experiment?

DESIGN YOUR OWN EXPERIMENT

1. In the original experiment using red cabbage indicator, only three different testing materials were used. Thus, a pH color scale for the indicator would look like Table 17.2.

TABLE 17.2 pH COLOR SCALE FOR RED CABBAGE INDICATOR

Testing Material	pH	Color of Indicator
Vinegar	2.8	red
Water	7	purple
Baking soda	8.5	blue

Design a more comprehensive pH color scale for red cabbage indicator as well as for one or more of the other food or plant indicators previously made. First test each indicator with testing materials of known pH, such as those in Table 17.3. Make an effort to create a scale with colors for the greatest pH range possible. See a chemistry text for the pH of other materials. *Note:* Mix about ½ teaspoon (2.5 ml) of solid materials with 1 tablespoon of water.

TABLE 17.3 pH DATA

Testing Material	pH
Lemon juice	2.3
Apple juice	3.2
Tomato juice	4.4
Bananas	5.3
Distilled water	7
Baking soda	8.5
Milk of magnesia	10.5
Ammonia	12

2. If you have access to a pH meter, design a pH color scale for red cabbage indicator and/or other food or plant indicators. With assistance from an adult, use an acid stronger than lemon juice or vinegar and a base stronger than ammonia to create a color pH scaled from 0 to 14. As you add drops of acid or base to the indicator, test the liquid's pH, then record the pH and color until you have determined colors for pH 0 to 14.

GET THE FACTS

The color of some flowers is an indication of the pH of the soil they grow in. Hydrangeas have pink flowers in soil with a high pH (basic) and blue flowers in soil with a low pH (acid). Find out more about soil pH by checking with a plant nursery, school agriculture department, or county agriculture department for information. What can be added to soil to change its pH? **Science Fair Hint:** Determine the range of colors of flowers containing acid-base indicators. Do this by growing plants, such as hydrangeas, in soils of various pH. Your control can be soil with a pH of 7.

18 Enzymes
Chemical Controllers

Advertisements for some detergents proclaim that their product is a miracle worker in a box. What is the ingredient in some detergents that makes them so effective at removing stains?

In this project, you will analyze the chemistry of enzymes, which are the chemicals added to detergents that make them such miraculous cleaners. You will examine the effect of water temperature and pH on the effectiveness of detergent enzymes. You will also determine the effectiveness of enzyme detergents on cleaning different stains.

GETTING STARTED

Purpose: To determine the effect of the enzymes found in a detergent on a protein.

Materials

twelve 1-quart (1-liter) jars
distilled water
marking pen
masking tape
1-tablespoon (15-ml) measuring spoon
powdered laundry detergent without enzymes (Ivory Snow)

stirring spoon
powdered laundry detergent with enzymes (such as Cheer)
12 eggs (fresh, hard-boiled, and peeled)
magnifying lens

Procedure

CAUTION: *When preparing the boiled eggs, wash your hands and any utensils used when handling the uncooked eggs. Raw eggs can contain a harmful bacteria.*

1. Fill the jars three-fourths full with distilled water.

2. Use the pen and tape to label and number the jars "Control-1," "Control-2," "Control-3," and "Control-4"; "With-1," "With-2," "With-3," and "With-4"; and "Without-1," "Without-2," "Without-3," and "Without-4."

3. Add 1 tablespoon (15 ml) of detergent without enzymes to each of the four jars labeled "Without." Stir.

4. Add 1 tablespoon (15 ml) of detergent with enzymes to each of the four jars labeled "With." Stir.

5. Divide the jars into four sets of three jars each. Each set will contain jars labeled "Control," "With," and "Without."

6. Observe and record a preliminary qualitative description of each egg in an Enzyme Data table, like Table 18.1. Then place one egg in each jar.

Set 1

Figure 18.1

7. Stand the jars together in an area away from drafts or direct sunlight and with relatively constant temperature.

8. For 7 days, make daily observations of the surface of the eggs. Each day, lift one of the eggs out of its jar, use the magnifying lens for close-up inspection, then replace the egg in its jar. Repeat this procedure for each egg. Make a point not to disturb the surface of the egg any more than necessary during the examination.

Results

The surface of each egg is smooth before being placed in the jars. For each set, as time passes, the surface of the eggs in the detergent with enzymes

Set	Observation							
1	Start	Day 1	Day 2	Day 3	Day 4	Day 5	Day 6	Day 7
Control-1								
With-1								
Without-1								
2								
Control-2								
With-2								
Without-2								
3								
Control-3								
With-3								
Without-3								
4								
Control-4								
With-4								
Without-4								

TABLE 18.1 ENZYME DATA

looks rough and may have a cratered appearance. But those in the detergent without enzymes, as well as the control, remain smooth.

Why?

Catalysts are chemicals that change (either speed up or slow down) the rate of a chemical reaction. **Enzymes** are **biological catalysts,** which means they are found in organisms (living things). The substance on which an enzyme acts is called a **substrate.** The specific part of an enzyme that attaches to a substrate is called the **active site.** Enzymes are **proteins,** which are any of a large number of complex **organic compounds** (chemicals containing carbon and found in living organisms) that make up living organisms and are essential to their functioning. Enzymes are different from other proteins because they cause a chemical change, which usually involves the forming or breaking apart of the substrate.

Enzyme action involves three basic steps: First, the enzyme binds to the substrate, then the chemical reaction occurs, and finally the changed substrate is released from the enzyme (see Figure 18.2). Enzymes are usually named after what they bind to (the sub-

strate), followed by the suffix *ase.* So the enzymes in detergent that break apart proteins are called **proteases.** Proteases change larger protein molecules in the egg into smaller molecules, causing the egg to break down. Some proteins, such as hemoglobin, exhibit color because they contain metals. Hemoglobin, for instance, is a blood protein and is red due to

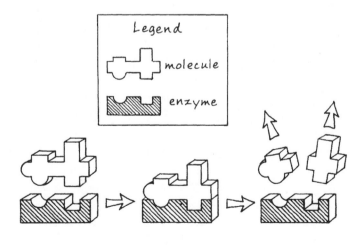

Figure 18.2

the iron attached to it. Proteins are made up of long twisted molecules, which can wind through the fibers of cloth and bind to them. In your wash, the proteases in laundry detergent break down protein, such as hemoglobin, thus making it easier for the water and detergent to wash the stains away. Stains that are not caused by colored proteins may not be affected by the proteases.

TRY NEW APPROACHES

How does pH affect proteases in detergent? Repeat the experiment with the hard-boiled eggs, omitting detergents without enzymes. Instead, have four sets of three jars. For each set 1, label and number the jars "Control-1," "Acid-1," and "Base-1." Fill the jars with distilled water as before. Add 1 tablespoon (15 ml) of detergent with enzymes to jars Acid-1 and Base-1. Use red and blue litmus to test the water in each jar. In the Base-1 jar, if necessary, add 1 teaspoon (5 ml) baking soda at a time so that the pH is high enough to turn the red litmus blue. In the Acid-1 jar, if necessary, add 1 teaspoon (5 ml) of vinegar at a time until the pH is low enough to turn blue litmus red. Repeat preparing sets 2, 3, and 4, then proceed as in the earlier experiment. *Note:* Litmus can be obtained at most teacher supply stores or your teacher can order it from a science supply company. See Appendix 8 for a list of science supply companies.

DESIGN YOUR OWN EXPERIMENT

Does temperature affect detergent enzymes? Design an experiment to determine how the temperature of wash water affects stain removal. One way is to use a permanent marker to label twelve 4-inch (10-cm) squares of white cotton cloth. Label 4 pieces "Cold," 4 pieces "Warm" and 4 pieces "Hot." Stain each by placing ⅛ teaspoon (0.72 ml) of yellow mustard in the cen-

ter of each cloth. Spread the mustard and allow it to dry. Prepare four sets of three 1-pint jars with lids. Each set will contain jars with cold distilled water, warm distilled water, and hot distilled water. Add 1 tablespoon (15 ml) of detergent with enzymes and 1 stained cloth to each jar of water. With the lids secured on each jar, vigorously shake each jar 5 times every 15 minutes for 1 hour. Then remove the cloth pieces, rinse in cold tap water, and allow to dry. Compare the stains. The cloth pieces in the warm water will be used as a control to compare with the cloth pieces in cold and hot water.

GET THE FACTS

1. The term *detergent* applies to materials that aid in the removal of dirt or other foreign matter from soiled items. Soap was the main detergent until the 1940s, when synthetic detergents were first developed. Now the term *soap* is usually used to refer to a cleanser made primarily from fat or oil, which doesn't clean well in hard water. Detergent is not made with fat or oil and is chemically active even in hard water. Find out more about the differences and similarities between soaps and detergents. Why are they called surfactants? Explain the hydrophilic and hydrophobic structures of each and how these structures aid them in cleaning. For information, see Carl H. Snyder's *The Extraordinary Chemistry of Ordinary Things* (New York: Wiley, 1997), pp. 323–329.

2. Discover more about the biochemistry of specific enzymes and the proteins they break down. One model that you could use to represent the specific nature of enzymes is the lock-and-key example. Each key fits only one lock, just as each enzyme "fits," or reacts with, only one protein, or a specific class of proteins. Information about the lock-and-key model can be found in a biology textbook.

19 Triglycerides
Saturated and Unsaturated

Fats and oils are naturally occurring organic compounds called triglycerides. While made of basically the same components, fats and oils can easily be distinguished by the fact that, at room temperatures, oils are liquid while fats are solid. Each molecule of fat or oil is composed of two different types of building-block compounds: glycerol and fatty acids. Both types of compounds are made of atoms of carbon, hydrogen, and oxygen.

In this project, you will study the difference between the molecular structure of saturated and unsaturated triglycerides. You will find out how to determine the iodine number of triglycerides and compare the degree of unsaturation of different oils with different iodine numbers. You will also study the effect of double bonds and length of fatty-acid side chains on the melting point of triglycerides.

GETTING STARTED

Purpose: To use iodine to determine whether a triglyceride is saturated or unsaturated.

Materials

tap water
2-quart (2-liter) cooking pot
heavy-duty aluminum foil
pencil
black permanent marker
5 test tubes

1-tablespoon (15-ml) measuring spoon
safflower oil
eyedropper
tincture of iodine
craft stick or stirring rod
heat mitten
test tube clamp

Procedure

CAUTION: *Keep the iodine out of reach of young children. It is poisonous and is for external use only. Tincture of iodine contains alcohol, which needs to be kept away from an open flame. Iodine will stain skin, clothes, and other materials.*

1. Fill the pot with 2 inches (10 cm) of water.

2. Cover the pot with a piece of aluminum foil that has been folded in half.

3. Use the pencil to make holes in the aluminum foil cover just large enough to stand the test tubes in.

4. Use the marker to label the test tubes "C," "1," "2," "3," "4."

5. Fill each test tube half full with oil. Make sure the height of the oil is the same in each tube.

6. Use the eyedropper to add two drops of iodine to test tubes 1 through 4. Use the craft stick to thoroughly stir the contents of each test tube. Tube C will be the control.

7. Record the initial color of the liquid in each test tube in the row for "0 minutes" in an Oil Data table like Table 19.1

8. Stand the test tubes in the pot by inserting one tube in each hole in the aluminum foil.

9. Turn the stove on to medium heat.

Figure 19.1

10. After 5 minutes, wearing the heat mittens, use the test tube holder to pick up each tube one at a time. Observe the color of the liquid in each tube and record it in the Oil Data table. Return the tubes to the pot of water.

11. Repeat step 10 twice or until no further color change occurs in tubes 1 through 4.

12. Compare the colors of the tubes recorded in the Oil Data table.

Time, min	Color of Oil				
	Test Tube 1	Test Tube 2	Test Tube 3	Test Tube 4	Test Tube C
0					
5					
10					
15					

TABLE 19.1 OIL DATA

Results

The addition of iodine to the pale yellow oil in tubes 1 through 4 turns the oil a pale reddish brown. At first small drops of iodine can be seen suspended throughout the liquid in these tubes. After heating, the reddish color of the liquid in the tubes slowly fades and the liquid returns to its original pale yellow color. The liquid in control test tube C does not change from its original color.

Why?

Molecules are two or more atoms bonded (linked) together. A **bond** is a force holding atoms together. Fats and oils make up a group of naturally occurring organic chemical compounds called triglycerides. **Triglycerides** are organic chemical compounds made of one molecule of **glycerol** (organic alcohol) with three molecules of **fatty acids** (organic acids). Each glycerol molecule has a structure of three carbon atoms with one fatty acid molecule branching from each carbon atom. Fatty acids are so named because they are commonly found in fats and oils. **Organic acids** or organic compounds with one or more acid groups are called the carboxyl group (COOH). Fatty acids have carbon "backbones," usually from 4 to 24 carbons or more, with one carboxyl group at the end. The three acid side chains can be alike or different from one another. Each carbon atom in an acid chain can be attached to another carbon by either a single or double bond. Organic compounds with single carbon-to-carbon bonds are called **saturated,** while **unsaturated** organic compounds have one or more multiple carbon-to-carbon bonds. Saturated fatty acid contains all the hydrogens they are capable of holding, thus the acid is said to be saturated with hydrogen. As the number of double bonds increases, the number of hydrogens attached to the carbons decreases. If the fatty acid has one double bond it is called **monounsaturated.** If there are two or more double bonds, it is called **polyunsaturated.** A **saturated triglyceride** has only saturated fatty acid chains; a **monounsaturated triglyceride** has one or more monounsaturated fatty acid chains; and a **polyunsaturated triglyceride** has one or more polyunsaturated fatty acid chains.

Tincture of iodine contains **elemental** (the natural, noncharged form of an element) iodine (I_2) dissolved in alcohol. When mixed with an unsaturated molecule, such as unsaturated triglycerol, the iodine causes the mixture to look reddish. After heating, the double bonds break and iodine bonds to the carbons. The elemental iodine, along with its color, disappears. (The heat speeds up the process.) The combination of iodine with ethene (an unsaturated organic compound) provides a simple illustration of how iodine bonds with an unsaturated molecule. The product resulting from adding iodine to ethene is colorless 1,2-diiodoethane, as shown in Figure 19.2. However, any remaining amounts of uncombined iodine generally are still present, causing the contents of the test tube to be yellow instead of clear.

Figure 19.2

TRY NEW APPROACHES

How does the amount of oil affect additions to carbon-to-carbon double bonds? Repeat the experiment twice, first using more oil. Keep the amount of iodine the same but use 3 tablespoons (45 ml) of oil. Then repeat using less oil, 1 tablespoon (15 ml).

Design Your Own Experiment

The degree of unsaturation of triglycerides is represented by a value known as the **iodine number,** which is the number of grams of iodine that will react with 100 grams of the triglyceride. Table 19.2 gives the iodine number of some common oils. Design an experiment to determine for yourself that oils with a low iodine number are less saturated and will react with a lesser amount of iodine than those with a higher iodine number. Try repeating the original experiment using different oils but start with less iodine, such as one drop. When the oil clears, add another drop. *Note:* Since tincture of iodine is flammable, hold tubes away from the heating source when adding the iodine. Continue to add measured amounts of iodine to each tube of oil until the reddish brown color no longer clears. **Science Fair Hint:** Construct and display a bar graph comparing the number of iodine drops added to each sample of oil.

TABLE 19.2 IODINE NUMBERS FOR SOME OILS

Oil	Iodine Number
Olive oil	75–95
Peanut oil	85–100
Cottonseed oil	100–117
Corn oil	115–130
Fish oils	120–180
Soybean oil	125–140
Safflower oil	130–145
Sunflower oil	130–145
Linseed oil	170–205

Get the Facts

1. The number of carbon-to-carbon double bonds in a triglyceride is known as its *degree of unsaturation.* The greater the number of double bonds the greater its degree of unsaturation and the lower the melting point of the triglyceride. How does the length or number of carbons in the fatty acids of a triglyceride affect melting point? For information about triglycerides, see Carl H. Snyder's *The Extraordinary Chemistry of Ordinary Things* (New York: Wiley, 1997), pp. 405–406.

2. *Hydrogenation* is the addition of hydrogen to an unsaturated molecule, which causes a decrease in saturation. If a product is made from a highly unsaturated oil, how does partial hydrogenation of the oil affect its physical and chemical properties? For information, see Snyder's *The Extraordinary Chemistry of Ordinary Things*, pp. 409–410.

20 Vitamin C Content
Analysis of Food by Titration

Vitamin C is required for good health. This vitamin is not produced by your body and must be obtained from foods or vitamin tablets.

In this project, you will use the titration method to determine the amount of vitamin C in various foods and vitamin tablets. You will also determine whether fruit drinks and fruit juices have comparable amounts of vitamin C. Vitamin C's antioxidant properties will be studied, and its part in an oxidation-reduction reaction will be examined. You will also look at the sources and uses of different vitamins.

GETTING STARTED

Purpose: To determine the amount of iodine needed to react with 25 mg of vitamin C.

CAUTION: *Be careful not to allow the vitamin C to touch your skin, in case you have any sensitivity to the chemical.*

Materials

100-mg **ascorbic acid** (vitamin C) tablet	marking pen
wax paper	masking tape
hammer	1-teaspoon (5-ml) measuring spoon
½ cup (125 ml) of distilled water	starch solution (see Appendix 6)
1-quart (1-liter) jar	sheet of white paper
spoon	eyedropper
4 baby-food jars	tincture of iodine

Procedure

CAUTION: *Keep the iodine out of reach of young children. It is poisonous and is for external use only. Tincture of iodine contains alcohol, which needs to be kept away from an open flame. Iodine will stain skin, clothes, and other materials.*

1. Prepare a standard vitamin C solution by:
   - crushing the vitamin C tablet (place it between two sheets of wax paper and hit it gently with a hammer).

   - pouring ½ cup (125 ml) of distilled water into the quart (liter) jar.

   - adding the crushed vitamin C powder to the water in the jar.

   - stirring until the powder dissolves.

2. Pour equal portions of the standard vitamin C solution into four baby-food jars.

3. With the marking pen, write "A," "B," "C," and "D" on pieces of masking tape and tape one label to each jar.

4. Add 1 teaspoon (5 ml) of the starch solution to each jar.

5. Place jar A on the sheet of white paper.

6. Fill the eyedropper with tincture of iodine. Slowly add the iodine in the eyedropper to jar A, counting each drop added (see Figure 20.1). Swirl the jar after each addition of five drops. Continue to add the iodine until the jar's contents remain a blue-black color.

7. Record the number of drops used in a Vitamin C Data table, such as Table 20.1.

Figure 20.1

8. Repeat the procedure using jars B, C, and D.

9. Add the results for the four jars and divide by four to compute the average number of drops of iodine needed to react with the 25 mg of vitamin C in each jar. This number will be used to calculate the concentration of vitamin C in other substances.

TABLE 20.1 VITAMIN C DATA					
	Vitamin C + Starch Solution				
	Jar A	Jar B	Jar C	Jar D	Average
Drops of I_2					

Results

The vitamin C–starch solution is unaffected by the initial drops of iodine, but adding more iodine results in a blue-black solution. The number of drops of iodine needed to react with the 25 mg of vitamin C in the solution will vary with the size of the eyedropper.

Why?

Titration is the process of combining a measured amount of a solution of known concentration with a measured amount of solution of unknown concentration. Tincture of iodine is a mixture of elemental (natural noncharged form of an element) iodine (I_2^0) and ethyl alcohol (C_2H_5OH). A chemical reaction in which electrons are transferred between reactants is known as an **oxidation-reduction reaction,** also called a redox reaction. Originally the term **oxidation** meant the combination of a substance with oxygen and **reduction** meant the loss of oxygen from a substance. Today, scientists extend these definitions to include all transfers of electrons. So oxidation is a loss of electrons or gain of oxygen and reduction is the gain of electrons or loss of oxygen. In the chemical reaction between vitamin C and elemental iodine (I_2^0), vitamin C is easily oxidized (loses electrons), forming **dehydroascorbic acid** and iodine is reduced (gains electrons) forming the **anion** (a negatively charged particle) called **iodide** (I^{-1}).

Elemental iodine reacts with starch to form a complex molecule that has a blue-black color. However, when the iodide anion (the reduced form) is present, the blue-black color is not seen. When starch, vitamin C, and elemental iodine are mixed, the iodine quickly reacts with the vitamin C. When all of the vitamin C has been oxidized by the iodine, additional drops of iodine react with the starch and the blue-black color is seen.

TRY NEW APPROACHES

Analyze a multivitamin tablet to determine the amount of vitamin C it it. Repeat the experiment substituting a multivitamin tablet for the vitamin C tablet. *Note:* Avoid using a multiple vitamin that contains vitamin E, which may affect the results.

The number of drops of iodine needed to react with the vitamin C mixture depends on the size of the drops, which is determined by the eyedropper. Thus, the same size eyedropper must be used throughout the experiment. Use the following equation and the calculated number of drops of iodine required to react with 25 mg of vitamin C to compute the amount of vitamin C in the test material (the multivitamin tablet). For example, if it takes 50 drops of iodine to react with 25 mg of vitamin C, determine the number of milligrams of vitamin C in a multiple vitamin tablet if 20 drops of iodine reacted with the multiple vitamin.

$$\frac{? \text{ mg of vit. C in multivitamin}}{20 \text{ drops of iodine}} = \frac{25 \text{ mg of vit. C}}{50 \text{ drops of iodine}}$$

$$? \text{ mg of vit. C in multivitamin} = \frac{25 \text{ mg of vit. C} \times \frac{20 \text{ drops of iodine}}{50 \text{ drops of iodine}}}$$

$$= 10 \text{ mg of vit. C}$$

DESIGN YOUR OWN EXPERIMENT

1. Commercial foods are generally heated when being prepared for packaging. Design an experiment to determine if heating affects the amount of vitamin C in foods. One way is to compare heated with unheated citrus juices. Prepare fresh orange juice by squeezing enough oranges to collect 1 cup of juice. Strain the juice through cheesecloth to separate out any pulp from the orange. Heat half of the juice to boiling, then let it cool to room temperature. Repeat the original experiment

twice, first substituting ½ cup (125 ml) of fresh orange juice for the vitamin C solution, and then using ½ cup (125 ml) of the heated orange juice. *Note:* Both juices need to be at room temperature when you test them.

2. Vitamin C is readily oxidized by combining with oxygen. Design an experiment to determine if storing orange juice in an open container affects its vitamin C content. One way is to store orange juice in two containers, one open (exposed to air, which contains oxygen) and one closed. Keep the containers in a refrigerator so the juice does not spoil. Each week for four or more weeks repeat the original experiment testing the vitamin C content in the juice in both containers. To determine the total amount of juice needed in each container, first decide on the number of days the testing will be done. Then multiply the total number of days by 1 cup (250 ml), the amount of juice needed for each day's testing.

GET THE FACTS

1. Vitamins contain a variety of complex chemicals. Like ascorbic acid (vitamin C), vitamins have names but are frequently identified by letters, such as A, B, C, D, E, and K. How all vitamins are used by the body is not exactly known, but we do know that many chemical reactions cannot occur in the human body if the proper vitamins are missing. For example, for calcium and phosphorous to be effective in the formation of teeth, vitamin D must be present. Use chemistry and biology texts to find out more about the uses of vitamins. Are chemists, such as Linus Pauling, correct about the role of vitamin C in helping to prevent colds? Is there any evidence to substantiate Pauling's views about the vitamin? What chemical reactions is vitamin C known to be involved in that keep your body functioning normally? What effect does the lack of individual vitamins have on the human body?

2. When skin is exposed to sunlight, the ultraviolet radiation in the light causes *cholesterol* (a fat-related compound) to be chemically converted to vitamin D. Fresh citrus fruits are a good source of vitamin C. Find out more about the natural sources of vitamins. How have the refining and the processing of foods affected their vitamin content?

3. The titration method was used in this project to determine an unknown concentration of vitamin C. Find out more about this process. Use a chemistry text to find the meaning of the following terms: *titration, end point, indicator,* and *standard solution.* You could use this information when preparing an oral presentation and a written report.

4. Combining vitamin C and tincture of iodine results in a redox reaction in which ascorbic acid is oxidized and iodine is reduced. Find out more about the following terms: *redox reaction, oxidized, reduced, oxidizing agent,* and *reducing agent.* What is the difference between the structure of vitamin C (ascorbic acid) molecules and the structure of dehydroascorbic acid, into which the vitamin C is changed as a result of the redox reaction?

21 Viscosity
A Difference in Stickiness

Liquids move to fill up the space of their containers. This ability to move or flow is a very important physical property of liquids. Viscosity is the measurement of the resistance of fluids to flow.

In this project, you will use the viscosity of common household liquids to make a viscometer, an instrument that measures the flow rate of liquids. The flow rate will be used to calculate the viscosity index, the viscosity of a fluid relative to the viscosity of water, of each testing liquid. You will also determine the effect of temperature on viscosity and look at the binding forces between liquid molecules.

GETTING STARTED

Purpose: To make and use a viscometer to determine the flow rate for a defined volume of water.

Materials

scissors
clear plastic dish detergent bottle with a pull top
marking pen
ruler
modeling clay
glass jar with a mouth slightly smaller than the upper part of the detergent bottle
water
timer

Procedure

1. Cut off the bottom of the detergent bottle.
2. Hold the bottle upside down. With the marking pen, make two straight lines, one about 1 inch (2.5 cm) below the cut-off bottom and the second 4 inches (10 cm) below the first line.
3. Label the first line "Start" and the second line "Stop."
4. Place a ring of clay around the top edge of the jar's mouth.
5. Close the pull top, then stand the bottle upside down inside the jar. Mold the clay ring so that the bottle stands upright, but do not secure the bottle with the clay.
6. Fill the bottle to about ½ inch (1.3 cm) above the start line with cold tap water.

7. Lift the bottle, and with the bottle above the jar, pull the top open.
8. Quickly set the bottle back on the jar (see Figure 21.1).
9. Start the timer when the water level reaches the, start line.
10. Stop the timer when the water level reaches the stop line. Record the time in a Viscosity Data table like Table 21.1.
11. Repeat the procedure three times and average the flow rate of the cold water.

Figure 21.1

TABLE 21.1 VISCOSITY DATA					
	Flow Time, minutes				
	Test 1	Test 2	Test 3	Test 4	Average
Cold Water					

Results

The author's flow rate for cold water was 39.3 seconds. *Note:* The flow rate will vary depending on the opening and size of the bottle used.

Why?

The amount of time it takes a liquid to flow out of a container depends on its viscosity. The **viscosity** of a liquid is the resistance of the liquid to flowing, because of the friction between the molecules. Viscosity depends on the structure of the liquid molecules. If the molecules are small and simple in structure, as in water, they move past one another quickly. But if they are large and intertwined, as in oil for example, they move slowly past one another. Liquid molecules that slide quickly past one another have a low viscosity; liquid molecules that move more slowly have a high viscosity.

TRY NEW APPROACHES

1. Does the temperature of water affect its viscosity? Repeat the experiment twice, first chilling the water in a freezer until its temperature is just above the freezing point, and then using warm tap water.

2. How does the viscosity of other liquids compare with the viscosity of water? The flow or viscosity of a liquid compared with the flow of cold water gives a relative viscosity for the liquid. A number measurement for the relative viscosity of a liquid is called its **viscosity index** (ratio of the rate flow of a fluid to the rate flow of water). Any number less than 1 indicates a lower viscosity than water; a number greater than 1 indicates a higher viscosity than water. Repeat the original experiment using liquids such as oil, dishwashing liquid, honey, and/or syrup. Prepare separate instruments for each liquid tested. Use the flow rate measurements and the following calculation to compute the viscosity index for each liquid. If the flow rate of a liquid is 573 seconds and the flow rate for the same volume of cold tap water is 39.3 seconds, then the viscosity index is determined as follows:

$$\text{viscosity index} = \frac{\text{flow rate of liquid}}{\text{flow rate of water}}$$

$$= \frac{573 \text{ seconds}}{39.3 \text{ seconds}}$$

$$= 14.58$$

This number indicates that the dishwashing liquid is 14.58 times as viscous as is water.

Science Fair Hint: Label and display, in order of viscosity index, photographs of each liquid as it flows from the viscometer.

3a. The viscosity of motor oil is rated by the Society of Automotive Engineers (SAE). The numbers assigned are called "weights" and are not exact viscosity values. Do higher weights of oil indicate a more viscous liquid? Repeat the original experiment using light, medium, and heavy weights of motor oil.

b. How does temperature affect the viscosity of oil? Vary the temperature of the motor oil previously tested and again use the viscometer to determine its flow rate. Place some samples in a freezer overnight to chill the oil. Heat other samples by placing containers of oil in hot tap water. Use a thermometer to determine the exact temperature of each sample tested.

Science Fair Hint: Construct and display a graph showing the relationship between temperature and flow rate.

DESIGN YOUR OWN EXPERIMENT

1a. As the thickness of a liquid increases there is an increase in its viscosity. Design an experiment to compare the viscosity of liquids using their thickness as a means of comparison. One way to compare viscosities is by dropping a glass marble into samples of the liquids. Fill identical slender jars with equal amounts of the liquids. Position the jars in front of a white background to increase your ability to clearly see the results. As you observe the contents of the jars, ask a helper to test two liquids at a time by holding a glass marble in each hand, and holding one hand over each jar. The helper should release both marbles from the same height and at the same time. Observe the movement of the marbles through the liquids. Continue to compare two liquids at a time until you can rate all the liquids in order of their viscosity.

b. Vary the temperature of the liquids. Prepare two jars of each testing sample. Chill one in a refrigerator and heat the second by setting it in a bowl of hot tap water. Measure and record the temperature of each liquid and then repeat the experiment. You could display drawings or photographs of the jars, showing them in order of viscosity.

GET THE FACTS

1. What happens to the *kinetic energy* (energy of motion) of molecules in liquids as the temperature is raised? How does this energy affect the binding forces between the molecules? See a physical science and/or physics text for information about the effect of kinetic energy on viscosity. Use this information to explain the effect of temperature on the viscosity of liquids.

2. Find out more about motor oil. Is there a difference between oil labeled SAE 30 and oil labeled SAE 30W? What does the label 10–W–30 mean? If temperature affects the viscosity of oil, why is it not necessary to change the oil in a car as the seasons change? A good resource is an automotive mechanic.

EARTH
SCIENCE

22 The Hydrologic Cycle

The Movement of Water from Place to Place

There is a continuous interchange of water between the oceans, land, plants, and clouds known as the hydrologic cycle, or water cycle. Most of this water is provided by the oceans.

In this project, you will model the sources of water in the hydrologic cycle, including transpiration (water from plants). You will also demonstrate whether dissolved pollutants in water are transported by the hydrologic cycle.

GETTING STARTED

Purpose: To model the hydrologic cycle.

Materials

½ cup (125 ml) of warm tap water

2-quart (2-liter) transparent heat-proof glass bowl

plastic food wrap

ice cube

resealable plastic sandwich bag

Procedure

1. Pour the warm water into the bowl.

2. Loosely cover the top of the bowl with plastic wrap so that about 2 inches (10 cm) of wrap extends past the edges of the bowl.

3. Put the ice cube in the bag and seal the bag.

4. Place the bag of ice in the center of the plastic wrap that covers the bowl.

5. Gently push the ice down about 1 inch (2.5 cm) so that the plastic wrap sags in the center. Then seal the plastic wrap by pressing its edge against the sides of the bowl (see Figure 22.1).

6. Observe the surface of the plastic wrap directly under the ice cube every 15 minutes for 1 hour or until the ice melts.

Results

At first, the underside of the plastic wrap becomes cloudy and water droplets form under the ice. Over time, the drops under the ice get larger and most of the plastic wrap looks clear. Some of these drops fall back into the water in the bowl.

Why?

The three common forms of matter, called **phases of matter,** are solid, liquid, and gas. The change from one form or phase of matter to another is called a **phase change.** Phase changes are generally the result of gain or loss of energy by a substance in the form of heat. The phase change from liquid to gas by a gain of heat is called **evaporation** and the phase change from gas to a liquid by a loss of heat is called **condensation.** In this experiment, the liquid water in the bowl evaporates, forming water **vapor** (gaseous phase of a substance, such as water that normally exists in the liquid phase). The energy needed for this phase change came from the warm water, but in nature, with phase changes such as evaporation of water from the surface of any body of water, the energy generally comes from the Sun. Water vapor in the bowl rises and comes in contact with the cool surface of the plastic wrap, where it loses energy and condenses, forming water droplets. In Earth's atmosphere (blanket of gases surrounding a celestial body), as water vapor rises it cools and condenses on tiny suspended particles. The tiny drops of water form **clouds** (visible mass of water drops that float in Earth's atmosphere), which are moved from one place to another by winds. Eventually the water in clouds falls as **precipitation** (liquid and solid phases of water that fall from the atmosphere). This movement of water from one place to another via changes in phase is called **hydrologic cycle,** or **water cycle.**

The primary source of water in the hydrologic cycle is the oceans, which contain about 97% of the Earth's water supply. The remain-

ice cube in bag

½ cup water

Figure 22.1

ing water comes from water evaporated from other sources such as lakes, rivers, and moist soil, and from water given off by plants in a process called **transpiration** (the process by which plants lose water through their leaves). About 75% of the precipitation falls back into the oceans, and much of the remaining 25% falls on the land.

Several things happen to the precipitation that reaches land. Some of it evaporates. In cold areas, snow and ice can remain on the ground for short or long periods before eventually melting. Rainwater soaks into the ground or runs along the surface in rivers and streams. Some collects in lakes and other bodies of standing water, but most finds its way back to the oceans. Rainwater that is unable to soak into the ground and that moves over its surface is called **runoff.** This moving water generally causes **erosion** (process by which materials are broken into smaller parts and moved) of the surface it flows over.

TRY NEW APPROACHES

Model the hydrologic cycle using moist soil as a source of water. Repeat the original experiment, but fill the bowl with about 1 inch (2.5 cm) of soil and add warm water to moisten the soil.

DESIGN YOUR OWN EXPERIMENT

1. Transpiration adds water to the hydrologic cycle. Demonstrate transpiration by placing a clear plastic bag over a group of leaves at the end of a stem of a tree or bush. (Do not cut or break the stem off the plant.) Secure the bag to the stem by wrapping tape around the open end of the bag. Observe the contents of the bag as often as possible for two to three days. The water leaving the plant's leaves evaporates, thus it is in the gas phase. Explain the phase change in the bag. For more information about transpiration, see *Janice VanCleave's Plants* (New York: Wiley, 1997), pp. 12–15.

2. Design a display to represent the hydrologic cycle. A sample diagram with labeled parts is shown in Figure 22.2. Colors and a legend can be used to show how **pollutants** (substances that destroy the purity of air, water, or land), such as chemical fertilizers added to the soil, can be added to waterways.

THE HYDROLOGIC CYCLE

Figure 22.2

3. Are pollutants transported by the hydrologic cycle? Design a way to analyze condensed water for dissolved materials. One way would be to repeat the original experiment, adding table salt to the water in the bowl. Collect the condensed water and taste it. Design a way to collect the water, such as placing a container inside the bowl beneath the plastic wrap. Remember that when tasting materials, all supplies used must be clean.

GET THE FACTS

1. *Deforestation* is the clearing of trees from land. Find out how this and other human activities, such as the growth of cities and the building of dams and reservoirs, affect the hydrologic cycle. For information, see *Weather,* The Nature Company Guides (Time-Life Books, 1996), pp. 120–121.

2. About 97% of all the Earth's water is contained in the oceans as salt water. Find out about the remaining 3%, which is fresh water. How much of fresh water is locked up as ice? How much is underground? What part of fresh water is on the surface in lakes and rivers? What part is in the soil and the air? For information, see Jack Williams's *The Weather Book* (New York: Vintage Books, 1992), pp. 86–87.

23 Minerals
Distinguishing Physical Characteristics of Minerals

The Earth's lithosphere is the solid part of Earth consisting of the crust and the upper mantle extending to a depth of about 60 miles (96 km). The lithosphere is made up mostly of minerals, which are naturally occurring inorganic solids with a definite chemical composition and physical characteristics.

In this project, you will learn a method to determine the specific gravity of a mineral and discover how heft can be used as a method of mineral identification. The difference between cleavage and fracture will be demonstrated. You will use minerals and everyday objects to demonstrate the hardness of minerals. You will learn how to test minerals for their streak and luster. All of this will then be used to prepare a display of minerals that represents their characteristics.

GETTING STARTED

Purpose: To determine the specific gravity of a mineral.

Materials

2-quart (2-liter) bowl

tap water

24-inch (60-cm) piece of string

fist-size sample of quartz, or any mineral of comparable size

metric spring scale

Procedure

1. Fill the bowl about three-fourths full with water.

2. Tie the string around the mineral and make a loop in the free end of the string.

3. Place the loop on the scale hook, suspend the mineral in air, and measure the mass of the mineral in grams (see Figure 23.1A). Record this as mass 1 (M_1).

4. With the mineral hanging from the scale, lower the mineral into the water in the bowl (see Figure 23.1B). Do not allow the mineral to rest on the bottom or sides of the bowl. Record this as mass 2 (M_2).

5. Determine the mass of the water **displaced** (pushed aside) by the mineral by calculating the absolute difference between M_1 and M_2. Record the answer as mass 3 (M_3).

Figure 23.1

Example:

$$M_3 = M_1 - M_2$$
$$= 530 \text{ g} \div 330 \text{ g}$$
$$= 200 \text{ g}$$

6. Use the following example to determine the mineral's **specific gravity (sp. gr.)** (the ratio of the mass of an object in air to the mass of the water displaced by the submerged object):

Example:

$$\text{sp. gr.} = M_1 \div M_3$$
$$= 530 \text{ g} \div 200 \text{ g}$$
$$= 2.65$$

Results

A method for determining the specific gravity of a mineral is used. The specific gravity of the mineral in the example is 2.65.

Why?

Most of the elements in the Earth's crust occur as minerals. A **mineral** is a single solid element or compound found in the Earth and has four basic characteristics: (1) it occurs naturally; (2) it is **inorganic** (not made from living things); (3) it has a definite chemical composition, meaning that it is not a mixture, but is made of the same substance throughout; and (4) it has a **crystalline structure** (atoms are arranged so that they form a particular geometric shape).

One way to distinguish one mineral from another is by comparing the specific gravities of the two minerals. To calculate the specific gravity of a mineral, divide the mass of the mineral by the mass of the water displaced by the mineral. Specific gravity tells how many times heavier the mineral is than water. The mineral in the example is 2.65 times as heavy as the same volume of water. Most minerals have a specific gravity from 2 to 5. Since every mineral has its own particular specific gravity, this characteristic can be used as a clue to the identity of a mineral.

Specific gravity is not always calculated with a scale. Instead, the heft of minerals is often used in identification. **Heft** is a subjective measurement. You measure heft by picking up minerals of equal volume and comparing their weights. Gold and pyrite are minerals that look alike, but the specific gravity of gold is 19.3 and the specific gravity of pyrite is 5.0. Thus, even though heft is not an exact measurement, the heft of gold is easily determined to be greater than that of pyrite.

TRY NEW APPROACHES

Would the size of a mineral sample affect its specific gravity measurement? Repeat the experiment two times. First, use a larger piece of quartz; then, use a smaller sample of the mineral. **Science Fair Hint:** use the mineral samples and their calculated specific gravities as part of a project display.

DESIGN YOUR OWN EXPERIMENT

1. **Cleavage** is a physical characteristic of a mineral which is the tendency to break along a flat surface called a **cleavage plane.** Minerals that break easily and cleanly are described as perfect. Less-clean breaks are described as distinct, indistinct, or none. Minerals can have cleavage in many different directions. Cleavage in one direction is called **basal cleavage.** Muscovite, the most common form of mica, is a mineral that has perfect basal cleavage. Examine a piece of muscovite. You should be able to peel the layers off with your fingers.

   Remove a thin layer of mica and break it in half. Observe the broken edges. This is a **fracture** (an irregular break) which is the way a mineral breaks when it doesn't split along a cleavage plane. Fracture surfaces are described as uneven, **conchoidal** (curved), **hackly** (jagged), or **splintery** (small, thin, and sharp or fibrous surface). Use a rock and mineral handbook to identify the type of fracture that muscovite has.

   Collect and display minerals having different types of cleavage and fractures. Use the handbook to find out more about how minerals break and to discover the identity of the cleavage and fracture type for each mineral specimen.

2a. **Hardness** is a physical characteristic of a mineral, which is the measure of its resistance to being scratched. The scale of hardness from 1 to 10 was devised in 1822 by Frederick Mohs (1773–1839), a German chemist. He arranged 10 common minerals from the softest to the hardest, giving the softest mineral, talc, the number 1, and the hardest mineral, diamond, the number 10. Minerals with higher Mohs' numbers will scratch those with lower numbers. Determine which has a higher Mohs' number, muscovite or quartz. First try to scratch the quartz with the muscovite. Then, try to scratch the muscovite with the quartz. Find the list of minerals for Mohs' scale of hardness in a rock and mineral handbook. Prepare a display showing specimens and/or pictures of the minerals for each Mohs' number.

   b. Everyday objects such as the following can be used to represent minerals' hardness:

fingernail	2½
copper coin (penny)	3½
paper clip	4½
pocketknife blade	5½
glass	6
sandpaper	7
steel file	7½

Make and display a chart of the Mohs' scale, similar to the one shown in Figure 23.2.

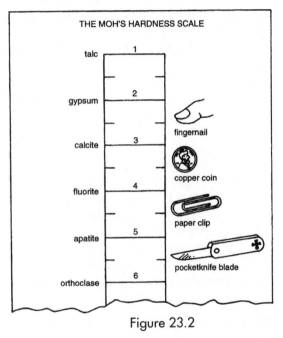

Figure 23.2

3. **Streak** is a physical characteristic of a mineral which is the color of the powder left when the mineral is rubbed against a rough surface that is harder than the mineral. An unglazed porcelain tile, called a **streak plate,** has a hardness of about 7 and is used to determine the streak of minerals with a hardness less than 7. Determine the streak of hematite by trying to scratch the plate with the edge of the hematite. Rub your finger over the powder left on the plate by the hematite and determine its streak color. Note that a mineral's color is not always its streak color. *Note:* A **streak test** is a test in which the streak of a mineral is determined.

4. All minerals have the physical characteristics of specific gravity, crystalline structure, cleavage, fracture, hardness, and streak. Use the previous tests to determine these characteristics of minerals you wish to display. For hints on how to label and display your minerals, see *Janice VanCleave's Rocks and Minerals* (New York: Wiley, 1996), pp. 80–83.

GET THE FACTS

Other than the previously listed physical characteristics, minerals have characteristics such as *luster* (the way a mineral reflects light) and color, and some have magnetism and fluorescence. A rock and mineral handbook is a good source to find out more about these characteristics. What determines a mineral's color or luster? What elements must be present in a mineral for it to have magnetic properties? What is phosphorescence?

24 The Rock Cycle
Processes That Change One Rock Type into Another

Volcanic rocks and fire rocks are common names for igneous rocks. These solidified masses are, as their names imply, the results of great temperatures within the Earth. Igneous rock is one of a trio of rock types—sedimentary, metamorphic, and igneous. Through different processes, each rock type can be changed into one of the other types in the trio. This process of change is called the rock cycle.

In this project, you will study and model the texture of different igneous rocks. The metamorphism of porphyritic rock (a kind of igneous rock) into foliated metamorphic rock will be demonstrated. You will also examine the relationship between the three rock types and model their transformation from one type to the other.

GETTING STARTED

Purpose: To model the difference between a porphyritic rock and other types of igneous rocks.

Materials

two walnut-size pieces of blue modeling clay
two walnut-size pieces of red modeling clay

Procedure

1. Break one red clay piece into four relatively equal size pieces.

2. Roll the four small pieces into balls.

3. Repeat steps 1 and 2 with one blue clay piece.

4. Lay the eight small balls in two rows next to each other, alternating the colors of the balls in the rows.

5. Gently press the clay balls just enough so that they stick together but retain as much of their shape as possible.

6. Break the other large red clay piece in half. From one half, form two relatively equal size balls, and from the other half form four relatively equal size balls.

7. Repeat step 6 with the remaining large blue clay piece.

8. Lay the twelve small balls in two rows next to each other, alternating the colors (and sizes) in the rows.

9. Repeat step 5.

10. Compare the appearance of the two clay rolls (see Figure 24.1).

Figure 24.1

Results

One of the clay rolls has large balls of clay pressed together. The second has large and small balls.

Why?

Rock is a solid, coherent **aggregate** (single mass) of one or more minerals. Rocks produced by the cooling and solidifying of molten rock are called **igneous rocks. Magma** (molten rock under the Earth's surface) at great depths cools slowly, and during this cooling process, large mineral crystals form. Igneous rocks that form within the crust and contain large uniform interlocking crystals are called **intrusive igneous rocks.** The **texture** of rocks is determined by the size of the mineral **grain** (hard particles) making up the rock. Intrusive igneous rocks are **coarse-grained** (having large hard particles). In this experiment, the clay roll made with large clay balls represents a coarse-grained intrusive igneous rock.

In **porphyritic rock,** like other types of intrusive igneous rock, large crystals form from magma cooling at great depths beneath the Earth's surface. However, during the formation of this rock, the magma is pushed to the surface before it completely hardens. There the final cooling occurs rapidly, producing small crystals. Thus, porphyritic rock contains two or more different sizes of interlocking crystals and can be said to have varied grain sizes. The clay roll with the large and small clay balls represents a porphyritic rock.

TRY NEW APPROACHES

Lava (molten rock from within the Earth that reaches the Earth's surface) cools quickly, producing rocks with small crystals or no crystals. Igneous rocks formed by the cooling of lava are called **extrusive igneous rocks.** Extrusive rocks are **fine-grained** (having very small hard particles) or have a **glassy** (smooth glasslike) texture. Repeat the experiment using only small balls of clay.

DESIGN YOUR OWN EXPERIMENT

1. **Metamorphism** is the change in structure, appearance, and composition of a rock in the solid state within the Earth's crust as a result of changes in temperature and/or pressure. **Regional metamorphism** occurs when large areas of rock are changed by pressure and heat, such as in mountain formation. What happens to grain arrangement during regional metamorphism when pressure is applied from one direction? Place a piece of paper on a table and position one of the clay rolls from the original experiment on the paper. Cover the clay with a second sheet of paper. Place a rolling pin on the top paper above one end of the clay roll. Pressing down firmly, roll the rolling pin across the clay roll. Repeat using the second clay roll.

   In nature, great pressure on rocks causes the temperature to rise. Together, the heat and pressure changes cause metamorphism, which produces **metamorphic rock.** Pressing the clay models of igneous rock represents the formation of **foliated metamorphic rock** (striped-looking metamorphic rock with grains arranged in parallel bands). **Science Fair Hint:** Make a display to show the clay rolls before pressure was applied to represent igneous rock and after pressure was applied in one direction to represent the resulting foliated metamorphic rock.

2a. Rocks come from other rocks. Igneous rock forms when sedimentary or metamorphic rock melts, cools, and solidifies. **Sedimentary rock** is made from **sediments** (materials deposited by water, wind, or glaciers) of metamorphic or igneous rocks that are **compacted** (packed together) and **cemented** (stuck together). Metamorphic rock forms when igneous or sedimentary rock is changed by metamorphism. This never-ending process by which rocks change from one type to another by a series of processes involving heat, pressure, melting, cooling, and sedimentation is called the **rock cycle.** Draw and display a diagram similar to the one shown in Figure 24.2 to represent the rock cycle. Note that sedimentary rocks are placed at the top of the diagram because these rocks are formed when the other rocks are lifted to or near the top of the Earth's surface, while the formation of metamorphic and igneous rocks is generally below the Earth's surface.

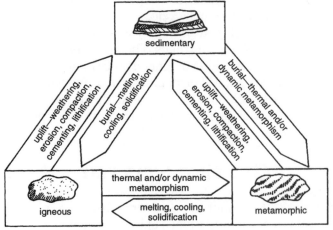

Figure 24.2

b. Use rock samples to prepare a display representing the rock cycle. Use found rocks or rocks purchased at rock and mineral shops or ordered from science catalogs. See Appendix 8 for a list of catalog suppliers and stores selling rocks and minerals.

GET THE FACTS

Thermal metamorphism includes changes due to heat. *Recrystallization* (enlargement of minerals) is one example of thermal metamorphism. Another example is *contact metamorphism,* which occurs when hot magma intrudes (penetrates) into the rock with which it comes in contact. How large an area is affected by contact metamorphism? What is a metasomatic change? How do contact and regional metamorphism compare? What are the names of different rocks before and after these metamorphic changes? To find out more about metamorphism, see John Farndon's *How the Earth Works* (New York: Reader's Digest Association, 1992), p.83.

25 Soil Texture
Effects of Regolith Size

Figure 25.1

A great part of the Earth's crust is covered with plant growth. The survival of theses plants depends on the physical and nutritional support they receive from a mixture of particles of weathered rock and humus called soil.

In this project, you will learn the differences between coarse-, medium-, and fine-textured soils. How the texture of soil and the shape of its particles affects a soil's porosity will be determined. You will also examine the relationship between soil texture and permeability. Soil profile and types will be studied.

GETTING STARTED

Purpose: To determine the texture of soil.

Materials

garden trowel
1-quart (1-liter) bowl
marker
masking tape
three identical 1-pint
  (500-ml) plastic transparent jars

newspaper
colander with large
  holes
large fine-mesh strainer

Procedure

1. Select a spot with soil, such as near a tree or where plants are growing. A bare soil area in a garden is also acceptable. Ask for permission to remove about 1 quart (1 liter) of soil.

2. Use the trowel to fill the bowl with soil.

3. Use the marker and tape to number the jars "1," "2," and "3."

4. Lay the newspaper on a table.

5. Spread the soil on the newspaper and pick out any live animals and parts of dead animals and plants, and return them to where the soil was collected.

6. Pour the soil into the colander, and shake the colander over the newspaper until no more particles fall through the holes in the colander (see Figure 25.1).

7. Put the particles left in the colander into jar 1.

8. Pour the particles on the newspaper into the fine-mesh strainer. Shake the strainer over the newspaper until no particles fall through.

9. Put the particles in the strainer into jar 2 and the particles on the newspaper into jar 3.

10. Compare the amount of material in each jar.

Results

The soil is separated into three sizes of particles—large, medium, and small. The amount of material in each jar will vary with different soil samples.

Why?

Soil is the top layer of the regolith (loose particles including soil, that cover Earth's surface) that supports plant growth. Soil composition includes small rock particles, **humus** (decayed animal and plant matter), air, and water. Soil provides support as well as nutrients for plants.

Not all soils are alike. Soil composition can vary by the type of rock and the amount and composition of humus it contains. Most soil contains particles of varying size. In this experiment, you separate the particles. Coarse-grained particles, as in jar 1, are larger than **medium-grained** particles, as in jar 2. Fine-grained particles, as in jar 3, are smaller than the other two particle types. The texture of soil depends on which type of particles predominates in the soil. For example, if there are more particles in jar 3, then your soil sample would be considered fine-textured.

TRY NEW APPROACHES

1a. Soil texture can be estimated by rubbing it between your fingers. Determine the feel of different textures, then collect a variety of soil samples from very coarse to very fine.

b. Compare the amount of the different-size particles in each sample collected in the previous experiment by repeating the original experiment. **Science Fair Hint:** Use photographs or diagrams of the jars of particles to represent the comparison of particles in different soil textures.

DESIGN YOUR OWN EXPERIMENT

1. **Porosity** is the percentage of a material's volume that is **pore space** (small, narrow spaces between particles in materials). How does the shape of soil particles affect porosity? Compare rounded and angular-shaped objects of comparable size. For example, compare smooth rocks or beads with aquarium gravel. Fill a measuring cup with the round objects. Note the visible spaces between the objects. Measure the volume of the spaces by filling the cup to the 1-cup (250-ml) mark with a measured amount of water. Repeat, replacing the rounded objects with the angular-shaped objects. Repeat again, using a mixture of equal parts of the rounded and angular objects.

2. **Permeability** is the measure of how easily a solid allows a **fluid** (any gaseous or liquid material that can flow) to pass through it. If a fluid, such as water, flows quickly through soil, the soil is said to have high permeability. How does texture relate to the permeability of soil? Use the point of a pencil to make six equal-size holes in the bottom of three 9-ounce (270-ml) paper cups. Cut circles from coffee filters to fit in the bottom of each cup. Label the cups "course," "medium," and "fine." Mark a line 2 inches (5 cm) from the bottom of each cup. Fill to this line with samples of the three soil textures corresponding to the labels on the cups. Lay two pencils parallel to each other across a measuring cup. Secure the pencils to the measuring cup with tape, then set the paper cup of coarse soil on the pencils, making sure that the pencils do not cover the holes in the cup (see Figure 25.2). Ask a helper to time you as you pour 100 ml of tap water into the cup. Stop timing when no more water drains from the cup. Record the draining time in a Soil Permeability Data Table like Table 25.1. Measure the amount of water that drained from the paper cup into the measuring cup. Record the amount of water in milliliters. Calculate the drainage rate by dividing the amount of water drained by the time it took to drain. Record this answer. Repeat the procedure with the other soil samples. The most permeable soil is the one with the highest drainage rate.

TABLE 25.1 SOIL PERMEABILITY DATA			
Soil Type	Draining Time	Amount of Water Drained	Drainage Rate
course-textured			
medium-textured			
fine-textured			

Figure 25.2

GET THE FACTS

1. A cutaway section of Earth would reveal a soil profile made up of layers called *horizons.* Mature soils have three basic horizons. What is the composition of each horizon? For information about horizons, see David Lambert's and the Diagram Group's *The Field Guide to Geology* (New York: Facts on File, 1988), p. 106.

2. *Pedologists* (soil scientists) divide soil into different types. Six basic types are tundra, desert, chernozem, ferralsol, brown forest, and red-yellow podzol. What types of plants grow in each soil type? How does climate affect soil types? What is the composition of the different soil types? For information about soil types, see *The Field Guide to Geology,* pp. 108–109.

3. Soils differ in the size of the particles they contain. Soil types in order of decreasing particle size are sand, silt, and clay. Most soils are not pure sand, silt, or clay, but mixtures of all the types. Such mixtures are called *loam.* How much sand is needed for the soil to be called sandy loam? What is a heavy soil? a light soil? See "soil" in various encyclopedias for information about soil.

26 Topography
Highs and Lows of the Earth's Surface

The Earth's surface has features with different elevations, such as mountains, valleys, and lakes, called topography. Three-dimensional (3-D) models, topographic maps, and profile diagrams can be used to show the elevation of surface features.

In this project, you will show how topographic maps use contour lines to indicate the elevation of a land area. You will determine the effect that changes in elevation have on the distance between the map's contour lines. You will use marks called hachures to indicate depressions and craters on your map. You will also measure the elevation of a gently sloping hill, draw a profile map of the hill, and make a 3-D model of the profile of the hill.

GETTING STARTED

Purpose: To produce a 3-D model of a mountain.

Materials

apple-size ball of clay
sheet of copy paper

metric ruler
about 30 toothpicks

Procedure

1. Lay aside a grape-size piece of clay. Use the remaining clay to mold a mountain with an uneven landscape. Make depressions in the side and/or a crater (a hollowed-out area at the top of a volcano) in the top.

2. Set the clay mountain in the center of the paper.

3. Insert the zero end of the metric ruler into the grape-size piece of clay, and stand the ruler vertically next to the clay mountain.

4. On one side of the clay mountain, use a toothpick to draw a straight vertical line from the top of the mountain to its base.

5. Align the vertical line drawn on the clay with the edge of the ruler, then mark heights 1 cm apart on the clay mountain: Holding the toothpick horizontally across the 1-cm mark on the ruler, insert the

end of the toothpick into the line on the clay. Repeat this procedure at each centimeter mark until you reach the top of the mountain (see Figure 26.1).

Figure 26.1

6. Turn the mountain one quarter turn and repeat steps 4 and 5. Repeat the procedure two more times so that heights are marked on four sides of the mountain.

Results

A mountain model with different indicated heights is made.

Why?

In this experiment, you made a 3-D model of a mountain. The toothpicks are placed at different heights to indicate **elevation** (height above ground level or sea level).

TRY NEW APPROACHES

Topography is the description of the size, shape, and elevation of a region of land. A **topographic map** is a flat map that shows the shapes and **elevations** (height above sea level) of a land area using **contour lines** (lines that connect points on a map that have the same elevation). The difference in elevation between one contour line and the next is called the **contour**

interval. The contour interval on the map in this experiment is 1 cm.

How can a topographic map of the clay mountain be made? Make the map by removing the ruler and following these steps:

1. Use a pen to trace around the base of the mountain. Make a mark on the paper at each vertical line on the clay model.

2. Wrap an 18-inch (45-cm) piece of dental floss around the mountain at the 1-cm height, letting the floss rest on the toothpicks. Cross the ends of the floss, then pull them in opposite directions to cut through the clay model.

3. Lift the top section of the clay straight up, remove the bottom slice without moving the paper, and lower the top section. The lines on the clay should match the marks on the paper. Trace around the base of the clay.

4. Repeat steps 2 and 3 for the remaining heights marked on the clay with toothpicks.

5. Remove the top, final section of the clay mountain from the paper and observe the tracings on the paper.

6. Label the contour lines with the appropriate elevations, as shown in Figure 26.2. Use **hachures** (short lines drawn inside a contour line) to indicate a depression or crater. The free ends of these lines always point downslope.

The closeness of the contour lines indicates the **slope** (the degree of steepness of an inclined surface) of the land. When the lines are far apart, the slope is gentle, but when they are close together, the slope is steep. **Science Fair Hint:** Stack the slices of the clay mountain and display the model along with the topographic map.

Figure 26.2

DESIGN YOUR OWN EXPERIMENT

1a. You can measure the elevation of a small, gently sloping hill by using two rods, such as dowels or plastic pipes, each 2 m long. Using a pen and a meterstick, mark a circle around the center of

one rod. Above and below this center mark, use the pen and the meterstick to mark every tenth of a meter, or decimeter (dm). With 0 at the center mark, first number every decimeter above zero as a positive number (1 to 10), then number every decimeter below zero as a negative number (–1 to –10). Tie a string at least 3 m long around the center of the unmarked rod. Stand the rods together so that the string around the unmarked rod is at the same height as the center mark on the marked rod. Secure the string with tape so that it cannot slide up or down the unmarked rod. Tie the free end of the string loosely to a ring, such as a jar ring, that is larger than the diameter of the marked rod. Place the ring over the marked rod. Stand the rods about 3 m apart and adjust the knot around the ring so the string is taut.

To measure a hill, stand on level ground at the base of the hill with your back to the hill. Hold the unmarked rod upright on the ground. Have your helper stand about 3 m away from you, facing you and the hill. Your helper should hold the marked rod upright so that the negative 10-dm mark is touching the ground and the string between the two rods is taut. Level the string by placing a line level (available in hardware stores) on the string near your rod. Instruct your helper to slowly move the ring up or down the marked rod until you can see the bubble in the center of the line level. This indicates that the string is level. Have your helper note the decimeter mark nearest the ring. The mark should be approximately zero. If the mark isn't zero, both you and your helper should very slowly move away from the hill until the ring at the end of the level string is at the zero mark (see Figure 26.3).

Figure 26.3

Profile of Hill 1

Figure 26.4

The base of the hill is interval 0, and the measurement is 0 dm. Record this measurement in a Hill Data table similar to Table 26.1. To take the measurement for interval 1, have your helper put his rod in place of yours at the base of the hill. Then move up the hill about 3 m until the string is again taut. Level the string as before, have your helper note the decimeter mark, and record this measurement as interval 1. This and all uphill measurements should be positive numbers. Repeat this procedure, recording each 3-m interval up the hill until you reach the top of the hill. To take downhill measurements, have your helper put his rod in place of yours at the top of the hill. Then move down the hill until the string is again taut. Level the string and record the measurement as before. This and all downhill measurements should be negative numbers. Measure each 3-m interval down the hill until the measurement is again approximately zero and your helper has reached the base of the hill.

TABLE 26.1 HILL DATA	
Interval (3m)	Measurement (dm)
0	0
1	5
2	10
3	2
4	8
5	–2
6	–10
7	–8
8	–5

b. To map the profile (side view) of the hill measured in the previous experiment, follow the procedure described here for the data in Table 26.1 and the graph in Figure 26.4. Each square on the graph paper is equal to 5 dm, and each six

squares across represent 30 dm, or 3 m, the measurement interval. The dots labeled 0 to 8 represent the measurements for intervals 0 to 8. Interval 0, the base of the hill, is marked by a dot labeled 0 in the bottom left corner. Each successive dot is placed six squares, or 3 m, to the right of the preceding dot. The dot is placed above the preceding dot depending on the interval measurement. Thus, because the measurement for interval 1 is 5 dm, the dot for interval 1 is placed one square, or 5 dm, above the dot for interval 0, and so on. The downhill or depression measurements are negative numbers and therefore are placed below the preceding dots. Thus, the dot for interval 5 is 2 cm below the dot for interval 4, and so on.

c. Make a 3-D model of the hill by measuring and graphing the hill at a 90° angle to the first path. Cut out the two profiles from the graph paper and use these as patterns to cut the shapes from stiff paper. Make a vertical cut on each profile so they fit together: Cut one profile halfway down from the highest point; cut the other halfway up from the bottom. Fit the profiles together at a 90° angel (see Figure 26.5).

Figure 26.5

GET THE FACTS

Cartography is the making or study of maps or charts. Find out more about mapping. What is a relief map? See H. J. de Blij's *The Earth: An Introduction to Its Physical and Human Geography* (New York: Wiley, 1995), pp. 15–26.

27 The Greenhouse Effect
Heat Transfer in the Atmosphere

The gases in the Earth's atmosphere are warmed by heat radiated from the Earth's surface. These warmed gases surround the Earth and act like a blanket, keeping the Earth warm.

In this project, you will demonstrate the greenhouse effect. You will discover how materials of the Earth's surface affect the greenhouse effect. You will examine the relationship between the greenhouse effect and surface temperatures at night. You will determine how composition and density of the atmosphere affect its ability to trap infrared energy. You will also show how cloud cover affects the surface temperatures at night.

GETTING STARTED

Purpose: To demonstrate the greenhouse effect.

Materials

two shoe boxes
ruler
soil

two thermometers
colorless plastic food wrap
timer

Procedure

1. Cover the bottom of each shoe box with about 2 inches (5 cm) of soil.

2. Lay a thermometer on the surface of the soil in each box.

3. Cover the opening of one box with a single layer of plastic wrap. Leave the other box uncovered.

4. Take readings from both thermometers.

5. Place both boxes side by side in a sunny place outdoors (see Figure 27.1).

6. Record readings from both thermometers every 15 minutes for 1 hour.

Results

The temperature readings show that the temperature inside the plastic-covered box was higher and increased faster.

Why?

Radiation, also called **radiant energy,** can move through space, and is not carried by matter. Radiation is also a term for the process by which this energy is transmitted. **Solar energy** is radiant energy from the Sun. Solar energy contains all the different forms of radiant energy, but most of the solar energy reaching Earth consists of **ultraviolet radiation** (causes skin to tan or even burn), **visible light** (radiant energy that can be seen and is divided into the rainbow colors of red, orange, yellow, green, blue, indigo, and violet), and **infrared radiation** (energy in the form of heat given off by all hot bodies).

Radiant energy from the Sun passes through the Earth's atmosphere and reaches the Earth's surface. However, about 30% of the Sun's total radiant energy reaching the Earth is reflected back into space by the atmosphere, the clouds, and the Earth's surface. About 20% is absorbed by the atmosphere, and the remaining 50% is absorbed by the Earth's surface. The radiant energy absorbed by Earth warms its surface, and this warm surface in turn warms the atmosphere above it. An object is warm because of its **internal energy,** which is also called its thermal energy. **Thermal energy** is the sum of all **kinetic energy** (energy possessed by an object because of its motion) and **potential energy** (stored energy of an object due to its condition or position) of particles in ran-

Figure 27.1

dom motion making up an object. The faster the particles are moving, the hotter the object. **Heat** is the transfer of thermal energy from one object or region to another due to differences in temperature. The three methods by which heat is transferred from one place to another are: conduction, radiation, and convection. **Conduction** (also called **thermal conduction**) is the method of transferring heat by the collision of one moving molecule with another. Conduction requires physical contact between the bodies or portions of bodies exchanging heat, but radiation does not require contact or the presence of any matter between the bodies. The method of heat transfer called **radiation** is the transfer of heat in the form of infrared radiation. **Convection** is the method of transferring heat by the movement of a heated fluid. Carbon dioxide and water vapor are gases in the atmosphere that help keep heat from being lost to space. They absorb heat from the Earth and then re-emit infrared radiation, some of which strikes and is absorbed by the Earth. Like the plastic covering that prevents the escape of some of the infrared radiation emitted from the soil, as well as the heated **air** (mixture of gases in Earth's atmosphere) inside the closed bowl, the Earth's atmosphere keeps the Earth warm. The absorption of infrared energy by the atmosphere and Earth, called the greenhouse effect, maintains a temperature range on Earth that is hospitable to life. The term **greenhouse effect** comes from the fact that the atmosphere is similar to a greenhouse in that it helps warm the Earth's surface by trapping infrared energy and heated air.

TRY NEW APPROACHES

1. What effect do surface materials have on the greenhouse effect? Repeat the original experiment, preparing boxes with different surfaces by covering the soil with different materials, such as sand, rocks, and grass. A surface of water could be prepared by lining the box with plastic and filling it with about 2 inches (5 cm) of water instead of soil. **Science Fair Hint:** Display photographs of the various boxes with the results of the experiment. Include a display, such as the one shown in Figure 27.2, indicating the percentage of radiant energy reflected back into space. For information about reflected radiant energy, see radiation in Jack Williams's *The Weather Book,* second edition (New York: Vintage Books, 1997).

REFLECTED SOLAR ENERGY

Figure 27.2

2. What is the relationship between the greenhouse effect and surface temperatures at night, in the absence of the Sun's radiant energy? Repeat the original experiment, taking temperature readings while the boxes are in direct sunlight outdoors. Then after dark, again take readings from both thermometers every 15 minutes for 1 hour.

3a. Could the composition of the atmosphere affect its ability to trap infrared energy? Compare different materials for their ability to trap infrared energy. Repeat the original experiment using plastic wrap and other materials, such as waxed paper, clear Plexiglas, and glass. **Science Fair Hint:** Display samples of the box covers with the results of the experiment.

b. **Density** is the mass of a substance per unit volume. The greater the density of a substance, the closer together its particles. How does the density of the atmosphere affect its ability to trap infrared energy? Repeat the previous experiment twice, first using two layers of covering material, then using three layers. **Science Fair Hint:** Compare the results of the experiment to surface environments on celestial bodies with little or no atmosphere, such as the Moon and Mars, and those with a dense atmosphere, such as Venus. Use an astronomy text to find out about the atmosphere of the different celestial bodies. Make charts showing the composition and density of their atmosphere and surface environment.

DESIGN YOUR OWN EXPERIMENT

1. Design a way to determine how the Earth's atmosphere affects the surface air temperature at night. One way is to record air temperature at sunset and again at sunrise for one or more weeks in a Day and Night Temperature Data table similar to Table 27.1. Calculate the difference between the two temperatures each day, and determine an average by adding the differences and dividing by the total number of days. *Note:* Your temperature measurements should be taken during a time of a constant weather pattern.

2. Repeat the previous experiment during a one-month time span to determine how cloud cover affects surface temperature during the night. Do this by recording air temperature during cloudy and noncloudy periods. On four or more days on which the weather forecast calls for the same amount of nighttime cloud cover, record the temperature at sunset and again at sunrise. Repeat by recording the day and night temperatures on four or more days with little or no nighttime cloud cover. Use the results to determine how the presence or absence of clouds in the troposphere leads to more heat escaping to space, thus causing a greater decrease in nighttime temperature.

TABLE 27.1 DAY AND NIGHT TEMPERATURE DATA

Day	Sunset Temperature, °F (°C)	Sunrise Temperature, °F (°C)	Temperature Difference, °F (°C)
1	80° (26.7°)	62° (16.7°)	18° (10°)
2	82° (27.8°)	61° (16.1°)	21° (11.7°)
↕			
7	80° (26.7°)	63° (17.2°)	17° (9.5°)

GET THE FACTS

Carbon dioxide, one of the greenhouse gases, is responsible for much of the warming of the Earth. Some scientists predict a rise in the average temperature of the Earth if the amount of carbon dioxide in the atmosphere continues to increase. Find out more about the production of carbon dioxide. How do fossil fuel emissions and deforestation affect the level of carbon dioxide in the atmosphere? What is insolation and how does it affect global warming? For information about the greenhouse effect and greenhouse gases, see *Janice VanCleave's Ecology for Every Kid* (New York: Wiley, 1996), pp. 139–146.

28 Soundings
Mapping a Profile of the Ocean Floor

The first scientific attempt to measure the depth of the ocean was made during an expedition by the British ship H.M.S. *Challenger* between 1872 and 1876. The measuring method on the *Challenger* was called sounding and involved lowering weighted ropes to the ocean bottom. Today investigators use echo-sounding sonar and other methods to determine ocean depths.

In this project, you will model the use of sonar to determine ocean depths. You will also determine how to use echo soundings to graph a profile of the ocean floor and learn how distances between echo soundings affect accuracies of profiles.

GETTING STARTED

Purpose: To model the use of sonar to determine ocean depth.

Materials

tennis ball
helper

stopwatch
calculator

Procedure

1. Hold your arms against the side of your body, then bend your elbows at a 90° angle so that your hands are held straight out in front of you.

2. Hold the ball in one hand.

3. Standing still and keeping your elbows against your sides, practice bouncing the ball several times until you can throw it with the least amount of force necessary to cause it to return to your other hand (see Figure 28.1).

4. Ask a helper to measure the time it takes for the ball to leave one hand and return to the other. When your helper says "go" and starts the stopwatch, throw the ball. When you

catch the ball, say "stop" and have your helper stop the watch and record the time that has passed as the echo time.

5. Repeat step 4 three more times and average the results by adding together the four recorded echo times and dividing the sum by 4.

Example:

0.56 sec + 1.02 sec + 0.59 sec + 1.0 sec = 3.17 seconds

3.17 sec ÷ 4 = 0.7925 = 0.79 seconds

6. The depth of the ocean floor (D) is one-half the average echo time (t) multiplied by the speed of sound in water (S). Use the average echo time to model how the depth in water could be determined by the following formula:

$$D = \tfrac{1}{2}t \times S$$

The speed of sound in ocean water is about 5,000 feet per second (1,500 meters per second), which can be written 5,000 ft/sec (1,500 m/sec).

Example:

$D = \tfrac{1}{2} \times 0.79$ sec $\times 5{,}000$ ft/sec (1,500 m/sec)

= 1,975 feet (592.5 m)

Results

The time for the ball to bounce and return will vary depending on the height of the person throwing it. For the example, the average time was 0.79 seconds. Using this as a model of the sonar echo time in the ocean, the ocean depth was calculated to be 1,975 feet (592.5 m).

Why?

Mapping the ocean floor requires methods different from those used on land. In the past, the depth was measured by a method called **sounding.** Sounding has nothing to do with sound. To take a sounding, knots were tied in a rope at intervals of 1 **fathom** (6 feet, or 1.8 m). A weight was tied at one end of the rope

Figure 28.1

and dropped over the side of the ship. The number of knots that went over the side before the weight struck bottom was counted. The number of knots equaled the depth in fathoms.

A modern method of measuring ocean depth is **echo sounding,** which is a method of sending out sound from a transmitter and measuring the **echo time** (time it takes sound leaving a transmitter to travel to an object, be reflected, and return to a receiver). Echo sounding is often called sonar. The term **sonar** is an acronym derived from *SO*und *Navi*-gation *A*nd *R*anging. Sonar is the method or the device used to determine ocean depth or distance by calculating the echo time of sound.

In this experiment, the bouncing ball represents sound bouncing off the ocean floor. The time for the round trip—the echo time—was measured and used to calculate the one-way distance—the depth.

TRY NEW APPROACHES

1a. Design a model for measuring the depth of different parts of the ocean floor by taping a 4-foot (120-cm) piece of adding machine tape to a tile floor. Write 0 at one end and mark each foot (30 cm) from 1 foot to 4 feet (30 cm to 120 cm), as shown. Position a stool on the zero mark and a chair at the 1-foot (30-cm) mark, and stack five or six thick books at the 2-foot (60-cm) mark and two or three books at the 4-foot (120 cm) mark (see Figure 28.2). Now, using the stool, chair, and the books as part of the ocean floor, repeat the original experiment, measuring the echo sound by bouncing the ball at each of the four marks. At zero, the stool that represents the shoreline, record the time as zero, then move to the 1 foot (30-cm) mark, drop the ball, and time the echo. Continue moving to each mark on the tape, dropping and timing the bouncing ball. Record the

Figure 28.2

measurements in an Ocean Depth Data table like Table 28.1. Use the depth equation to calculate the depth at each distance from the shoreline, and record it in the data table.

TABLE 28.1 OCEAN DEPTH DATA		
Distance from Shoreline	Average Echo Time	Calculated Depth
0 foot	0 second	0 foot (0 m)
1 foot (30 cm)	0.35 second	875 feet (262.5 m)
2 feet (60 cm)	0.52 second	1,300 feet (390 m)
3 feet (90 cm)	0.80 second	2,000 feet (600 m)
4 feet (120 cm)	0.68 second	1,700 feet (510 m)

b. Use the calculated depths from the data table to plot a graph representing the profile of the ocean floor (see Figure 28.3).

OCEAN MODEL PROFILE

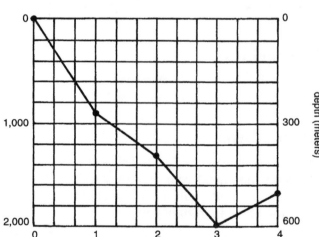

distance from shoreline (feet)

Figure 28.3

c. How does the distance between the echo soundings affect the accuracy of the profile? Repeat parts 1a and 1b taking echo soundings every 6 inches from the model's shoreline. Compare the profiles made with 1-foot (30-cm) soundings and 6-inch (15-cm) soundings to determine which better represents a profile of the ocean model.

DESIGN YOUR OWN EXPERIMENT

1a. Design another ocean model representing a section of the ocean, and use sounding to map the ocean model's profile. One way is to place two identical chairs, with backs at least 30 inches (70 cm) tall, 4 feet (1.2 m) apart. Represent the surface of the ocean by tying a string horizontally between the highest points of the chairs. Use a black marking pen to mark off 3-inch (7.5-cm) intervals along the "surface" string. Place stacked books, a stool, and an upturned pot and bowl under the string as shown in Figure 28.4. These objects represent features on the ocean floor.

Cut a second string 12 inches (30 cm) longer than the height of the chairs. Tie a washer to one end. Use the pen to mark off a 1-inch (2.5 cm) scale along this second string. This string will be called the scale. Holding the free end of the scale, position it against the surface string, next to the back of one chair (this is the 0-inch, or 0-cm, mark) and slowly lower the scale until the washer touches an object or the floor. Use the marks on the scale to determine the depth of the ocean at that point. Round off the measurement to the nearest scale marking. Measure the depth of the ocean every 3 inches (7.5 cm) along the length of the surface string, and record the depth measurements and the distances from the shoreline (the zero mark) in a data table like Table 28.1.

b. Use the data table to make a graph of your measurements. Title the graph "Ocean Model Profile." Display the graph and a photograph of the profile of the ocean model.

GET THE FACTS

1. The profile of the ocean floor is divided into four areas: the continental shelf, the continental slope, the continental rise, and the abyss. Which areas make up the *continental margin* (water-covered area from the shoreline of the continents to the abyss)? What is the location and size of each area? For information about these four ocean areas, see Don Groves's *The Oceans* (New York: Wiley, 1989), pp. 96–97. Display a diagram of the ocean profile showing the four areas.

2. On December 21, 1872, H.M.S. *Challenger* embarked from Portsmouth, England, and changed the course of scientific history. Physicists, chemists, and biologists collaborated with expert navigators to map the sea. During the 4-year journey, the voyager circumnavigated the globe and sounded the ocean bottom to a depth of 26,850 feet. Find out about this historic journey. What equipment was used to make the soundings? Information can be found by searching for H.M.S. *Challenger* on the Web.

Figure 28.4

PHYSICS

29 Resonance
Sympathetic Vibration

As soldiers walk across a bridge, they cause the bridge to vibrate. If the soldiers march in rhythm with the natural frequency of the bridge, each step will cause the bridge to vibrate at a higher amplitude. If the amplitude is great enough, the bridge could actually collapse. This phenomenon in which a small, repeated force causes the amplitude of a vibrating object to become very large is called resonance.

In this project, you will demonstrate sympathetic vibration, or resonance, and determine how distance affects sympathetic vibration. You will investigate how building size and stiffness affect the resonance caused by earthquakes. You will also learn how the application of a force at the same natural frequency of an object affects the amplitude of the object's motion.

GETTING STARTED

Purpose: To demonstrate sympathetic vibration.

Materials

2 identical empty 1-liter plastic soda bottles

Procedure

1. Blow across the mouth of one soda bottle to produce a constant sound. Note the pitch and the loudness of the sound.

2. As you blow across the mouth of the bottle, place the mouth of the other bottle near your ear as shown in Figure 29.1. Note any change in the pitch and the loudness of the sound.

Results

When you blew across the mouth of the first bottle alone, you heard a sound. When you

Figure 29.1

blew across the mouth of the first bottle while the second bottle was held next to your ear, you heard a sound that had the same sound but was louder.

Why?

Frequency is a term used in physics to denote the number of times that any regularly recurring event, such as **vibrations** or **oscillations** (swinging or back-and-forth movements) occur in one second. **Resonance** is the condition of starting or amplifying vibrations in a body at its natural frequency by a vibrating force having the same frequency; this is also called **sympathetic vibration.** All objects have a natural frequency depending on their size and shape. Since the two soda bottles are alike in size and shape, they share the same natural frequency. Blowing across the first bottle causes the air inside the bottle to vibrate, which makes the air around the bottle's mouth vibrate as well. This vibrating air moves outward and causes the air in the second bottle to start vibrating. Resonance occurs when the natural frequencies of two objects are the same or if one has a natural frequency that is a multiple of the other. For example, if the natural frequency is 4 vibrations/1 sec, a multiple that is two times the natural frequency would be 8 vibrations/1 sec. The second bottle in this experiment, vibrated even without air being blown across its mouth because the air entering it was vibrating at the same frequency as its natural vibration. Since the rate of vibration for the two bottles was the same, there was **constructive interference,** meaning the vibrations added together producing a vibration with a larger **amplitude** (the farthest displacement of an object from its resting position), and thus a louder sound. The vibrating air makes a sound that you can hear when the vibrations reach your ears. So the combined vibrating air from the two bottles produced a louder sound but at the same **pitch** (how high or how low a sound is).

Try New Approaches

How does the distance of a vibrating source affect resonance? Repeat the experiment asking a helper to hold a bottle near his or her ear while you blow across your bottle's mouth. First repeat the experiment standing about 3 feet (1 m) from your helper, then standing about 6 feet (2 m) away. Reverse positions and ask your helper to blow across the mouth of one of the bottles while you hold the second bottle near your ear.

Figure 29.2

Design Your Own Experiments

1a. An **earthquake** (violent shaking of the Earth caused by the sudden movement of rock beneath its surface) can cause more resonance in some buildings than in others. Is the difference because of the size of buildings? Design a way to show how size affects resonance. One way is to verify that as the circumference of paper rings decreases the frequency at which they strongly vibrate or resonate increases. Prepare the paper strips by cutting two 1-inch (1.25-cm)-wide strips from a sheet of copy paper. One strip should be 10 inches (25 cm) long and the other 8 inches (20 cm) long. Tape the ends of each strip together to form two circular rings. Tape each ring to the center of a 4-by-4-inch (10-by-10-cm) piece of cardboard so that they are about 1 inch (2.5 cm) apart as shown in Figure 29.3. Shake the cardboard from side to side. Start at a low frequency by slowly moving the cardboard back and forth. Then gradually increase the frequency of your

Figure 29.3

shaking by increasing the speed at which it is shaken. Notice when each of the paper rings starts to vibrate.

b. What effect does stiffness of a material have on resonance? Repeat the previous experiment, using stiff paper to make the circles. Attach the stiff circles to the ends of the cardboard used in step 1a so that you have the different types of paper on the same piece of cardboard. Observe the same-size rings while you shake the cardboard and determine if their frequency varies.

2. Resonance also can be induced when a small force is applied at the right frequency. An example of this is pumping a swing. Design an experiment to demonstrate that when you apply a force at intervals close to the natural frequency of an object, the amplitude of the object will increase. Since the frequency of a **pendulum** (a suspended object called a **bob** that swings back and forth) depends on its length, create three or more pendulums from different lengths of string. Stretch and tie a 1-yard (1-m) string between two chairs. Tie a washer (bob) to the ends of three strings of 12 inches (30 cm), 10 inches (25 cm), and 8 inches (20 cm) long. Tie the free ends of these strings to the horizontal string between the chairs. At regular intervals, very gently tap the side of the horizontal string, near one of the chairs. Change the frequency of the tapping (increasing or decreasing) until one of the pendulums starts to swing. Once a pendulum starts to swing, continue tapping at this frequency for 20 swings. You can determine the frequency of the pendulum by timing the 20 swings. Then calculate the frequency using this equation: F = vibrations (swings)/time.

For example, if the time for 20 swings is 10 seconds, the frequency would be:

$$F = 20 \text{ vibrations}/10 \text{ sec}$$
$$= 2 \text{ vibrations/sec}$$

3a. Determine how the movement of one pendulum can affect the movement of another pendulum with the same frequency. Tie a fourth pendulum 12 inches (30 cm) long, on the horizontal string from the previous experiment next to the other 12-inch (30-cm) pendulum. Pull one of the 12-inch (30-cm) pendulums toward you and release. Observe the movement of each pendulum.

b. Does the position of pendulums of the same length affect their movement? Repeat the previous experiment twice, using three pendulums, each 12 inches (30 cm) long. First tie the pendulums on the horizontal string 2 inches (5 cm) apart, then repeat by tying the pendulums 6 inches (15 cm) apart.

GET THE FACTS

1. A natural vibration is also called a *free vibration*. What is a forced vibration? For information see Sir James Jeans's *Science and Music*. (New York: Dover Publication, Inc., 1968), pp. 53–54.

2. How did resonance destroy the Tacoma Narrows Bridge in Washington State on November 7, 1940? For information see P. Erik Gundersen's *The Handy Physics Answer Book* (Detroit: Visible Ink, 1999), pp. 197–198.

Figure 29.4

30 Thermal Conduction
Transfer of Vibrational Energy

The term heat is often used very loosely. It is commonly said that hot objects possess more heat than do cold objects but technically the energy in the hot object is not heat, it is thermal energy. Heat is the movement of thermal energy from one object to another as a result of differences in temperature. The process by which heat is transferred from one particle to another due to collisions of the particles is called thermal conduction or conduction.

In this project, you will determine the effects of distance, time, cross-sectional area, and types of materials and temperature on thermal conduction. You will also compare the efficiency of different thermal insulators.

GETTING STARTED

Purpose: To determine how distance affects thermal conduction.

Materials

lemon-size piece of modeling clay
one small birthday candle
metal cookie sheet or baking pan
1 small paper clip
permanent marker

metric ruler
margarine
18-by-30-inch (45-by-75-cm) piece of aluminum foil
transparent tape
kitchen matches

Procedure

1. Use a grape-size piece of clay to stand the candle on the metal cookie sheet, as shown in Figure 30.1.

2. Unbend the paper clip to form a metal wire that is as straight as possible.

3. Use the marker and the ruler to make marks on the wire at 2 cm, 4 cm, and 6 cm starting from one end.

4. Use the remaining clay to form a cylindrical holder for the wire that is about 3 inches (7.5 cm) tall. You should be able to stick one end of the wire into the side of the clay holder so that when the wire is held parallel to the table the free end of the wire will be positioned above the candlewick (in the top of the flame when the wick is lit, as shown in Figure 30.1).

5. Place balls of margarine about ½ inch (1.25 cm) in diameter on the marks on the wire.

6. Fold the aluminum foil in half placing the long sides together. Then connect the ends with tape, forming a circle about 4 inches (10 cm) high.

7. Place the circle of aluminum around the candle, wire, and cylindrical clay holder. This will shield drafts from the materials.

8. Use a match to light the candle.

9. With the end of the wire in the tip of the flame, observe the samples of margarine. Make note of the order in which the samples show any sign of melting. When all of the samples show signs of melting, blow out the flame.

Figure 30.1

Results

The samples of margarine melt in order of placement from the flame, with the first margarine sample closest to the flame showing the first signs of melting with the sample farthest from the flame melting last.

Why?

Thermal conduction is the movement of heat through a substance from a region of high temperature to a region of lower temperature. Conduction occurs in fluids when their moving molecules collide. But conduction is more commonly the method of heat transfer through a solid material without the movement of the solid material itself. Materials through which heat flows readily are called **thermal conductors** or **conductors.** Metals, such as the paper clip in this experiment, are particularly good conductors of heat because of a high concentration of **free electrons** (electrons in some solids, particularly metals, that are attracted relatively equally to all nearby atoms and thus are not tightly bound to a single site and are relatively free to move through the solid), which transfer heat when they collide with the atoms of the metal. The measure of the ability of a material to conduct heat is called **thermal conductivity.**

If a substance is heated, such as the wire in this investigation, the heat is conducted from the heated end to the cooler end. The fact that the margarine sample closest to the heated end of the wire melts first, followed by the second sample, and then the third, shows that it takes time for the heat to be conducted from the hotter end of the wire to the cooler end. Thus the amount of heat conducted through the metal wire from the warmer end to the cooler end is proportional to the time during which conduction has been taking place.

TRY NEW APPROACHES

1. How does the cross-sectional area of a metal affect the heat conducted through it? Repeat the experiment using a paper clip with a larger cross-sectional area. Determine if the amount of heat conducted is proportional to or inversely proportional to the cross-sectional area of a material.

2. How does the type of metal affect heat conduction? Repeat the original experiment using different types of wire with the same cross-sectional area thus the same **gauge** (a measure of a standard size). Wire strippers have gauge sizes that can be used to measure the circumference of the wire. Generally, a small paper clip is 22 gauge and is made of steel. Use a piece of wire of equal gauge and length but made of different material, such as

copper. Be sure to strip away all of the insulation from the wire. Prepare two clay holders and place them on opposite sides of the candle. Position both wires so they are at the same height and have the same amount of metal in the flame. A large-diameter circle will be needed. Compare the time it takes for each margarine sample to melt. For information about good thermal conductors see Mary Jones's *Physics* (New York: Cambridge University Press, 1997), pp. 82–83.

DESIGN YOUR OWN EXPERIMENT

1. Does length of a wire affect heat conduction? Design an experiment to show the effect of length of a conduction material on heat conduction. One way is to repeat step 2 in "Try New Approaches," using two wires of the same gauge but different lengths. When the first sample of margarine shows signs of melting, blow out the candle. Continue to observe the remaining blobs of margarine. Use the results to determine if the same amount of heat is transferred from one end of the wire to the other.

2. How is temperature difference between two materials related to heat conduction between them? Design a way to determine if a larger temperature difference causes more or less heat to flow from one material to another. One way is to fill two Styrofoam cups one-fourth full with water. Put hot tap water in cup A and cold tap water in cup B. Measure the temperatures of the hot and the cold water. Place two metal washers in the hot water. After 3 minutes, use a spoon to remove the washers from the hot water and place them in cup B, the cup of cold water. At the end of 1 minute, stir the water in cup B, then measure the temperature of the water in the cup. Note the difference between the original temperature of the cold water and the temperature after the warm washers had been in the water for 1 minute. Repeat twice, first use warm water in cup B made warm by mixing equal amounts of hot and cold tap water. Then use water in cup B made colder by adding one or more ice cubes to the water. Allow the ice to remain in the water for 2 minutes, stir, then remove the ice before adding the washers. For more information

Figure 30.2

about a material's **temperature gradient** (the temperature change with distance along a material), see Corine Stockley's *Illustrated Dictionary of Physics,* (London: Usborne, 2000), p. 28.

3. **Insulators** are materials with a low concentration of free electrons, and **thermal insulators** are poor conductors of heat. These materials, such as glass, paper, and Styrofoam, depend on the interaction of vibrating atoms and molecules to transfer heat, which is a less efficient method than by movement of free electrons in conductors. Thus less heat is conducted by thermal insulators. Design an experiment to compare the insulating properties of materials used to hold hot liquids. One way is to use cups each made of different insulating materials. Add equal amounts of hot water to each cup. Place a thermometer in each container. Measure the temperature of the water in each container every 2 minutes for 30 minutes or until no further temperature changes occur. Record the temperature in a Temperature/Insulation Data table like Table 30.1. Use the data to prepare a graph recording the information, using a different color ink for each material on the graph.

GET THE FACTS

1. *Specific heat* of a substance is the amount of energy that must be added to raise the temperature of a unit mass one temperature unit. When 1 calorie of heat is added to 1 gram of water, the water's temperature rises 1° C. What are the specific heats of other materials, such as aluminum? How can specific heat be used to determine the amount of heat transferred through metal? For information see specific heat in a physics text.

2. There are temperature-sensitive nerve endings in your skin that can detect differences between the temperature inside and outside your body. You perceive an object as feeling cold when heat is transferred from your body to that object. Why do some things that are the same temperature but made from different materials, such as a carpet and a tile floor, feel as if they have different temperatures from each other? For information, see Annabel Craig's *Science Encyclopedia* (London: Usborne, 1988), p. 14.

Materials	TABLE 30.1 TEMPERATURE/INSULATION DATA									
	Temperature, °F (°C)									
	Time, minutes									
	2	4	6	8	10	12	14	16	18	20
Glass										
Paper										
Styrofoam										

31 Static Electricity
Stationary Charges

Electricity is the name given to an effect resulting from the presence of stationary or moving electric charges and the effects they cause. The word *electricity* was coined by William Gilbert (1544–1603), an English physicist and physician known primarily for his original experiments on the nature of electricity and magnetism (the force around a magnet). Rubbing two materials together, such as your feet against a carpet, causes the separation of two kinds of electric charges in the atoms that make up the materials. A buildup of stationary charges are called static charges. If enough charges separate, a spark, called static discharge, is produced when the charges recombine. American scientist and statesman Benjamin Franklin (1706–1790) named the two kinds of charges positive and negative. He also experimentally demonstrated that lightning, like the small spark created when you touch a metal doorknob after rubbing your feet on the carpet, is an example of static discharge, which is a loss of static charges. Static electricity is specifically the effect produced by static charges.

In this project, you will learn about two methods by which materials are charged: friction and conduction. You will discover the effects of electrostatic induction. You will also determine how materials and distance between charged materials affect the electric force.

GETTING STARTED

Purpose: To charge materials electrically by friction and induction.

Materials

9-inch (22.5-cm) round balloon
pencil
9-ounce (270-ml) paper cup
tap water
helper
wool cloth (scarf or sweater)

Procedure

1. Inflate the balloon to a size that is easily held in one hand. Tie a knot in the neck of the balloon.

2. Use the pencil point to punch a small hole in the side of the cup near its bottom.

3. Ask a helper to hold his or her finger over the hole in the cup, fill the cup with water, then set the cup on the edge of a sink with the hole pointing toward the sink.

4. Rub the balloon on the cloth five or more times.

5. Ask your helper to remove his or her finger from over the hole and observe the direction of the water coming from the hole in the cup.

6. Hold the balloon near but not touching the stream and observe any change in the direction of the stream of water.

Figure 31.1

Results

The stream of water bends toward the balloon.

Why?

Electricity is any effect resulting from the presence of stationary or moving electric charges. A **charge** (**electric charge**) is the property of particles within atoms that causes a **force** (a push or pull on an object) between the particles. The force between particles due to their charges is called an **electric force.** The two forms of charges are called positive and negative. When two like charges (positive and positive or negative and negative) are near each other, they **repel** (push apart) each other. But when two unlike charges (positive and negative) are near each other, they **attract** (pull together) each other. The property of space around a charged object that exerts an electric force on other charged objects is called an **electric field.** The source of positive and negative charges are the protons and electrons in atoms, which contain a nucleus. **Protons** are positively charged particles inside the **nucleus** (central part), and **electrons** are negatively charged particles outside the nucleus.

Physical contact, such as rubbing, between uncharged material is one method, called the **friction method,** of electrically charging them. **Friction** is the name of forces that oppose the motion of two surfaces in contact with each other, such as the rubbing of the balloon and cloth together. Before the balloon and the cloth are rubbed together, they are **neutral** (having an equal number of positive and negative charges, thus having no electric charge). This is because the atoms they are made of have an equal number of protons (positive charges) and electrons (negative charges). Atoms can become charged by either losing or gaining electrons. This happens because electrons, unlike protons, are free to move. If an atom loses an electron, the atom then has more positive charges (protons) than negative charges (electrons), and is therefore positively charged. If an atom gains an electron, it has more negative charges (electrons) than positive charges (protons), and is consequently negatively charged.

When two objects are rubbed together, one of them tends to lose electrons more than the other. The loss of electrons in one object results in its becoming positively charged, and the gain of electrons by the other object results in that object becoming negatively charged. In this experiment, when the rubbing stops and the balloon and cloth are separated, the electric charges stop moving. The balloon has a negative charge and the cloth a positive charge. An object with more of one kind of charge than another is said to be **charged.** These electric charges remain stationary, thus are called **static charges** (a buildup of stationary electric charges). **Static electricity** is the effect of static charges.

While water molecules are neutral, they are **polarized,** meaning their positive and negative charges are separated so that they have a positive and negative end. The presence of the negatively charged balloon causes the negative end of the water molecules to be repelled. Because water is a liquid, its molecules have more freedom of motion, so the water molecules rotate until the positive ends of the molecules are facing the balloon. Thus the side of the stream of water facing the balloon becomes more positively charged. Since unlike charges are attracted to one another, the positively charged water stream is attracted to the negatively charged balloon. The process of polarizing a neutral material by separating its positive and negative charges due to the proximity (nearness) of a charged object is called **electrostatic induction.** The rotation of the polarized water molecules by the charged balloon is an example of electrostatic induction.

TRY NEW APPROACHES

How would using a positively charged object affect the results? Since the balloon stripped away electrons from the wool scarf, the scarf becomes positively charged. Repeat the original experiment, again rubbing the balloon with the scarf, but this time using the scarf instead of the balloon.

DESIGN YOUR OWN EXPERIMENT

1. Two charged objects that have different charges attract each other, while two charged objects that have the same charge repel each other. So if a negatively charged object is brought near a neutral, nonpolarized solid, will the solid be polarized by induction because of the separation of its positive and negative charges? Design a way to determine if neutral solids can be polarized by electrostatic induction. One way is to prepare a pendulum using a bob (the suspended object on a pendulum) made of aluminum foil. Crush a small piece of aluminum foil to make the bob, then tie it to a 12-inch (30-cm) piece of string. Using tape, secure the free end of the string to the edge of a table. Charge a balloon as in the original experiment by rubbing it on a wool scarf. Hold the charged balloon under the hanging aluminum bob so that the charged balloon is near but not

touching it. Slowly move the charged balloon to the left, then move it to the right. Observe the motion of the hanging bob.

Figure 31.2

2a. Electrical conduction is the movement of electric charges through a substance. **Electrical conductivity** is the measure of the ability of a substance to conduct an **electric current** (the flow of electric charges). Conductors or **electrical conductors,** such as metals, are substances with a high concentration of free electrons and are good conductors of electric charges. **Insulators** or **electrical insulators** are substances with a low concentration of free electrons and are poor conductors of electric charges. **Charging by conduction** is the method of charging a neutral object by touching it with a charged object. Design an experiment to determine which would hold a static charge longer, a conductor such as aluminum, or an insulator such as paper. One way is to prepare two sets of pendulums: set one with two aluminum bobs, and set two with two paper bobs equal in size to the aluminum bobs. Use the procedure in the previous experiment to make the four bobs. First hang the pendulums from set one by taping the free ends of their strings to a table so that the bobs are slightly separated. Charge the aluminum bobs by conduction. Do this by touching them simultaneously for 1 to 2

seconds with a charged balloon. The bobs will have like charges, so they will separate. Measure the length of time of separation between the bobs. Make note of how many times you rub the balloon against the cloth when charging it. Then repeat the procedure with the paper bobs from set two.

b. Electric discharge is the loss of static electricity. Does the magnitude of the charge on the balloon affect electric discharge? Repeat the experiment twice, first rubbing the balloon more times, then rubbing it fewer times against the cloth. Make sure that all materials start with a neutral charge. Allowing the bobs to hang undisturbed and away from charged materials for 10 or more minutes should give them time to electrically discharge. This happens as excess electrons on the bobs are picked up by molecules in the air, especially water molecules.

c. What effect would bobs made of insulating material have on the results? Repeat the experiment using insulating materials, such as paper and cotton. Be sure that the only variable you change is the type of material used; keep the size and shape of the bobs as similar as possible.

3. An instrument called an **electroscope** is used to determine the presence of an electric charge on an object. As shown in Figure 31.3, an electroscope has a conducting metal rod with two thin metal leaves attached. If the rod is charged by conduction, the leaves separate. Design a way to determine any difference in the effect of charging the electroscope with a positively or negatively charged object. One way is to build an electroscope and test it first with a positively charged object (wool scarf after it has been rubbed with a balloon) then with a negatively charged object (balloon after it has been rubbed on a wool scarf). The electroscope can be made using a glass jar with a circle of cardboard to cover its top. Use pliers to reshape a large paper clip into a U-shaped loop. Punch two holes in the center of the cardboard circle about ½ inch (1.25 cm) apart. Push the ends of the loop of wire through the holes and mold a small piece of modeling clay around the base of the loop to hold the wire in place. The bent section of the loop should stand up above the cardboard about ½ inch (1.25 cm). Bend both ends of the wire loop outward to form hooks. Hang a small light-weight aluminum foil strip on each wire

Figure 31.3

hook. The strips should jiggle back and forth freely. If they do not, enlarge their holes. Place the cardboard circle over the mouth of the jar with the foil strips hanging down inside the jar. Tape the cardboard cover to the jar. Charge the foil strips by conduction (touching the metal top with a charged object). Variables that could affect the results of your experiment include size and weight of the aluminum foil strips, humidity, and separation of the foil strips. Electroscopes can also be charged by induction. See a physics book for information on this method of charging as well as instructions on how to charge an electroscope by induction.

GET THE FACTS

1. Static electricity has many uses, for example, electrostatic copying machines make duplicates of printed material by attracting negatively charged particles of powdered ink to positively charged paper. But static electricity also causes problems, such as sparks produced in a grain bin that can cause explosions. Find out more about the positive uses and negative problems of static electricity. For information see Mary and Geoff Jones's *Physics* (New York: Cambridge University Press, 1997), pp. 63–68.

2. In 1785, French physicist Charles Coulomb (1736–1806) used a type of balance to measure the force between two charged spheres. Use a physics text to find out more about Coulomb's experiment and the equation he used to describe the relationships among electric forces, charge, and distance. This equation is called *Coulomb's law*. Another source of information is Karl F. Kuhn's *Basic Physics: A Self-Teaching Guide.* (New York: Wiley, 1996), p. 139.

3. The triboelectric series ranks materials according to the amount of energy needed to remove their electrons. This listing provides information about predicting the charges of two materials that are rubbed together. For information about the triboelectric series see Kuhn's *Basic Physics*, p. 143.

32 Electromagnetism
Magnetism from Electricity

In 1820, the Danish physicist Hans Oersted (1777–1851) noticed that a compass needle was deflected at right angles to a wire carrying an electric current. Since a compass needle is deflected by a magnet, he concluded that the electric current somehow caused a magnetic field around the wire. Further studies by Oersted proved that any wire carrying an electric current has a magnetic field around it. Oersted's discovery started the study of electromagnetism and the use of an electromagnet (device that uses an electric current to produce a concentrated magnetic field).

In this project, you will determine the direction of a magnetic field around a current-carrying wire. You will determine the effect of the direction of an electric current in a current-carrying wire on the pattern of the magnetic field around it. You will also make an electromagnet, determine its polarity, and test its strength.

GETTING STARTED

Purpose: To determine the direction of a magnetic field around a current-carrying wire.

Materials

pencil	wire stripper
ruler	18-inch (45-cm) piece of 20- or 22-gauge insulated single-strand wire
sheet of copy paper	
compass	
1.5-volt D battery	

Procedure

1. Use the pencil and the ruler to draw two perpendicular lines in the shape of a plus sign across the center of the paper. Label the longer line N, S, and the short one E, W as shown in Figure 32.1.

2. Place the paper on a wooden table and set the compass in the center of the paper, where the lines cross.

3. Allow the needle to come to rest in line with Earth's magnetic field.

4. First rotate the compass so that N on the compass is in line with the needle pointing north. Then lift the compass and rotate the paper so that its compass directions match those on the compass. Replace the compass on the paper.

5. Place the battery on the east side of the paper, with the negative terminal of the battery pointing south.

6. Using the wire stripper, remove about 1 inch (2.5 cm) of insulation from each end of the wire.

7. Bend the wire so that it has a straight center piece slightly wider than the battery's length.

8. Holding the insulated part of the end of the wire, position the wire so that the center section is about 1 inch (2.54 cm) above the compass, and across the compass from north to south. Then touch the bare ends of the wire to the ends of the battery for about 1 second. Notice the direction in which the north end of the compass needle moves. **CAUTION:** *For your safety, hold the insulated part of the current-carrying wire so that you do not get burned or shocked. Holding the wires against the battery terminals for longer than 3 seconds can result in the wire becoming hot enough to burn your skin.*

Figure 32.1

9. Move the battery to the opposite (west) side of the compass. With the negative terminal of the battery pointing south as before, repeat step 8.

Results

With the battery's negative terminal pointing south, and the battery on the east side of the compass, the north end of the compass needle deflects from its north position toward the east.

Why?

An electric current is the flow of electric charges through a conductor such as a metal wire. The motion of electric charges also produces a force called a **magnetic force.** The property of a space in which a magnetic force can be detected is called a **magnetic field.** A magnetic field is made up of imaginary lines called **magnetic field lines** that indicate the direction and magnitude of the field. The straight current-carrying wire in this experiment produces a magnetic field as indicated by the movement of the compass needle. The direction of the magnetic field produced by the the current-carrying wire is the direction to which the north pole of the compass points when placed in the magnetic field. The compass needle is a **magnet** (a material with magnetic forces that attracts other magnetic material and is attracted to another magnet). Every magnet has two **magnetic poles** (the regions around a magnet where the magnetic forces appear strongest) called south and north poles. For a freely swinging straight magnet, such as the compass needle, its **south pole** (south-seeking pole) is attracted in the direction of geographical South. Its **north pole** (north-seeking pole) is attracted in the direction of geographical North. The direction of the current flow in the wire is from the battery's negative terminal to its positive terminal. With the current flowing in a south-to-north direction, the magnetic field lines below the wire are directed toward the east as indicated by the deflection of the north end of the compass needle toward the east. The relationship between a magnetic field and an electric current is called **electromagnetism.**

Try New Approaches

What effect would changing the direction of the current through the wire have on the deflection of the compass needle? Rotate the battery 180° so that the terminals of the battery have been reversed.

Design Your Own Experiment

1. A straight current-carrying wire is said to have magnetic field lines encircling it. Design a way to show that the direction of the magnetic field lines are in a circle around a current-carrying straight wire. One way is to compare the direction of the magnetic field above and below the wire in the original experiment. Design a way to raise the compass and place the wire below it, such as forming a stand for the compass by bending the ends of an index card to form a table shape.

2. Design a way to show the pattern of the magnetic field lines around a magnet. One way is to place a piece of insulated wire through a piece of cardboard, such as the top of a small cardboard box. Sprinkle a thin layer of iron filings on the cardboard around the wire in a circle with about a 4-inch (10-cm) diameter. Connect the ends of the wire to the terminals of a 1.5-volt battery. Observe the pattern of concentric circles (circles with a common center) around the wire.

3. An **electromagnet** is a device that uses electric current to produce a concentrated magnetic field. An electromagnet is made of a **solenoid** (coil of wire through which a current can pass) with a core of magnetic material such as iron. The current-carrying wire in a solenoid produces a magnetic field, which **magnetizes** (causes a substance to become a magnet) the iron core. Design an experiment to determine the **polarity** (the direction of the magnetic poles) of an electromagnet. One way is to wrap a 3-foot (90-cm) piece of 22-gauge insulated wire around a 16d finishing nail (also called a 16-penny nail) (see Figure 32.2). Leave about 4 inches (10 cm) of free wire at each end. Use a wire cutter to strip about 1 inch (2.5 cm) of insulation from the ends of the wire. Allow the compass to align with Earth's magnetic north. With a 1.5V battery in a battery holder, twist together the bare end of one solenoid wire and the bare end of one battery-holder wire. Hold the electromagnet so that the pointed end of the nail is near but not touching the west

side of the compass. While in this position, touch the free solenoid wire and the free battery wire together for 1 second. Note the direction in which the north end of the compass needle moves. If the end of the nail pointing toward the compass attracts the north end of the compass needle, the end is the south pole of the electromagnet. If the north end of the needle is repelled, the nail's end is the north pole of the electromagnetic. Reverse the direction of the battery and repeat the procedure.

Figure 32.2

4. How does the number of wire coils in an electromagnet affect the strength of its magnetic field? Design an experiment to test the magnetic strength of an electromagnet. One way is to use the electromagnet from experiment 3 made of 3 feet (90 cm) of insulated wire. Assemble a circuit using the electromagnet, a 1.5-volt D battery in a battery holder, and a switch. Tape the electromagnet to the edge of a wooden table as shown in Figure 32.3. Use metal paper clips to test the strength of the electromagnet. Bend one paper clip to form a hook that other paper clips can be hung on. Close the switch and touch the paper clip hook to the pointed end of the nail. Add paper clips to the hook one at a time until the weight of the clips causes the hook to pull away from the nail. Then repeat the experiment using twice as much—6 feet (180 cm) of wire to make the electromagnet. If all the coils will not fit on the nail, wind them as tightly as possible, then wind the next layer over the top, still turning in the same direction. **CAUTION:** *If you feel any*

Figure 32.3

warmth through the insulated area of the nail, open the switch. Do not touch the bare nail or bare ends of the wire because electric current flowing through the wire can cause these areas to get hot enough to burn your skin.

GET THE FACTS

1. Television images are the result of thousands of electrons hitting the television screen. What effect do electromagnets play in the direction in which the electrons move? For information see P. Erik Gundersen's *The Handy Physics Answer Book* (Detroit: Visible Ink, 1999), pp. 329–330.

2. *MAGLEV* stands for "magnetically levitated." How are MAGLEV trains different from conventional trains? For information see Gundersen's *The Handy Physics Answer Book*, pp. 330–331.

3. *Left-hand rules* are used to find the force on current or moving particles in a magnetic field. They are also used to find the direction of a magnetic field caused by current in straight wires as well as in solenoids. What are the left-hand rules? How do left-hand rules compare? For information see physics texts.

33 Static Fluids
Fluids at Rest

Static means no motion, and fluids are liquid or gaseous materials that can flow. Thus static fluids is the study of the characteristics of liquids and gaseous materials that are at rest.

In this project you will experimentally compare air pressure in different directions at a given point. You will experimentally determine the relationship between pressure and depth in a static liquid. You will also experimentally test Pascal's law, which states that pressure applied to an enclosed fluid is transmitted equally in all directions and to all parts of the enclosing vessel.

GETTING STARTED

Purpose: To compare air pressure in different directions at a given point.

Materials

1-pint (500-ml) jar   1 index card
tap water   large bowl

Procedure

1. Fill the jar with water.

2. Cover the mouth of the jar with the card.

3. Hold the jar over the bowl.

4. With one hand over the card, invert the jar.

5. Carefully remove your hand from the card.

6. Keeping the mouth of the jar at relatively the same height, slowly rotate the jar through a complete 360° circle, so that the mouth of the jar faces down, then up, and then down again.

7. Observe the surface of the card over the jar.

Results

The card remains over the mouth of the jar through the entire rotation. The part of the card over the mouth of the jar has no noticeable change in its slight concave (curved inward) shape throughout the rotation.

Figure 33.1

Why?

The water around the mouth of the jar wets the paper, and **cohesion** (the force of attraction between like molecules) between the water molecules and **adhesion** (the force of attraction between unlike molecules) between the water molecules and the paper molecules forms a seal. But this seal alone is not enough to overcome the force of gravity. The **concave** (inward curve like the surface of a plate) shape of the card over the mouth of the jar indicates that the card is being pushed into the jar by an outside pressure. This is **atmospheric pressure** (force that gases in the atmosphere exert on a particular area).

At a given point in a fluid, such as air (the name for the mixture of gases in earth's atmosphere), pressure exerted by the fluid acts at right angles at every point on a submerged object. The card stays in place over the mouth of the jar regardless of orientation, showing that an equal air pressure is exerted on the card from all directions. In the same way, at a specific height above Earth, atmospheric pressure is the same on all sides of an object as indicated by no noticeable change in the concave shape of the paper covering.

TRY NEW APPROACHES

1. Does the size of the jar affect the results? Repeat the investigation using jars of different sizes, but with the same mouth size as the original jar.

2. Does the size of the mouth of the jar affect the results? Repeat the investigation using jars with the same size but with different mouth sizes.

DESIGN YOUR OWN EXPERIMENT

1. The relationship between the pressure of a liquid and the depth (height) of that liquid is expressed by the formula $P_{liquid} = dgh$, where d is the density of the liquid, g is the **acceleration** (an increase in velocity) due to gravity (9.8 m/s^2), and h is the height of the fluid column above the point in question. For a specific fluid such as water, if the density of water ($1 \times 10^3 \text{ kg/m}^3$) remains the same throughout, since gravity is relatively constant, the only variable is depth. Thus the pressure on the liquid is directly related to the depth or height of the liquid in the cup.

   Design a way to test this. One way is to fill a container with water and make holes of identical size in the container at various depths (see Figure 33.2). The length (L) of the stream of water spurting from each hole can be used to compare pressure. The greater the depth of the liquid, the greater the pressure. Use a tall paper cup and make a hole near the bottom with the point of a pencil. Put a piece of tape over the hole and fill the cup. Measure the height from the hole to the top of the water's surface. Record this as the depth of hole A in a Pressure Data table like Table 33.1. Use this height and the equation $P_{water} = dgh$ to determine the pressure of water with a density of $1 \times 10^3 \text{ kg/m}^3$ at the depth of hole A measured in meters. Example: The pressure of water at a depth (h) of 0.03 m is:

$$P_{water} = dgh$$
$$P_{water} = 1 \times 10^3 \text{ kg/m}^3 \times 9.8 \text{ m/s}^2 \times 0.03 \text{ m}$$
$$= 0.294 \text{ kg·m·m/m}^3\text{·s}^2$$
$$= 0.294 \times 10^3 \text{ N/m}^2$$
$$= 0.294 \text{ kPa}$$

Note that the units $\text{kg·m·m/m}^3\text{·s}^2$ can be grouped forming $\text{kg·m/s}^2\text{·m}^2$.

Since $1 \text{ kg·m/s}^2 = 1 \text{ N}$, then $0.294 \text{ kg·m·m/m}^3\text{·s}^2 = 0.294 \times 10^3 \text{ N/m}^2$, and since $1000 \text{ N/m}^2 = 1 \text{ kPa}$, then $0.294 \times 10^3 \text{ N/m}^2 = 0.294 \text{ kPa}$. Kilopascal (kPa) is a practical metric unit for measuring pressure since Pascal (Pa) is generally too small.

Elevate the cup on an inverted rectangular container at one end of a tray so that the hole points toward the tray. Remove the tape, and mark where the water squirting out of the hole first lands. Measure the distance from the hole to this mark and record it as the length of the water stream for hole A. Repeat this procedure for two other holes, B and C, above hole A, making sure you open only one hole at a time and that all the holes are of equal size.

Figure 33.2

TABLE 33.1 PRESSURE DATA			
	h = Depth of Hole (m)	Pressure (kPa)	L = Length of Water Stream (m)
hole A (bottom)			
hole B (middle)			
hole C (top)			

2. Blaise Pascal (1623–1662), a French mathematician and inventor, was the first to discover that fluids at rest exert pressure equally in all directions. **Pascal's law** states that the pressure applied to an enclosed fluid is transmitted equally in all directions and to all parts of the enclosing vessel, if the

fluid is incompressible. Design an experiment to test Pascal's law. One way is to squeeze a 2-liter plastic soda bottle containing both water and a transparent condiment with an air bubble. The bubble of air in the condiment will increase or decrease depending on the pressure applied to it. When the bottle is squeezed, the liquid is not compressed but transmits the pressure in all directions, resulting in the compression of the air bubble inside the packet; thus the average density of the packet increases and the packet is less buoyant. Prepare the bottle by first selecting the best condiment packet. Do this by filling a quart (liter) jar about three-fourths full of water and dropping several condiment packets into the water. Select the packet that just barely sinks below the water's surface. Insert the condiment packet into an empty 2-liter plastic soda bottle. Fill the bottle to overflowing with tap water. Secure the cap on the bottle. Then squeeze the bottle with your hands.

Figure 33.3

The condiment packet will sink when the bottle is squeezed and rise when the bottle is released. Note the size of the air bubble in the condiment as it sinks and rises.

3. Earth's atmosphere is kept around Earth by gravity. Atmospheric pressure, which is created by air molecules hitting and bouncing off surfaces, including one another, keeps gravity from pulling all of the air molecules to Earth's surface. Gravity pulls the atmosphere downward and air pressure pushes the atmosphere upward. The result of the original experiment showed equal air pressure from all directions. Design another experiment to measure atmospheric pressure from different directions. One way is to use a **manometer** (an instrument used to measure the pressure of fluids). See Appendix 7 for instructions on how to make a manometer. Test atmospheric pressure by holding one end of the manometer tube in different directions: right, left, up, and down. The water level in the tubes will be even if the pressure on both sides is equal.

GET THE FACTS

1. In physics, pressure is defined as a force measured over an area. In the International System of Units (SI), one unit of pressure is newtons (N) per square meter. In honor of Pascal, the Pascal (Pa) unit is also used to measure pressure. It is equal to one newton per square meter. There are other units of measuring pressure, such as atmosphere, millimeters of mercury, bar, milibar, barye, and torr. Find out more about Pascals and other units of pressure. How do the other units compare to the Pascal unit? For information see a physics text.

2. How does Pascal's law explain the workings of a hydraulic jack? For information see Karl F. Kuhn's *Basic Physics* (New York: Wiley, 1996), pp. 75–76.

34 Newton's Third Law of Motion
Action-Reaction

Isaac Newton (1642–1727), the famous British scientist credited with discovering gravity, also gave us three laws describing motion. Newton's first law of motion states that a force is needed to change the motion of an object. In other words, a force either starts an object moving or causes a moving object to stop. His second law of motion explains how the force needed to accelerate (a change in velocity) an object depends on the mass of the object. His third law explains that forces act in pairs.

In this project, you will demonstrate Newton's third law of motion, that every action has an equal and opposite reaction due to the action of paired forces. You will also determine how pairs of forces that are equal but acting in opposite directions can produce motion.

GETTING STARTED

Purpose: To demonstrate Newton's third law of motion.

Materials

pencil
5-ounce (150-ml) paper cup
40 to 50 pennies
12-inch (30-cm) piece of string
1 handheld spring scale

Procedure

1. Use the pencil to make two holes across from each other just beneath the rim of the cup. Place the coins in the cup.

2. Loop the string through the holes, then tie the ends of the between the holes.

3. Hold the scale and adjust it so that it reads zero.

4. While holding the scale, attach the cup so that the cup hangs freely. Observe the reading on the scale.

Results

The cup pulls the scale down so that the measurement on the scale indicates the weight of the cup and the coins.

Figure 34.1

Why?

Newton's third law of motion states that for every action there is an equal and opposite reaction due to pairs of forces. In other words, Newton realized that if one object exerts a force on another, the second object exerts an equal force but in the opposite direction on the first object. You can be sure that two forces are action-reaction pairs of forces if the reverse description of one force describes the other force. In Figure 34.1, the three identified action-reaction pairs of forces are A/A_1; B/B_1; C/C_1. The description of force A is "the hand acts on the scale," and the description of force A_1 is "the scale acts on the hand." One description is the reverse of the other, so the forces are equal in magnitude, opposite in direction, and act on different objects. Thus forces A and A₁ are an action-reaction pair.

TRY NEW APPROACHES

The scale attached to the cup measures the downward force of the cup (the action). How can the upward force of the hand be measured (the reaction)? Repeat the experiment using two scales. First hang one scale from the other. So that the weights of the scales are not considered, while holding the top scale (called A), adjust the scales so each reads zero. Let the top scale be A and the bottom scale be B. Attach the cup to the bottom scale (called B) as before. The reading on scale A measures the upward force (the reaction force) and scale B measures the downward force (the action force). **Science Fair Hint:** A diagram showing the action-reaction pairs can be used as part of a project display.

Figure 34.2

DESIGN YOUR OWN EXPERIMENT

1. Every force on an object causes the object to be compressed to some degree. Design an experiment to demonstrate that an object compresses

until the action-reaction forces are equal. For example, fill a 3-ounce (90-ml) cup with coins. Lay two similar-size books about 10 inches (25 cm) apart on a table. Support the ends of a thin, flexible, plastic ruler on the books. Set the cup of coins in the center of the ruler. **Science Fair Hint:** Make a diagram showing the compression of the ruler, the action-reaction pairs of forces, such as in Figure 34.3. Three legends describing the force pairs of the books and the cup can be added to the drawing. For example:

Force Pairs for Book A

- Ruler acts on book A.
  Book A acts on ruler.

- Book A acts on table.
  Table acts on book A.

- Table acts on Earth.
  Earth acts on table.

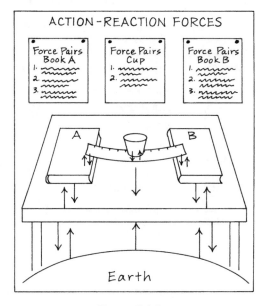

Figure 34.3

2. Unaccompanied forces do not exist. Since all forces are in pairs of equal strength, acting in opposite directions, and acting on different objects, what causes motion? A **resultant force,** is the single force that has the same effect as the sum of two or more forces acting simultaneously on one object. When forces simultaneously act on an object and the resultant force is zero, the forces are said to be **balanced forces** and produce no acceleration. When the resultant force of a group

of forces acting simultaneously on an object is not equal to zero, the forces are said to be **unbalanced forces. Newton's first law of motion** explains that an unbalanced force acting on an object is needed to cause acceleration. In this law, the resultant force is the **net force** (the sum of all forces acting simultaneously on an object).

Design an experiment to demonstrate that a pair of action-reaction forces are unbalanced because they act on different objects. One way is with two identical balloons. Inflate one of the balloons and tie a knot in its open end. Lay the balloon on a table and observe any motion of the balloon. **Science Fair Hint:** Prepare a diagram representing the action-reaction forces for the open and closed balloons, such as in Figure 34.4. Write the calculations for determining the net force of the gas inside the closed balloon on the balloon, represented by forces A as well as the net force of the balloon on the gas inside the balloon, represented by forces B. The equation for net force is:

$$F_{(net\ force)} = (F\uparrow + F\downarrow) + (F\rightarrow + F\leftarrow)$$

The calculation for determining the net force of the gas on the balloon in the closed balloon is:

$$\begin{aligned} F_{(net\ force)} &= (F\uparrow + F\downarrow) + (F\rightarrow + F\leftarrow) \\ &= (A_1\uparrow + A_3\downarrow) + (A_2\rightarrow + A_4\leftarrow) \\ &= 0 + 0 \\ &= 0 \end{aligned}$$

The equation representing the net forces of the gas acting on the open balloon is:

$$\begin{aligned} F_{(net\ force)} &= (F\uparrow + F\downarrow) + (F\rightarrow + F\leftarrow) \\ &= (A_1\uparrow) + (A_2\rightarrow + A_3\leftarrow) \\ &= A_1\uparrow + 0 \\ &= A_1\uparrow \end{aligned}$$

In the closed balloon, the net force is zero, therefore there is no unbalanced force and thus no motion. In the open balloon, the net force is equal to force $A_1\uparrow$. Thus there is an unbalanced force in the up direction causing the balloon to move upward. Use the net force equation to calculate the net force of the balloon on the gas inside the open

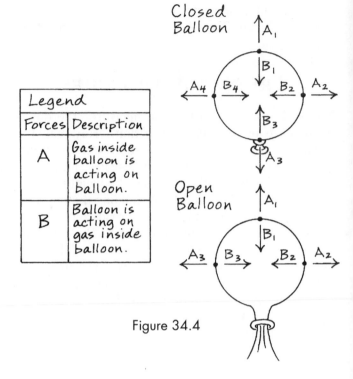

Legend	
Forces	Description
A	Gas inside balloon is acting on balloon.
B	Balloon is acting on gas inside balloon.

Figure 34.4

and closed balloons to determine why the gas moves out of the open balloon.

GET THE FACTS

1. The use of steam as a source of power can be traced back to a toy invented by a Greek engineer named Hero of Alexandria (20?–62?). This toy turned as a result of action-reaction forces. For information about the construction of Hero's toy and how the action-reaction forces were produced, see Struan Reid's and Patricia Fara's *Inventors* (Tulsa, Okla: EDC, 1994), p. 10.

2. A simple Hero's engine can be made from a soda can. For information about building this simple Hero's engine and making predictions about its movement see Robert Ehrlich's *Why Toast Lands Jelly-Side Down* (Princeton, N.J.: Princeton University Press, 1997), pp. 69–71.

35 Polarization
Vibrations in One Direction

Unpolarized light consists of waves with electric fields vibrating in all directions. In some cases, however, all the waves in a beam vibrate in one direction or in one plane. Such light is said to be polarized.

In this project, you will investigate polarized and unpolarized light. You will determine what effect an analyzer has on polarized light. You will determine if the angle of incidence (angle at which light strikes a surface) affects the degree of horizontal polarization. You will also test the optical activity of different solid materials and of different concentrations of water solutions.

GETTING STARTED

Purpose: To polarize light.

Materials

desk lamp with incandescent bulb
inexpensive plastic polarized sunglasses

Procedure

1. Turn on the lamp and position it so that the bulb is visible to you. Stand at a distance of about 3 feet (1 m) from the bulb. Look at the bulb and make note of its brightness.

2. Remove the lenses from the sunglasses by twisting the frames and popping the plastic lenses out.

3. At a distance of about 3 feet (1 m), close one eye and look through one of the polarized lenses at the lit bulb and again note the bulb's brightness. This will be called lens A.

4. Hold the second lens (called lens B) in front of but not touching lens A and while still closing one eye look at the light through both lenses. Hold lens A in place while rotating lens B until the bulb appears at its brightest as viewed through both lenses. Then slowly rotate lens B 90°, observing any change in the brightness of the bulb.

Figure 35.1

Results

The bulb is less bright when viewed through one lens than with the naked eye. Viewing the bulb through two lenses further decreases its brightness. As one of the lenses is rotated in front of the other lens, the light decreases still further until it is no longer visible or only partly visible.

Why?

Visible light is a form of radiation, which is energy that travels in the form of **electromagnetic waves** (transverse waves consisting of an electric field and a magnetic field vibrating at right angles to each other and to the direction of the propagation of the wave). A **transverse wave** is one in which the vibrations are perpendicular to the direction in which the waves are traveling, like the up-and-down or vertical motion of water waves. But unlike water waves, light waves can vibrate in all directions perpendicular to the direction of motion. **Polarized light** is light in which the electric fields of the light waves vibrate in a direction parallel to each other. A light wave whose electric field is vibrating in the vertical direction is said to be

vertically polarized. A light wave whose electric field is vibrating in the horizontal direction is said to be **horizontally polarized. Unpolarized light** contains light waves with electric fields vibrating in directions that are not parallel with one another, such as the light from the bulb in this experiment. (See Figure 35.2.) A polarized lens acts as a **polarizer,** which is a material that allows electric fields of light vibrating in only one direction to pass through it. When unpolarized light strikes a polarized lens, part of the light is **reflected** (bounced off of), part is absorbed by the lens, and part of the light with electric fields vibrating in one specific plane passes through. The light that emerges from the other side of the polarizer contains light waves with electric fields vibrating only in one direction or in one plane and is said to be **polarized** (also called **plane polarized**). Figure 35.2 represents vertical polarization. Polarized sunglasses are generally made of plastic material in which needlelike microscopic crystals are embedded. These crystals line up parallel to one another and make the polarized lens act as though it consists of many slitlike openings parallel to one another. So only those light waves with electric fields vibrating in the same plane as the parallel slits in the polarizer can get through.

Placing the two lenses together demonstrates the effect of using two polarizers aligned with each other. The first lens in line with the light is called the polarizer, and the second lens is called the **analyzer** (a polarizer used to determine if light is polarized). When the crystals in the two lenses are lined up parallel to one another, the greatest amount of light possible passes through. In this position, rotating the analyzer 90° results in the crystals in the separate

lenses being at right angles to one another. None of the polarized light is able to pass through the analyzer in this position, as shown in Figure 35.3. **Science Fair Hint:** Use diagrams such as the ones shown to represent the results of this investigation.

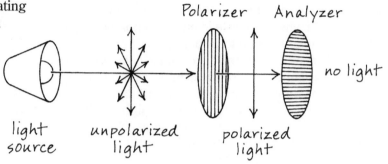

Figure 35.3

TRY NEW APPROACHES

How is light affected by nonpolarized lenses? Repeat the experiment using the lenses from an inexpensive pair of nonpolarized sunglasses.

DESIGN YOUR OWN EXPERIMENTS

1a. Unpolarized light becomes partially polarized when reflected from nonmetallic surfaces, such as water or glass, while some is transmitted and/or absorbed. The parallel components of the **incident light** (the light striking a surface) is largely reflected. The reflected light is partially polarized in a direction parallel with the surface it reflects from. Thus for lakes and other surfaces parallel to Earth's surface, the reflected light is said to be horizontally polarized. There is a special **angle of incidence** (the angle between the incident light and a line perpendicular to the surface it strikes) called **polarization angle** at which the reflected light from a nonmetallic surface is completely polarized. Design a way to determine the approximate magnitude of the polarization angle for light reflecting from water. One way is to fill a large bowl with water and set

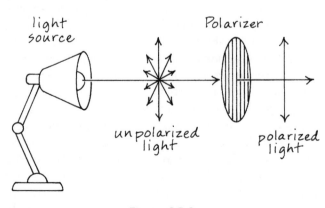

Figure 35.2

it on a table. In a darkened room, hold a flashlight above the water so that its light is perpendicular (normal or 90°) to the water's surface, then slightly tilt the flashlight. Sit facing the bowl and view the water's surface through a polarized lens. Since the water acts as a polarizer, the lens acts as an analyzer. Part of the light will enter the water and form a light spot on the bottom of the bowl, and part will reflect, thus forming an **image** (a representation of a physical object formed by light reflected from a surface) of the end of the flashlight. Rotate the analyzer to determine if the reflected light from the water's surface is polarized. The degree of polarization will be determined by how much of the reflected light (the image) disappears. If you see no change in the image, it indicates that the reflected light is not polarized. If all of the image disappears, then the reflected light is 100% polarized. Increase the angle of incidence by tilting the flashlight from its perpendicular position and analyze the reflection at the new angle. Continue this until the flashlight is held parallel to the water's surface. Estimate the angle of the flashlight from perpendicular (the incidence angle) and devise a way to compare the degree of polarization for each angle, such as a rating of 0 to +5, with +5 being the greatest polarization. For information about polarized angles see Craig F. Bohren's *What Light through Yonder Window Breaks?* (New York: Wiley, 1991), pp. 37–40. For information about horizontal and vertical polarization see Louis A. Bloomfield's *How Things Work* (New York: Wiley, 1997), pp. 494, 498, and 529–530.

b. How does the material of the reflective surface affect polarization? Repeat the previous investigation using different materials including a smooth metal, such as a flat baking pan. For information about polarization from reflected surfaces, see of Karl F. Kuhn's *Basic Physics* (New York: Wiley, 1996), pp. 79–80.

2a. A material is said to be **optically active** when it rotates the plane of the electric light waves pass-ing through it. Design a way to test the optical activity of materials, such as by placing a material between two polarized lenses. For example, to test the optical activity of a plastic cup, place the lamp, cup, and analyzer in a straight line with one another. Rotate the analyzer and observe the changing patterns of color. To test the optical activity of transparent tape, you can stretch some of the tape across a small, open frame cut from poster board. Repeat the experiment replacing the cup with the frame of tape. For information about the colors seen in optically active materials when viewed through an analyzer see Hazel Rossotti's *Colour: Why the World Isn't Grey* (Princeton, N.J.: Princeton University Press, 1993), pp. 49–51.

b. Sugar and tartaric acid (cream of tartar) are known to be optically active. Design a method of testing different concentrations of solutions of water and these chemicals. Note that the container used to hold the solutions must not be optically active. Test light passing through empty containers for optical activity and select one that is not optically active. Devise a method of comparing the degree of optical activity of each concentration.

GET THE FACTS

When two polarized lenses are placed together, the amount of light passing through the analyzer is greatest when their crystals are parallel and least when they are perpendicular, such that no light gets through. Since the light exiting the polarizer is polarized, why does any of it pass through the lenses when the crystals in one lens are positioned between 0° and 90° relative to the crystals in the second lens? What are photons and how does their spin affect polarization? For information see John Gribbin's *In Search of Schrödinger's Cat* (New York: Bantam, 1984), pp. 218–229.

1

Random Error of Measurement

Purpose: To determine the uncertainty of experimental measurements.

Materials

calculator

Procedure

1. Calculate the average of the measurements. For example, the average of the same measurements in Table A1.1 is:

$$\text{average} = (28° + 30° + 31° + 29° + 30°) \div 5$$

$$= 29.6°$$

2. Calculate the random error (E) of the average measurement using these steps:

TABLE A1.1 ANGLES OF MEASUREMENTS	
Measurement	Angle, °
1	28
2	30
3	31
4	29
5	30

- Calculate the range (R) of the measurements by finding the difference between the largest and smallest measurement values. In Table A1.1, the difference between the largest and smallest measured angle is:

$$R = 30° - 28°$$

$$= 2°$$

- Calculate the random error by dividing the range by $\sqrt{(n-1)}$, where n is the number of measurements. The equation that expresses this is:

$$E = R \div \sqrt{(n-1)}$$

For the sample data, the random error would be:

$$E = 2° \div \sqrt{(5-1)}$$

$$= 2° \div \sqrt{4}$$

$$= 2° \div 2$$

$$= 1°$$

- To express the random error of your measurements, you would say that the value of the angle is 29.6° ± 1°. This means that the measurement is between 28.6° and 30.6°.

2

Relative Error: Percentage Error

Purpose: To calculate the relative error of experimental measurements.

Materials

calculator

Procedure

1. Calculate the average of the measurements. For example, the average of the sample experimental measurements in Table A2.1 is:

$$average = (28° + 30° + 31° + 29° + 30°) ÷ 5$$
$$= 29.6°$$

TABLE A2.1 ANGLES OF MEASUREMENTS	
Measurement	Angle, °
1	28
2	30
3	31
4	29
5	30

2. Use the following equation to determine the relative error (also called percentage error) of the measurements. For example, if the accepted (true) value for the angle measurement is 29.8°, the relative error for the experimental measurement would be:

$$E_r = E_a ÷ A \times 100\%$$

where E_r is the relative error, E_a is the absolute error (the difference between the true and experimental measurements), and A is the true measurement. Note that E_a is the experimental measurement minus the accepted true measurement. For this sample, the absolute error is 29.6° − 29.8° E_r = −0.2°.

$$E_r = −0.2° ÷ 29.8° \times 100\%$$
$$= −0.67\%$$

The sign of the absolute or relative error merely indicates whether the result is low (–) or high (+).

3

Planet Facts and Figures

Planet Facts and Figures							
Celestial Body	Diameter, miles (km)	Average Density g/ml (water = 1)	Albedo	Aphelion, or Greatest Distance from Sun, millions of miles (millions of km)	Perihelion or Least Distance from Sun, millions of miles (millions of km)	Average Distance from Sun, millions of miles (millions of km)	Period of Rotation, hours
Mercury	3,047 (4,878)	5.4	0.1	44 (70)	29 (46)	36 (58)	1,407.5
Venus	7,562 (12,100)	5.3	0.76	68 (109)	67 (107)	68 (108)	5,832
Earth	7,973 (12,757)	5.5	0.39	95 (152)	92 (147)	93 (149)	24
Mars	4,247 (6,796)	3.9	0.16	156 (249)	129 (207)	143 (228)	24.6
Jupiter	89,875 (143,800)	1.3	0.52	510 (816)	463 (741)	486 (778)	9.8
Saturn	75,412 (120,660)	0.7	0.61	942 (1,507)	842 (1,347)	892 (1,427)	10.2
Uranus	31,949 (51,118)	1.2	0.35	1,875 (3,000)	1,712 (2,740)	1,794 (2,870)	15.2
Neptune	30,937 (49,500)	1.7	0.35	2,838 (4,540)	2,782 (4,452)	2,810 (4,497)	16
Pluto	1,434 (2,294)	2.0	0.5	4,604 (7,366)	2,771 (4,434)	3,688 (5,900)	153

4

Random Sampling in an Open Ecosystem

Use the following procedure to calculate the abundance of plant life in each sampling area.

1. Count the number of each plant type.

2. Determine the total number of all plants.

3. Determine the abundance of each plant type as a percentage of the total number of all the plants.

Example

If there are 30 woody plants and 300 total plants in a sampling area, the abundance of woody plants is calculated as follows:

$$\text{abundance} = \frac{30 \text{ woody plants}}{300 \text{ total plants}} \times 100\%$$

$$= \textbf{10\% woody plants}$$

Use the following procedure to calculate the density of plant life in each sampling area.

1. Count the number of each plant type.

2. Determine the area of the sampling plot.

3. Divide the total number of each plant type by the area of the sampling plot.

Example

If there are ten trees in a 100-square-yard (100-square meter) area, the density of trees is calculated as follows:

$$\text{density} = \frac{10 \text{ trees}}{100 \text{ yd}^2 \text{ (m}^2)} = \textbf{0.1 tree/yd}^2 \textbf{ (m}^2)$$

Use the following procedure to calculate the frequency of each plant type.

1. Determine how many of the subplots have each type of plant.

2. Determine the frequency by dividing the number of subplots with a specific plant type by the total number of subplots, which is 9 for the projects in this book.

Example

If six subplots have trees, the frequency of trees in the total test plot is calculated as follows:

$$\text{frequency} = \frac{6}{9} \times 100\% = 67\%$$

5

Cross-Staff

Materials

pen   stapler
white copy paper   yardstick (meterstick)
scissors

Procedure

1. Trace or photocopy the crosspiece pattern (see Figure A5.1).
2. Cut along the solid lines.
3. Fold the paper away from you along the dashed lines.

CROSSPIECE

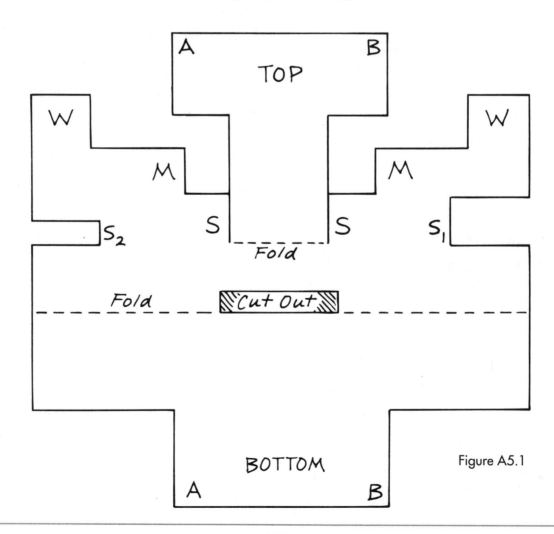

Figure A5.1

4. Position the T-shaped top so that its A and B sides meet the A and B sides of the bottom. Staple the A sides together first, then staple the B sides.

5. Slip the yardstick (meterstick) through the rectangular cutout section and between the top and bottom sections that are stapled together. The side labeled "W," "M," and "S" should face the zero end of the measuring stick. The paper is the crosspiece. It has a wide sight, "W," 4 inches (10 cm) across; a medium sight, "M," 2 inches (5 cm) across; and a small sight, "S," 1 inch (2.5 cm) across (see Figure A5.2). The notches in each side of the crosspiece are smaller sights and will be used in a later experiment.

Figure A5.2

6

Preparing Test Solutions

RED CABBAGE INDICATOR

Materials

red cabbage
knife
cutting board
1-cup (250-ml) measuring cup
electric blender
4 cups (1000 ml)
   distilled water

large strainer
large bowl
tape
marking pen
refrigerator

Procedure

1. Cut enough red cabbage into small pieces to fill the cup.

2. Pour the cabbage pieces into the blender. Then add 4 cups (1000 ml) of distilled water.

Figure A6.1

3. Blend the water and cabbage.

4. Hold the strainer over the bowl and empty the contents of the blender into the strainer.

5. Pour the cabbage juice from the bowl into the jar and discard the solid pieces of cabbage left in the strainer.

6. Use the tape and marking pen to label the jar "Red Cabbage Indicator."

7. To prevent spoilage, store the indicator in a refrigerator until needed. It should be discarded after seven days.

STARCH SOLUTION (1%)

Materials

$\frac{1}{2}$ teaspoon (2.5 ml)
   cornstarch
1 cup (250 ml) distilled
   water

small saucepan
1-pint (500-ml) jar with
   lid

Procedure

1. Mix the starch with 1 tablespoon (15 ml) of the water to form a paste.

2. Boil the remaining water in the saucepan and slowly add the starch paste.

3. Cook for two minutes, stirring constantly. Allow to cool.

4. Pour into the jar and secure the lid.

5. To prevent spoilage, store the indicator in a refrigerator until needed. It should be discarded after seven days.

7

Manometer

Materials

pencil

ruler

6-inch-by-30-inch (15-cm-by-75-cm) piece of poster board

transparent tape

scissors

9-inch (23-cm) round balloon

2- to 3-inch (5- to 7.5-cm) funnel

48-inch (120-cm) piece of aquarium tubing

cup

tap water

red food coloring

spoon

walnut-size piece of modeling clay

Procedure

1. Use the pencil and the ruler to mark lines across the poster board at 6 inches (15 cm) and 18 inches (45 cm) from one short side as shown in Figure A7.1.

2. Fold the poster board on these lines and tape the ends together to form a 3-sided stand as shown in Figure A7.2.

Figure A7.1

3. Tape the ruler vertically in the middle of one side of the stand.

4. Cut off the neck of the balloon. Discard the neck and stretch the bottom section of the balloon across the mouth of the funnel.

Figure A7.2

5. Fill the cup about one-fourth full with water.

6. Add about 20 drops of red food coloring to the cup of water. Stir.

7. Place one end of the aquarium tubing in the cup of colored water. Fill about 18 inches (45 cm) of the tube using your mouth to suck the water into the tube as you would draw liquid into a straw. Tap the tube to release any air bubbles in the water.

8. Tape about half of the tubing to the poster board so that it forms a U shape around the ruler as shown in Figure A7.3. Note the colored water is in the U shape of the tube.

Figure A7.3

9. Insert the free end of the tubing into the end of the funnel and secure with modeling clay. You have made a manometer.

10. To use the manometer, place the balloon-covered funnel in an area where pressure is to be measured. A rise in the column of water on the open side of the U tube indicates an increase in pressure.

8

Science Project and Experiment Books

ASTRONOMY

VanCleave, Janice. *A+ Astronomy*. New York: Wiley, 2001.

———. *Astronomy for Every Kid*. New York: Wiley, 1991.

Wood, Robert W. *Science for Kids: 39 Easy Astronomy Experiments*. Blue Ridge Summit, PA: TAB BOOKS, 1991.

BIOLOGY

Bonnet, Robert L., and G. Daniel Keen. *Botany: 49 Science Fair Projects*. Blue Ridge Summit, PA: TAB Books, 1989.

———. *Botany: 49 More Science Fair Projects*. Blue Ridge Summit, PA: TAB books, 1995.

Cain, Nancy Woodard. *Animal Behavior Science Projects*. New York: Wiley, 1995.

Dashefsky, H. Steven. *Zoology: 49 Science Fair Projects*. New York: Wiley, 1995.

Hershey, David R. *Plant Biology Science Projects*. New York: Wiley, 1995.

Kneidel, Sally. *Pet Bugs*. New York: Wiley, 1994.

Russo, Monica. *The Insect Almanac*. New York: Sterling, 1992.

VanCleave, Janice. *A+ Biology*. New York: Wiley, 1993.

———. *Animals*. New York: Wiley, 1993.

———. *Biology for Every Kid*. New York: Wiley, 1990.

———. *Foods and Nutrition for Every Kid*. New York: Wiley, 1999.

———. *The Human Body for Every Kid*. New York: Wiley, 1995.

———. *Insects*. New York: Wiley, 1998.

———. *Microscopes and Magnifying Lenses*. New York: Wiley, 1993.

———. *Plants*. New York: Wiley, 1997.

Wood, Robert W. *Science for Kids: 39 Easy Animal Biology Experiments*. Blue Ridge Summit, PA: TAB Books, 1991.

———. *Science for Kids: 39 Easy Plant Biology Experiments*. Blue Ridge Summit, PA: TAB Books, 1991.

CHEMISTRY

Johnson, Mary. *Chemistry Experiments*. London: Usborn Publishing, 1981.

VanCleave, Janice. *Chemistry for Every Kid*. New York: Wiley, 1989.

———. *A+ Chemistry*. New York: Wiley, 1993.

———. *Molecules*. New York: Wiley, 1993.

EARTH SCIENCE

Levine, Shar, and Allison Grafton. *Projects for a Healthy Planet*. New York: Wiley, 1992.

VanCleave, Janice. *A+ Earth Science*. New York: Wiley, 1999.

———. *Dinosaurs for Every Kid*. New York: Wiley, 1994.

———. *Earthquakes*. New York: Wiley, 1993.

———. *Earth Science for Every Kid*. New York: Wiley, 1991.

———. *Ecology for Every Kid*. New York: Wiley, 1995.

———. *Geography for Every Kid*. New York: Wiley, 1993.

———. *Oceanography for Every Kid*. New York: Wiley, 1995.

———. *Rocks and Minerals*. New York: Wiley, 1996.

———. *Solar Systems*. New York: Wiley, 2000.

———. *Volcanoes*. New York: Wiley, 1994.

———. *Weather*. New York: Wiley, 1995.

Wood, Robert W. *Science for Kids: 39 Easy Geology Experiments*. Blue Ridge Summit, PA: TAB Books, 1991.

———. *Science for Kids: 39 Easy Meteorology Experiments*. Blue Ridge Summit, PA: TAB Books, 1991.

MATH

VanCleave, Janice. *Geometry for Every Kid*. New York: Wiley, 1994.

———. *Math for Every Kid*. New York: Wiley, 1991.

PHYSICS

Amery, Heather, and Angela Littler. *The How Book of Batteries and Magnets*. London: Usborn Publishing, 1989.

Cobb, Vicki. *Science Experiments You Can Eat*. New York: HarperTrophy, 1994.

VanCleave, Janice. *A+ Physics*. New York: Wiley, 2002.

———. *Electricity*. New York: Wiley, 1994.

———. *Gravity*. New York: Wiley, 1993.

———. *Machines*. New York: Wiley, 1993.

———. *Magnets*. New York: Wiley, 1993.

———. *Physics for Every Kid*. New York: Wiley, 1991.

Wiese, Jim. *Roller Coaster Science*. New York: Wiley, 1994.

Wood, Robert W. *Sound Fundamentals*. New York: Learning Triangle Press, 1997.

GENERAL PROJECT AND EXPERIMENT BOOKS

Amato, Carol J. *Super Science Fair Projects*. Chicago: Contemporary Books, 1994.

Bochinski, Julianne Blair. *The Complete Book of Science Fair Projects,* revised edition. New York: Wiley, 1996.

Bombaugh, Ruth. *Science Fair Success*. Hillside, NJ: Enslow, 1990.

Cobb, Vicki. *Science Experiments You Can Eat*. New York: HarperTrophy, 1994.

Frekko, Janet, and Phyllis Katz. *Great Science Fair Projects*. New York: Watts, 1992.

Levine, Shar, and Leslie Johnstone. *Everyday Science*. New York: Wiley, 1995.

———. *Silly Science*. New York: Wiley, 1995.

Markle, Sandra. *The Young Scientist's Guide to Successful Science Projects*. New York: Beech Tree Books, 1990.

Murphy, Pat, Ellen Klages, Linda Shore, and the Staff of the Exploratorium. *The Science Explorer*. New York: Henry Holt and Co., 1996.

Potter, Jean. *Science in Seconds for Kids*. New York: Wiley, 1995.

Smolinski, Jill. *50 Nifty Super Science Fair Projects*. Los Angeles: Lowell House Juvenile, 1995.

VanCleave, Janice. *Guide to the Best Science Fair Projects*. New York: Wiley, 1997.

———. *Guide to More of the Best Science Fair Projects*. New York: Wiley, 2000.

———. *200 Gooey, Slippery, Slimy, Weird, and Fun Experiments*. New York: Wiley, 1993.

———. *201 Awesome, Magical, Bizarre, and Incredible Experiments*. New York: Wiley, 1994.

———. *202 Oozing, Bubbling, Dripping, and Bouncing Experiments*. New York: Wiley, 1996.

Vacchione, Glen. *100 Amazing Make-It-Yourself Science Fair Projects*. New York: Sterling, 1994.

Wood, Robert W. *When? Experiments for the Young Scientist*. Blue Ridge Summit, PA: TAB Books, 1995.

9

Sources of Scientific Supplies

CATALOG SUPPLIERS

Carolina Biological Supply Company
2700 York Road
Burlington, NC 27215
(800) 334-5551

Cuisenaire
10 Bank Street
P.O. Box 5026
White Plains, NY 10606
(800) 237-3152

Delta Education, Inc.
P.O. Box 915
Hudson, NH 03051-0915
(800) 258-1302

Fisher Scientific
Educational Materials Division
485 South Frontage Road
Burr Ridge, IL 60521
(708) 655-4410
(800) 766-7000

Frey Scientific Division of Beckley Cardy
100 Paragon Parkway
Mansfield, OH 44903
(800) 225-3739

NASCO
901 Janesville Avenue
P.O. Box 901
Fort Atkinson, WI 53538
(800) 677-2960

Sargent-Welch
911 Commerce Court
Buffalo Grove, IL 60089
(800) 727-4368

Showboard
P.O. Box 10656
Tampa, FL 33679-0656
(800) 323-9189

Ward's Natural Science
5100 West Henrietta Road
Rochester, NY 14586
(800) 962-2660

SOURCES OF ROCKS AND MINERALS

The following stores carry rocks and minerals and are located in many areas. To find the stores near you, call the home offices listed below.

Mineral of the Month Club
1290 Ellis Avenue
Cambria, CA 93428
(800) 941-5594
cambriaman@thegrid.net
www.mineralofthemonthclub.com

Nature Company
750 Hearst Avenue
Berkeley, CA 94701
(800) 227-1114

Nature of Things
10700 West Ventura Drive
Franklin, WI 53132–2804
(800) 283-2921

The Discovery Store
15046 Beltway Drive
Dallas, TX 75244
(214) 490-8299

World of Science
900 Jefferson Road
Building 4
Rochester, NY 14623
(716) 475-0100

GLOSSARY

abiotic factors   Nonliving things including water, soil, climate, light, and oxygen.

abstract   In reference to science fair projects, it is a brief overview of the project.

acceleration   An increase in velocity.

acid   A substance that has opposite characteristics of a base. A substance that makes red cabbage indicator turn from purple to red and makes bromthymol blue turn from blue to yellow; aqueous solution containing hydronium ions—H_3O^{+1}; a substance with a pH less than 7.

acid/base indicator   An indicator that changes color in the presence of an acid or base.

acoustics   The study of sound.

active site   The specific part of an enzyme that attaches to a substrate.

adhesion   The force of attraction between unlike molecules.

aerobic respiration   See **internal respiration.**

aggregate   A single mass, such as a rock.

agricultural chemistry   The science that deals with farming concerns, such as the makeup of soil, the application of fertilizer and insecticides, the analysis of agricultural products, and the nutritional needs of farm animals.

"aha!" response   See **insight response.**

air   The name for the mixture of gases in Earth's atmosphere.

algae   A plantlike organism with no leaves, stems, or roots, but that has chlorophyll.

altitude   (1) The angular distance above the horizon. (2) The distance above a surface, such as Earth's surface.

amplitude   The farthest displacement of an object from its resting position.

anabolic process   A process in living organisms in which larger molecules are built from smaller ones; energy is required.

analytical chemistry   The science of determining the qualitative and/or quantitative amounts of the chemical components of a substance.

analyze   To critically examine.

analyzer   A polarizer used to determine if light is polarized.

anatomy   A branch of biology dealing with the structural organization of living things.

angiosperm   A flowering seed plant.

angle of incidence   In reference to light, it is the angle from perpendicular which light strikes a surface.

angular distance   See **angular separation.**

angular separation   Apparent distance expressed in radians or degrees.

angular velocity   The angular displacement per unit time of an object moving in a curved path, expressed in degrees or radians.

anion   A negatively charged particle; an atom that has gained one or more electrons.

anthocyanins   Red pigments found in some foods, such as red cabbage.

apex   Tip.

apical meristem   Meristem at the apex of plant stems.

apparent distance   How large the linear measurement between two points appears to be.

apparent magnitude   A measure of how bright a celestial body appears as viewed with the naked eye from Earth.

aquatic   Pertaining to water.

aqueous solution   A mixture in which one or more substances are dissolved in water.

arc   Segment of a circle.

artificial satellites   Any object purposely placed into orbit around Earth, other planets, or the Sun; man-made satellites.

asterism   A group of stars with a shape within a constellation.

asteroid   An irregularly shaped rocky chunk of matter that rotates as it orbits the Sun; generally found in an orbit between Mars and Jupiter; also called minor planet.

astrometry   The observational study concerned with the measurement of the position of celestial bodies.

astronautics   The science and technology of space exploration.

astronomical unit (AU)   A unit of measurement used to measure distance in the solar system, based on the average distance between Earth and the Sun—93 million miles (149 million km).

astronomy   The science dealing with all the celestial bodies in the universe, including the planets and their satellites, comets and meteors, the stars and interstellar matter, the star systems known as galaxies, and clusters of galaxies.

astrophysics   The study concerned particularly with the production and expenditure of radiation in systems such as stars and galaxies and in the universe as a whole.

atmosphere   A gaseous layer surrounding any celestial body that has gravity strong enough to prevent the gases from escaping.

atmospheric pressure   The force that gases in the atmosphere exert on a particular area.

atoms   The building blocks of matter.

attract   To pull together.

autotrophs   Organisms, such as plants, that can make their own food.

axis   The imaginary line through the center of a body.

balanced forces   Forces that act simultaneously on an object with a resultant force of zero.

bar graph   A diagram that uses solid bars to represent data.

barycenter   The point between binary bodies where their center of mass is located; the point around which binary bodies rotate.

basal cleavage   Cleavage in one direction.

base   A substance that has opposite characteristics of an acid. A substance that makes red cabbage indicator turn from purple to green; an aqueous solution containing hydroxide ions—OH^{-1}, a substance with a pH greater than 7.

behaviorism   The study of actions that alter the relationship between an animal and its environment.

binary bodies Two celestial bodies held together by mutual gravitational attraction.

biochemistry The study of the substances found in living organisms, and of the chemical reactions involved in life processes.

biological catalysts Enzymes.

biology The study of organisms and their life processes.

biotic factors Living organisms.

bob The suspended object on a pendulum.

bond A force holding atoms together.

botany The study of plants and plant life.

breathing The mechanical process of moving gases into and out of the body.

calcium propionate A food additive on the U.S. Food and Drug Administration's GRAS list used to preserve foods, such as bread.

capillaries The tiniest blood vessels.

catabolic process A process in living organisms in which large molecules are broken into smaller ones, usually with the release of energy.

catalysts Chemicals that change the rate of a chemical reaction.

celestial bodies The natural objects in the sky, such as stars, moons, suns, and planets.

celestial mechanics The study of the motion of celestial bodies due to gravity.

cemented Stuck together.

center of mass The point on a body where its mass seems to be concentrated.

charge The property of particles within atoms that causes an electric force between the particles; the two kinds of charges are called positive and negative; also called an **electric charge.**

charged The condition of an object with more of one kind of charge than another.

charging by conduction The method of electrically charging a neutral object by touching it with a charged object.

chart Data or other information in the form of a table, a graph, or a list.

chemical reaction A change that produces one or more new substances.

chemicals Substances made of a combination of elements.

chemistry The study of the composition, structure, properties, and interactions of matter. See **agricultural chemistry, biochemistry, inorganic chemistry, organic chemistry,** and **physical chemistry.**

chlorophyll A green coloring substance in plants; pigment that absorbs light and is necessary for photosynthesis.

chlorosis The loss of the green color in plants due to the loss of chlorophyll.

chromosphere The layer of the Sun's atmosphere between the photosphere and the corona.

circle graph A chart that uses a circle divided into wedge-shaped sections to display data.

cleavage A physical characteristic of a mineral, which is the tendency of a mineral to break along a cleavage plane.

cleavage plane Flat surface along which a mineral can be split apart.

cloud In reference to Earth, it is a visible mass of water drops floating in Earth's atmosphere.

coarse-grained The texture of a material having large hard particles.

cohesion The force of attraction between like molecules.

column The space between vertical lines in a table.

comet A celestial body made of dust, rock, sand, gases, and ices (mainly water and carbon dioxide) that moves in an extremely elongated orbit about the Sun.

compacted Packed together.

computer science The study of and development of all aspects of computers, including hardware and software.

concave An inward curve like the surface of a plate.

concentration The amount of one substance dissolved in a given volume of another.

conchoidal A type of fracture with a curved shell-like surface.

condensation The phase change from a gas to a liquid.

conduction (1) The method of transferring heat from a region of high temperature to a region of lower temperature by the collision of one particle with another. Also called **thermal conduction.** (2) The movement of electric charges through a substance. Also called **electrical conduction.**

conductor A substance that allows heat and an electric current to easily flow through it; a substance with a high concentration of free electrons. See **electrical conductor** and **thermal conductor.**

constant factors The factors of a scientific experiment that are held unchanging while the study is being completed. Also called controlled variables or constants.

constellation A group of stars that appears to make a pattern in the sky.

constructive interference Vibrations that when added together produce a vibration with a larger amplitude.

contour interval Difference in elevation between one contour line and the next.

contour lines Lines that connect points on the Earth that have the same elevation.

control A standard for comparison. It is a test in which the independent variable is absent or is kept constant in order to measure changes in the dependent variable.

convection A method of transferring heat by the movement of a heated fluid.

convection zone The layer of the Sun between the radiation zone and the photosphere.

core The center of a celestial body, such as the Sun.

corona The outermost layer of the Sun's atmosphere.

cotyledon Part of a seed where nutrients required for the seed to grow and develop are stored; also called a seed leaf.

cross-staff An instrument used to measure angular separation.

crystalline structure The characteristics of a substance, such as a mineral, in which atoms of the substance are arranged so that they form a particular geometric shape.

data As used in this book, data means observations and/or measured facts obtained experimentally; quantitative (numerical) as well as qualitative (adjectives) facts obtained experimentally. See **raw data.**

debris Scattered pieces of something that has been broken.

density The measure of the mass per unit volume of a substance.

dependent variable A factor being observed in an experiment that changes in response to the independent variable.

dicot See **dicotyledon.**

dicotyledon One of the two groups of flowering plants whose seeds have two cotyledons; also called a dicot.

diffused Spread out in different directions.

displace To push aside, as in the displacement of water.

dissolve To break into very small particles and mix thoroughly with a liquid.

earthquake The violent shaking of the Earth caused by a sudden movement of rock beneath its surface.

earth science The study of the Earth from the outermost limits of its atmosphere to the innermost depths of its interior.

echo sounding Method of ending out sound from a sound transmitter and measuring its echo time.

echo time Time it takes sound leaving a transmitter to travel to an object, be reflected, and return to a receiver.

ecology The study of the relationships of living things to other living things and to their environment.

ecosystem A unit of nature that includes all organisms living in a particular environment, such as a forest or desert, and the physical parts of the environment that affect them.

electrical conduction The movement of electrical charges through a substance as a result of the movement of free electrons.

electrical conductivity The measure of the ability to conduct electric charges.

electrical conductor A substance that has a high electrical conductivity; a substance with a high concentration of free electrons that allows electric charges to move easily through it.

electrical insulator Materials with a low concentration of electrons that are poor electrical conductors.

electric charge See **charge.**

electric current The flow of electric charges through a conductor, such as a metal wire.

electric discharge The loss of static electricity.

electric field The property of space around a charged object that exerts an electric force on other charged objects.

electric force The force between charged particles.

electricity Any effect resulting from the presence of stationary or moving electric charges.

electrodynamics The study of electric and magnetic force fields; the behavior of electrically charged particles in electromagnetic fields; and the propagation of electromagnetic waves.

electromagnet A device that uses electric current to produce a concentrated magnetic field; a device made of a solenoid with a core of magnetic material such as iron.

electromagnetic wave A transverse wave consisting of an electric field and a magnetic field vibrating at right angles to each other and to the direction of the wave motion.

electromagnetism The relationship between a magnetic field and an electric current.

electron Negatively charged particle outside an atom's nucleus.

electroscope An instrument used to determine the presence of an electric charge on an object.

electrostatic induction The process of polarizing a neutral material by separating positive and negative charges due to the proximity (nearness) of a charged object.

elemental Natural form of an element.

elementary particle physics The study of properties of elementary particles, such as electrons in static electricity.

elements The basic chemical substances of which all things are made; composed of building blocks called atoms; only one kind of atom makes up each specific element.

elevation Height above ground level or sea level.

embryo Organism in its earliest stage of development.

energy Ability of matter to make changes.

engineering The application of science for practical purposes.

environment All the external factors affecting an organism, including abiotic and biotic factors.

enzymes A biological catalyst found in living organisms.

epicotyl The end of the embryo that develops into the shoot.

erosion The process by which materials are broken down and moved off the surface it flows over.

evaporation Phase change from liquid to gas; requires energy.

exploratory experiments As defined in this book, experiments in which the data is used as part of the project research.

external respiration Process used by organisms to exchange gases with the environment; respiration in animals.

extrusive igneous rock Fine-grained igneous rock formed at the Earth's surface.

factor One of the conditions contributing to the results of an experiment.

fathom Measurement of length equal to 6 feet (1.8 m).

fatty acids Organic acids commonly found in fats and oils; compounds with relatively long carbon chains, usually from 4 to 24 carbons or more.

filter A material that allows a liquid, but not solids, to pass through.

filtrate The liquid that passes through a filter.

fine-grained Texture of a material having very small hard particles.

fluid Any gaseous or liquid material that can flow.

fluid dynamics The study of the properties and behavior of moving fluids.

foliated metamorphic rock Striped-looking or layered metamorphic rock with grains arranged in parallel bands.

food additives Natural and synthetic chemicals added to food to supply nutrients, to enhance color, flavor, or texture, and to prevent or delay spoilage.

food preservative A food additive such as calcium propionate used to maintain freshness and extend the shelf life of package food.

force A push or pull on an object.

fracture A characteristic of a mineral, which is the way in which a mineral breaks when it doesn't split along a cleavage plane; an irregular break; **see conchoidal, hackly,** and **splintery.**

free electrons Electrons in some solids, particularly metals, that are attracted relatively equally to all nearby atoms and thus are not tightly bound to a single site and are relatively free to move through the solid.

frequency A term used in the physics to denote the number of times that any regularly recurring event, such as vibrations, waves, or swings occurs in one second.

friction The name of forces that oppose the motion of two surfaces in contact with each other.

friction method The method of electrically charging materials by physical contact, such as rubbing them together.

fungi (singular **fungus**) A group of plantlike organisms that have no leaves, flowers, or chlorophyll, including mildew, mold, mushrooms, and toadstools.

Galilean satellites Any of the four largest moons of Jupiter: Io, Europa, Ganymede, and Callisto.

gauge   A measure of a standard size; used to measure the diameter of wire.

geosynchronous satellites   Artificial satellites that remain above one place on Earth during their orbit.

germination   The process by which a seed grows.

gills   Organs through which fish breathe.

glassy   A very smooth glasslike texture.

glucose   A type of sugar; reactant in aerobic respiration.

glycerol   Organic alcohol found in fats and oils.

grain   A hard particle.

granulation   In reference to the Sun, it is the grainy appearance of the Sun's photosphere due to granules.

granules   In reference to the Sun, it is a bright spot on the Sun's surface that is the top of a rising current of hot gases from the convection zone, measuring about 900 miles (nearly 1,500 km) across.

graph   A diagram used to compare the independent and dependent variables in an experiment.

GRAS list   The acronym for Generally Recognized As Safe. The GRAS is a list of food additives whose use is permitted by the U.S. Food and Drug Administration.

gravity   A force of attraction between all objects in the universe.

greenhouse effect   The warming of the Earth by the trapping of infrared radiation from the Sun, just as the glass or plastic of a greenhouse traps infrared radiation.

gymnosperm   A nonflowering seed plant.

hachure   One of a set of short lines drawn inside a contour line to indicate a depression or crater. These lines always point downslope.

hackly   A type of fracture with a jagged surface.

hardness   A physical characteristic of a mineral, which is the measure of its resistance to being scratched.

heat   The transfer of thermal energy from one object or region to another due to differences in temperature.

heft   Subjective measurement of how heavy an object is. Heft is determined by picking up objects of equal volume and comparing their weights.

heliology   The study of the Sun.

herbaceous plants   See **nonwoody plants;** also called herbs.

hilum   The scar on the seed coat of some seeds, such as beans; point where the seed was attached to the plant during development.

horizon   Imaginary line where the sky appears to touch Earth.

horizontally polarized   A characteristic of light waves with electric fields that are vibrating in the horizontal direction.

humus   Soil material formed by decayed plants and animals.

hydrologic cycle   Continuous interchange of water between the ocean, the land, plants, and clouds. Also called water cycle.

hydrology   The science concerned with the quality and distribution of water on Earth.

hypocotyl   The part of the embryo below the epicotyl that attaches the embryo to the cotyledon. The end of the hypocotyl, called the radicle, develops into the root.

hypothesis   A prediction to the solution to a problem, based on knowledge and research. See **research hypothesis** and **null hypothesis.**

igneous rock   Rock produced by the cooling and solidifying of molten rock. See **extrusive igneous rock** and **intrusive igneous rock.**

image   A representation of a physical object formed by light reflected from a surface.

incandescent   Glow with heat.

incident light   Light striking a surface.

independent variable   The factor purposely manipulated in an experiment.

indicator   A natural or synthetic chemical substance that changes color in response to other chemicals. See **acid/base indicator.**

infrared radiation   A form of radiant energy commonly called heat rays; energy in the form of heat given off by all hot bodies; part of light energy.

innate behavior   Behavior that is inherited, not learned.

inorganic   Not made from living things.

inorganic chemistry   The study of the structure, properties, and reactions of the chemical elements and their compounds. (except for hydrocarbons).

inquiry question   An introductory problem for investigation about a project topic.

insight response   New response to a situation that depends upon previously learned responses; also called the "aha!" response.

instrumental conditioning   See **operant conditioning.**

insulator   A substance that is a poor conductor of heat and electricity; a substance with a low concentration of free electrons; see **electrical insulator** or **thermal insulator.**

intergranular lanes   In reference to the Sun, they are dark areas between granules where cooler gases return to the convection zone.

internal energy   See **thermal energy.**

internal respiration   A process by which plants and animals combine oxygen with glucose to produce energy as well as carbon dioxide and water; a catabolic process; also called aerobic respiration.

interpret   To explain or restate.

intrusive igneous rock   Coarse-grained igneous rock formed underground: See **porphyritic rock.**

iodide   The reduced form of elemental iodine.

iodine number   A value describing the degree of unsaturation of triglycerides; the number of grams of iodine that will react with each 100 grams of triglycerides.

ion   An atom or group of atoms that has lost or gained one or more electrons.

kinetic energy   Energy possessed by an object because of its motion.

lava   Molten rock from within the Earth that reaches the Earth's surface.

leaching   Process of removing the soluble chemicals from a material, such as soil, by filtering water through the material so that water-soluble substances are extracted.

legend   Words written on a diagram, such as a graph, to explain it.

lichen   A plantlike organism made of fungus and algae.

line graph   A graph that uses a line to compare or express patterns of change.

luminosity   The amount of light energy given off by a light source, such as a star, in a given amount of time.

lunar   A term referring to the Moon, Earth's natural satellite.

magma   Molten rock under the Earth's surface.

magnet   A material with magnetic forces that attracts other magnetic material and is attracted to another magnet.

magnetic field   The property of a space in which a magnetic force can be detected.

magnetic field lines   Imaginary lines making up a magnetic field that indicate the direction and magnitude of the field.

magnetic force   Force produced by the motion of electric charges.

magnetic poles   The region around a magnet where the magnetic forces appear strongest; see **north pole** and **south pole.**

magnetize   To cause a substance to become a magnet.

magnitude   A measure of how bright a celestial body appears to be.

magnitude scale   Numerical values indicating the range of apparent magnitudes of celestial bodies; expressed as magnitudes denoting an inverse relationship between brightness and magnitude number.

manometer   An instrument used to measure the pressure of fluids.

mass   The measure of the amount of matter in an object.

mathematics   The development and application of formal logical systems of computations.

matter   The substance from which all objects are made.

mechanics   The study of forces, interactions, and motions of material.

medicine and health   The study of diseases and health of humans and animals.

medium-grained   Texture of a material having particles that are a size between coarse-grained and fine-grained.

meristem   The main growing regions of a plant's stem and roots with specialized clusters of cells that produce growth by mitosis.

metamorphic rock   Rock that has been changed by great heat and pressure within the Earth's crust. See **foliated metamorphic rock.**

metamorphism   Change in structure, appearance, and composition of rock in the solid state within the Earth's crust as a result of changes in temperature and pressure. See **regional metamorphism.**

meteor   A meteoroid that enters Earth's atmosphere and burns up; also the light a meteor emits because it is heated to a state of incandescence.

meteorite   A meteor that strikes a surface, such as Earth's.

meteoroid   A solid particle that has broken off a celestial body and that orbits the Sun.

meteoroid stream   Debris from a comet traveling in or near a comet's orbital path.

meteor shower   An increase in the rate of meteors; occurs when Earth passes through debris left by comets.

meteor storm   Many meteors occurring in a short period of time.

meteoritics   The study of meteors.

meteorology   The study of Earth's atmosphere and especially of Earth's weather.

microbes   Microscopic organisms.

microbiology   The study of microbes or microscopic parts of living things.

mineral   A single, solid element or chemical compound found in the Earth. It has four basic characteristics: (1) it occurs nat-

urally; (2) it is inorganic; (3) it has a definite chemical composition; (4) it has a crystalline structure.

mineralogy   The study of the composition and formation of minerals.

minor planets   Asteroids.

mitosis   The process of cell duplication, in which cell parts duplicate themselves and then divide into two separate cells.

molecule   Two or more atoms bonded together.

monocot   See **monocotyledon.**

monocotyledon   A plant whose seed has one cotyledon; also called a monocot.

monounsaturated   A fatty acid with one double carbon-to-carbon bond.

monounsaturated triglyceride   A triglyceride that has one or more monounsaturated fatty acid chains.

moon   A celestial body in orbit about a planet; a natural satellite. When capitalized, it refers to Earth's moon.

morphology   The study of plant forms, development, and life histories. Plant developmental morphology is the study of plant growth and development.

natural satellites   Celestial bodies that orbit about another larger celestial body; generally refers to moons about planets.

net force   The sum of all forces acting simultaneously on an object.

neutral   (1) Having no acidic or basic properties. (2) Having an equal number of positive and negative charges, thus having no electric charge.

Newton's first law of motion   A law that states that a force is needed to change the motion of an object.

Newton's third law of motion   A law that states that for every action there is an equal and opposite reaction.

nonwoody plants   Plants containing stems with a small amount of wood, also called herbaceous plants.

north pole   The north-seeing pole of a magnet; magnetic pole attracted in the direction of geographical north.

nuclear fusion   The combining of the nuclei of atoms, resulting in the release of enormous amounts of radiant energy.

nucleus   The center of an atom; where protons are located.

null hypothesis   A statement of no predicted change as to the outcome of an experiment.

nutrients   Nourishing materials needed for the life and growth of living organisms.

observations   Information about events or things; acts of collecting information. See **qualitative observations** and **quantitative observations.**

oceanography   The study of oceans and marine organisms. (The study of marine organisms is generally called marine biology.)

opaque   Not allowing light to pass through.

operant conditioning   Method of using rewards to train an animal to perform tasks that are not innate behavior.

operculum   Protective flap of skin over a fish's gills.

optically active   A material that rotates the plane of light waves passing through it.

optics   The study of light.

orbit   To move in a curved path around another body; the curved path of one body around another.

orbital period   The time per revolution of a revolving celestial body.

orbital velocity   The reciprocal of an object's orbital period.

organic acid   An organic compound with one or more carboxyl acid group (COOH).

organic chemistry   The study of hydrocarbons (compounds composed of carbon and hydrogen) and their reactions.

organic compounds   Chemicals containing carbon and found in living organisms.

organism   A living thing.

organs   Structures in organisms that perform a function, such as lungs or gills.

oscillation   To swing or move back and forth; a vibration.

oxidation   The loss of electrons by a substance; a gain of oxygen by a substance.

oxidation-reduction reaction   A chemical reaction in which electrons are transferred between reactants.

Pascal's law   A law that states that the force exerted by a fluid acts at right angles at every point on a submerged object.

pendulum   Suspended object called a bob that swings back and forth.

penumbra   The grayish outer part of a sunspot or of a shadow.

permeability   The measure of how easily a solid allows fluids to pass through it.

petrology   The study of the composition and formation of rocks.

phase change   The change from one form or phase of matter to another.

phases of matter   The three common forms of matter: solid, liquid, and gas.

pH   A number used to indicate the acidic or basic nature of a solution.

pH scale   A scale used to measure the acidic or basic nature of a substance.

photoperiod   The interval during a 24-hour period in which an organism is exposed to light.

photoperiodism   The response of an organism to changes in the photoperiod.

photosphere   The layer of the Sun outside the convection zone that is the first layer of the Sun's atmosphere and appears to be the visible surface of the Sun.

photosynthesis   A process by which plants capture light energy and store it in glucose molecules; chemical process by which in the presence of light, carbon dioxide, and water combine forming glucose, oxygen, and energy; an anabolic process.

physical chemistry   The study of the physical properties of substances, such as viscosity and molecular structure.

physical geology   The study of the nature of Earth in its present state. See **hydrology, mineralogy, petrology, soil,** and **topography.**

physics   The study of forms of energy and the laws of motion.

physiology   The study of physical and chemical processes that take place in living organisms during the performance of life functions.

pie chart   A circle graph that shows information in percentages.

pigment   A substance that absorbs visible light; gives color to materials.

pitch   How high or low a sound is.

plane polarized   A characteristic of light in which the electric field is vibrating in one direction.

planetary satellite science   The study of moons.

planets   Celestial bodies that orbit a sun and shine only by reflected light.

planetology   The study of planets of the solar system, and especially how they differ.

plumule   The embryonic shoot tip that consists of several tiny, immature leaves that at maturity form the first true leaves; the tip of the epicotyl that looks like folded leaves.

polarity   The north or south pole of a magnet.

polarization angle   The angle of incidence at which light reflected from a nonmetallic surface is completely polarized.

polarized   (1) In reference to light, it is light in which the electric fields of all the light waves vibrate in a direction parallel to each other. (2) In reference to objects, it is an object that has a negative and a positive end, such as a water molecule.

polarizer   A material that allows electric fields of light vibrating in only one direction to pass through it.

pollutants   Substances that destroy the purity of air, water, or land.

polyunsaturated   An organic compound with one or more multiple carbon-to-carbon double bonds.

polyunsaturated triglyceride   A triglyceride with one or more polyunsaturated fatty acid chains.

pore space   Small spaces between particles in materials such as soil, sand, or rocks.

porosity   Percentage of a material's volume that is pore space.

porphyritic rock   Intrusive igneous rock containing two or more different sizes of interlocking crystals; thus it is said to have varied grain sizes.

potential energy (PE)   Stored energy possessed by an object due to its condition or position.

precipitation   Liquid and solid phases of water that fall from the atmosphere.

primary research   Information you collect on your own, such as data from exploratory experiments and interviews.

product   A substance produced in a chemical reaction.

project conclusion   A summary of the results of the project experiment and a statement of how the results relate to the hypothesis.

project experiment   An experiment designed to test a hypothesis.

project journal   A written progress record of your science fair project.

project problem   The scientific question for a science project that will be solved.

project report   The written record of your science fair project from start to finish.

project research   An in-depth study of the project topic with the objective of expressing a project problem, proposing a hypothesis, and designing a project experiment to test the hypothesis.

project title   A descriptive heading for your science fair project.

project topic   The subject of a science fair project.

protease   A group of enzymes that break large protein molecules into smaller molecules.

proteins   Any of a large number of complex organic compounds that make up living organisms and are essential to their functioning.

proton   Positively charged particle in the nucleus of atoms.

qualitative observation   A description of the physical properties of something, including how it looks, sounds, feels, smells and/or tastes.

quantitative observation   A description of the amount of something.

radiant energy   See **radiation.**

radiation   Energy that can move through space, and is not carried by matter; also called **radiant energy;** energy traveling in the form of electromagnetic waves. Process by which radiant energy is transmitted.

radiation zone   The area outside the core of the Sun.

radicle   The end of the hypocotyl that develops into the root.

random error of measurements   The uncertainty of experimental measurements.

raw data   The information collected during a scientific study.

reactant   A substance that is changed during a chemical reaction.

reduction   The gain of electrons by a substance; the loss of oxygen by a substance.

reflected   Bounced off of.

regional metamorphism   Metamorphism that occurs when large areas of rock are changed by pressure and heat, such as in mountain formation.

regolith   All the loose rock particles, including soil, that cover Earth's surface.

relative error   The percentage error as compared with a known value.

repel   To push apart.

research   The process of collecting information and data; the facts collected about a topic.

research hypothesis   The hypothesis for an experiment containing measurable results. It is a specific and testable prediction, and must contain the independent and dependent variable.

resonance   The condition of starting or amplifying vibrations in a body at its natural frequency by an outside vibrating force having the same frequency; also called **sympathetic vibration.**

respiration   See **external respiration** and **internal respiration.**

resultant force   The single force that has the same effect as the sum of two or more forces acting simultaneously on an object.

revolution   One turn around an orbit.

revolve   To move in a curved path around another object.

rock   A solid, coherent aggregate of one or more minerals. See **igneous rock, metamorphic rock,** and **sedimentary rock.**

rock cycle   Changing of rocks from one type to another by a series of processes involving heat, pressure, melting, cooling, and sedimentation.

rotation   The turning of a body about its axis.

row   The space between horizontal lines in a table.

runoff   Rainwater that is unable to soak into the ground and that moves over its surface.

sampling plot   A select area of an ecosystem that allows you to study the biotic and abiotic factors in it.

satellite   A natural or man-made body that revolves about a celestial body. See **artificial satellite** and **natural satellite.**

saturated   An organic compound with single carbon-to-carbon bonds.

saturated triglyceride   A triglyceride with only saturated fatty acids.

scale   A ratio between the measurements of a model and the actual measurements of an object.

scale model   A replica made in proportion to the object it represents.

science   A system of knowledge as well as the pursuit of knowledge about the nature of things in the universe.

science fair   An organized contest in which science fair projects compete.

science fair project   An entry in a science fair; an investigation in finding the answer to one science related question.

scientific method   The technique of solving a scientific problem by conducting research, identifying a specific problem, stating a hypothesis, testing the hypothesis through experimentation, and summarizing the results in a conclusion.

secondary research   Information and/or data that someone else has collected, such as in written records in books and magazines.

sediment   Materials transported and deposited by water, wind, or glaciers.

sedimentary rock   Rock formed by deposits of sediment.

seed coat   Protective covering around a seed.

shoot   The part of a plant growing above ground consisting of parts including a stem and leaves.

shrubs   Plants with several low, woody stems branched near the ground that are able to stand erect without support. Also called bushes.

slope   The measure of the steepness of an inclined surface.

soil   The top layer of the regolith that can support the growth of rooted plants.

soil science   The study of soil.

solar energy   Radiant energy from the Sun.

solar system   A group of celestial bodies that orbit a sun.

solenoid   A coil of wire through which a current can pass.

soluble   The ability of a substance to break up and thoroughly mix with another substance.

sonar   An acronym derived from *So*und *N*avigation *A*nd *R*anging.

sounding   Early method of measuring depth with a weighted line marked with distance measurements.

south pole   The south-seeking pole of a magnet; magnetic pole attracted in the direction of geographical south.

species   A group of similar organisms.

specific gravity (sp. gr.)   The ratio of the mass of an object in air to the mass of the water displaced by the submerged object.

splintery   A type of fracture producing surfaces that are small, thin, and sharp or fibrous.

spoilage   The ruining of food as a result of chemical changes in the food, often from the presence of organisms, such as fungi and bacteria.

star   A celestial body; a glowing sphere of gas.

static charges   A buildup of stationary electric charges.

static electricity   The effect of static charges.

stem   The part of a plant that supports other plant parts, including the leaves, flowers, and fruit.

stereomicroscope   A dissecting microscope that allows thick specimens to be observed.

streak A physical characteristic of a mineral, which is the color of the powder left when a mineral is rubbed against a rough surface harder than the mineral.

streak plate Surface of unglazed porcelain or other material against which a mineral is rubbed in a streak test.

streak test A test in which the streak of a mineral is determined.

substrate The substance on which an enzyme acts.

sun A star at the center of a solar system. When capitalized, refers to the star at the center of our solar system.

sunspots Large dark spots on the Sun's photosphere.

sympathetic vibration See **resonance.**

table A diagram that uses words and numbers in columns and rows to represent data.

tangent Touching at a single point.

temperature gradient The temperature change with distance along a material.

tendrils The slender spiraling stems of some vines that attach themselves to supporting structures.

texture In reference to rocks, it is the size of mineral grains making up the rock; the size of particles in soil; See **coarse-grained, medium-grained, fine-grained,** and **glassy.**

thermal conduction The transfer of heat when energetic particles collide with some of their less energetic neighboring particles; also called **conduction.**

thermal conductivity The measure of the ability of a material to conduct heat.

thermal conductor Materials with a high concentration of free electrons through which heat flows readily; also called **conductors.**

thermal energy or **internal energy** The sum of the kinetic and potential energy of random motion of particles making up an object.

thermal insulator Materials with a low concentration of free electrons that are poor thermal conductors.

thermodynamics The study of temperature and energy; heat flow; the transformation of energy; phases of matter.

third law of planetary motion Kepler's law that states that the more distant a planet's orbit from the Sun, the greater the planet's period of revolution.

titration The process of combining a measured amount of a solution of known concentration with a measured amount of solution of unknown concentration.

topic research As defined in this book, it is research done with the objective of selecting a project topic.

topography The study of the layout of natural and artificial features on the surface of the Earth; description of the size, shape, and elevation of a region of land.

topographic map Flat map that shows the shapes and heights of land areas using lines that connect points on the Earth that have the same elevation.

translucent Allows some light to pass through, but the light is diffused.

transparent Allows light to pass through.

transpiration The process by which plants lose water from their surface, especially through their leaves.

transverse waves Waves in which the vibrations are perpendicular to the direction in which the waves are traveling.

trees Large plants with a single tall, woody stem called a trunk that grows from the ground and is able to stand erect without support. Other wood stems branch from the trunk.

triglycerides Fats and oils; organic chemical compounds made of one molecule of glycerol with three fatty acid side chains. See **monounsaturated triglyceride, polyunsaturated triglyceride,** and **saturated triglyceride.**

turgor pressure The internal pressure of plant cells due to the presence of water.

ultraviolet radiation A form of radiant energy in solar energy that causes skin to tan or burn.

unbalanced forces Forces that act simultaneously on an object with a resultant force that is not equal to zero.

umbra A dark area, especially the darkest part of a sunspot or a shadow.

universe Everything in space including Earth.

unpolarized light Light waves with electric fields that are vibrating in directions that are not parallel with one another.

unsaturated An organic compound with one or more multiple carbon-to-carbon bonds.

vapor Gaseous phase of a substance such as water that is normally in a liquid phase.

vaporize To change to a gas.

variables Changeable factors in an experiment. See **dependent variable** and **independent variable.**

velocity Speed in a specific direction.

vertically polarized A characteristic of light waves with electric fields that are vibrating in the vertical direction.

vines A flexible, weak-stemmed plant whose long, fast-growing shoots rely on other plants or objects for support. The stems of vines may wind around supporting structures, and/or use thorns, tendrils, or hooks on the stems to climb and anchor to a structure. Some are woody and some are nonwoody.

vibrations Swinging or back-and-forth movements; also called **oscillations.**

viscosity Measurement of thickness of a fluid; resistance to flow.

viscosity index A ratio of the rate flow of a fluid to the rate flow of water.

visible light A form of radiant energy in solar radiation that can be seen and is divided into the rainbow colors of red, orange, yellow, green, blue, indigo, and violet.

vitamin C Ascorbic acid.

waning To grow smaller.

waxing To grow larger.

water cycle See **hydrologic cycle.**

wood The part of a plant made of xylem tubes.

woody plant A plant containing stems with a large amount of wood.

x-axis The horizontal axis on a line graph. The independent variable is often recorded on the x-axis.

xylem tubes Tubes in a plant that transport water and other nutrients from the root throughout the plant and provide support.

y-axis The vertical axis on a line graph. The dependent variable is often recorded on the y-axis.

zenith The position of a celestial body, such as the Moon, when it is at its highest in the sky.

zoology The study of animals and animal life, including their structure and growth.

INDEX